EASTERN EUROPEAN

GOVERNMENT

AND POLITICS

Harper's Comparative Government Series

MICHAEL CURTIS, EDITOR

EASTERN EUROPEAN
GOVERNMENT
AND POLITICS

VACLAV BENES
Indiana University

ANDREW GYORGY
The George Washington University

GEORGE STAMBUK
The George Washington University

HARPER & ROW
Publishers
NEW YORK, EVANSTON, AND LONDON

CONTENTS

JN
96
.B4

Eastern Europe

PREFACE

THIS VOLUME on Eastern European Government and Politics is the product of a truly collaborative venture. Four authors have shared in its planning, preparation, writing, and editing. Each of the coauthors is a native of the region, a specialist in its political development, and a practicing professor and scholar. For purposes of this volume, the coverage of the complex Eastern European area has been selective rather than encyclopedic. The authors have emphasized illustrative case studies rather than an across-the-board coverage of the eight countries which comprise this stormy "shatter zone" of the European continent.

The six countries selected present ideologically important variations on the Eastern European political theme. Three (Poland, Czechoslovakia, and East Germany) clearly fall into the geopolitical "Northern Tier" of the region. They are industrialized, technologically advanced, possess important strategic and human resources, and have been historically and culturally Western-oriented. They have also formed an extremely vulnerable buffer area and have an exceptionally long history of military and political exploitation. Hungary, in turn, is portrayed here as a transitional country linking north and south and forming a bridge between the Danubian countries of Eastern Europe and the southeast. Once the core of a vast Austro-Hungarian Empire, Hungary is now more of a clearing house and connecting channel between two diverse patterns or clusters of nations.

Finally, Yugoslavia and Rumania are components of the "Southern Tier." In their analysis the authors present prototypes of a characteristically Balkan political development. The evolution of these two nations has been determined by an eastern exposure, an overwhelmingly agricultural base and a consequent industrial weakness, a great resource potential and—last but not least—by hopelessly turbulent domestic politics and equally unstable foreign relations. Since so much attention is being devoted to these two fascinating Balkan countries, the authors decided to omit the drab and less representative political patterns of Bulgaria and Albania. We must add, however, that although they are not centrally treated, these two countries appear peripherally throughout the book, directly and by means of cross-referencing.

The task of writing the individual chapters was so allocated that Vaclav Benes of Indiana University prepared Chapters Two (Poland), Three (Czechoslovakia), and Five (Hungary); Andrew Gyorgy of The George Washington University wrote the Introduction (Chapter One) and Chapter Four (East Germany); while George Stambuk, also of The George Washington University, was responsible for Chapter Six (Yugoslavia) and Stephen Fischer-Galati of the University of Colorado for Chapter Seven (Rumania). Although the book is a collective venture, in the last analysis each author is responsible for his particular sector.

VACLAV BENES
ANDREW GYORGY
GEORGE STAMBUK

April, 1966

CHAPTER ONE

Eastern Europe in Historic Perspective

THE HISTORIC evolution of the region broadly labelled Eastern Europe has been conditioned by two major processes: inner political fragmentation and outer geographic accessibility. The complex interplay of these two factors produced, in turn, the *Balkanization* of the whole area as probably its most distinctive single geopolitical feature through the centuries.

This introduction cannot examine all the historic and economic ramifications of Eastern Europe's internal "fragmentation" process; the following six chapters analyze in some detail the turbulent political evolution of both its "Northern" (or Danubian) and "Southern" (or Balkan) Tiers. However, it is appropriate to review here in brief sequence the various imperialistic waves of occupying powers which, as a result of the area's vulnerability and immense external accessibility, have victimized its peoples and shaped their historic development. In his distinguished *The Balkans in Our Time*, Robert Lee Wolff characterized these outside pressures:

> The peoples of our . . . countries, separated from each other and divided among themselves, were deeply affected by the radiations of military power and of political, economic, cultural, and religious influence which emanated from certain great centers of Europe, from which armies, diplomats, merchants, scholars, and priests always found it easy to penetrate into the heart . . . of the region.[1]

Keeping in mind this portrayal of imperialistic pressures, we must note the particular impact of four external "waves." The "wave" analogy is most suitable: each of these powers "washed

[1] See Robert L. Wolff, *The Balkans In Our Time* (Cambridge: Harvard University Press, 1956), pp. 19–20.

1

over" the area, enveloped it for a while, and then began to recede slowly—yielding to the next inexorable wave which was already gathering its strength for the appropriate moment. All four patterns of external influence had certain basic features in common: they combined political, economic, military, and cultural weapons in an effort to establish and maintain control over the key countries of Eastern Europe. By the skillful use of a wide assortment of imperialistic instruments, Turkey's significant domination of the Danubian-Balkan area set the stage for subsequent colonial exploits. Turkish rule cast its long and oppresive shadow for several centuries, from the historic battle of Kossovo (June, 1389) in which the backbone of a determined Serbian resistance was broken, all the way to the late nineteenth century when Bulgaria was finally liberated. Turkish influence actually stretched into the twentieth century, punctuated by the "liberation" of Albania, the Balkan Wars of 1912–1913, and finally by the collapse of the Turkish Sultanate (by then the very "sick man of Europe") in 1918.

Although Turkish influence has been most pervasive in those Balkan provinces (Bulgaria, Rumania, Serbia, Albania) where Ottoman control lasted from 400 to 500 years, its impact has also been obvious in Hungary and discernible in parts of the "Northern Tier." Among its most disastrous features the following have to be stressed:

First, Turkish rulers insisted on keeping the political and military administration of the occupied provinces in their own hands. Their single-minded interest centered on inexorable tax collection and the maintenance of tight military supervision; the result was that native political elites, true leadership groups, could not emerge in Eastern Europe because political control was concentrated in the hands of a tiny *foreign* elite. This considerably handicapped the rise of an educated, self-reliant bourgeois middle class, thus producing a social weakness which seriously affected the nineteenth- and twentieth-century socioeconomic development of Eastern Europe. We find here a peculiar atomization of society into two sharply divided groups: a small political elite (lawyers, a handful of professional politicians, businessmen,[2] and—last but

---

[2] These were often considered "outsiders" since under Turkish occupation commerce and industry were handled largely by Greeks, Armenians, and Jews rather than by the natives of these countries.

not least—the owners of large estates) facing an immense, practically enslaved and largely illiterate mass of peasants. Hence the proliferation and perpetuation of truly feudal conditions in Danubia and the Balkans, with disastrous implications for their twentieth-century social evolution.

Second, this catastrophic retardation of political development in turn created in Eastern Europe a perfect hotbed for any and all revolutionary social ideas which happened to sweep the European continent. Since there were few indigenous leadership groups capable of guidance and moderation, the element of ideological resistance had been missing or had proved ineffective in a showdown action. Not only the Turks, but such subsequent conquerors as the Germans and Russians, took full advantage of the fact that there was a deep-seated revolutionary tradition in the Balkans and that there was little willingness on the part of the entrenched political elites to resist the recurrent sweep of exciting revolutionary ideas. The older elite groups usually preferred to flee, loaded with their precious possessions, or they meekly and unconditionally surrendered to the revolutionary forces. The new leaders then skillfully posed as the "liberators" of the Eastern European peoples from an oppressive Turkish yoke.

The struggle for liberation from Turkey was an immense one. Countless small revolts and bloody, but localized, peasant uprisings had been staged through the centuries, and while they did not produce national independence, at least they helped to project the image of the intrepid Balkan guerrilla or freedom fighter. This image subsequently gained in importance as the guerrilla fighter became the carrier of military traditions and a central figure in the promise of effective political leadership. By the time of the Balkan Wars (1912–1913), effective Turkish domination had ended over southeastern Europe, and the traditions described here had sufficiently crystallized to produce new revolutionary heroes.

The second impact was less external and less of a wave than that of Turkey. Nevertheless, the *Austrian* rule of the Habsburgs has been considered oppressive and imperialistic by millions of Eastern Europeans for the many centuries of its duration. In terms of length of control, Austria's overlordship stretched with few interruptions from the end of the thirteenth century (when the obscure Prince Rudolph was first elected king) all the way to 1918, when the Monarchy collapsed in the wake of World War I, along with its German, Turkish, and Russian czarist equivalents.

In terms of occupation techniques the Austrian emperors' rule can be portrayed as wholly unpredictable, ranging from the ugly oppression of various minority groups at one end of the spectrum to indolent, inefficient "enlightened despotism" at the other. Belligerence and the waging of aggressive warfare were definitely not Austrian traits—the Habsburgs preferred to consolidate their control over European royalty by ambitious matrimonial designs linking most of these royal families to Austria by marrying off the numerous Habsburg daughters. On the whole, Austro-Hungarian rule was the least disastrous in Eastern Europe and, in effect, the long reign of Emperor Francis Joseph (1848–1916) seems in retrospect as a fairly happy and economically prosperous period for the 75 million people of the so-called "Dual Monarchy." The Austrian empire was defeated in the end by certain inexorable forces of history; vacillating, irrational, and often cruel treatment of the diverse and large ethnic groups led to the inevitable explosion of 1918. The obsolete edifice of the Austro-Hungarian Monarchy collapsed in the wake of a disastrous world war and was forced to yield to such "successor" states as Czechoslovakia and Yugoslavia. Clearly, the Slavic peoples' long and successful struggle for self-determination was the key historic process which spelled the doom of the Habsburg era and ushered in the short-lived and transitional interwar period from 1919 to 1939.

A third major wave was represented by Germany. The German impact on Eastern Europe must be divided into two sectors: first the nineteenth- and early twentieth-century influence of Bismarck's and Kaiser William II's "Imperial" Germany, and more recently Adolf Hitler's disastrous Third Reich and the Nazi occupation of the area from 1933 to 1945. Briefly summarized, the first phase had the primary characteristic of economic domination. Both the nationalistic school of German social scientists (represented by such able but aggressive economists as Friedrich List and the forerunners of the "geopoliticians," such as Friedrich Ratzel), and the belligerent operators of an expansionist German foreign policy (particularly the "Iron Chancellor," Prince von Bismarck) increasingly regarded Danubia and the Balkans as their primary sphere of influence. As such, this region was to be treated as an extractive, raw-material producing colony into which German industry could, in exchange, freely dump its own manufactured products. In addition to this systematic economic exploitation, the *Drang nach Osten* ("Push toward the East") of the 1880–1914 period, noisily articulated in such slogans as the "Berlin to Baghdad" line, the demand for increased *Lebensraum* (living space), for a German "place in the sun," for colonies in the Middle East and Africa, also considered Eastern Europe as an essential geopolitical staging area from which these aggressive moves were to be launched.

Thus economic control was merely a harbinger of more ominous imperialistic policies—the road to Baghdad unfortunately led through Vienna, Prague, Budapest, Belgrade, and Bucharest! In the long run, Emperor William's clumsy and irrational execution of Bismarck's cleverly conceived diplomatic strategies involved the whole area in the terrible conflagration of World War I.

The second wave of German influence materialized in the tragic aspects of Hitler's 12 years of the "New Order" for Eastern Europe. Nazi Germany not only continued and accelerated the earlier policies of economic exploitation, but also left complete political disruption in the wake of its military occupation of the region. Pursuing their fanatical genocide aimed at Jews, Slavs and, in effect, at all non-Germans, the Nazi rulers and their various local puppet—or quisling—regimes ruined the bases of constitutional government and murdered or drove into exile the most valuable and constructive statesmen. In short, in the course of a few brief years they produced a political, moral, and social vacuum which allowed Communism first to seep into, and later to engulf, the whole area. The atmosphere of distrust and hatred which originally opened the door to swift conquest and total military occupation, was eventually enhanced by the slow retreat of the German armies, by a "scorched earth" type of punitive treatment, and by such bloody military stands as the vicious battles of Warsaw, Berlin, and Budapest. Here Germans, Russians, and various underground resistance forces were locked in combat during the dreadful "last gasp" months of the winter of 1944 and the spring of 1945.

Russia is the fourth major power whose past imperial interests and current colonial tactics have left a permanent imprint on the "body politic" of Eastern Europe. Again, we must divide

Russian influences into two chronological parts. The first covers most of the nineteenth century and stretches to World War I, while the second covers the period since 1945, the appearance of Stalin's armies and the establishment of Soviet Communist control in Eastern Europe. To understand the first phase, it must be stressed that Russian historic ambitions and dynastic rivalries have asserted themselves in the Balkan Peninsula and the lower Danube Valley ever since 1812, when Russian troops occupied the strategic province of Bessarabia, which assured them temporary control over the delta region of the Danube. Starting from this geopolitically modest nucleus, czarist Russia then steadily enlarged its sphere of interest until, in the latter part of the century, it actually assumed the function of protector of small states in the Danubian-Balkan area. For some of these countries it developed and exploited its role of liberator from Turkish rule (as in the cases of Serbia, Rumania, and Bulgaria) while for such essentially Slavic countries as Bulgaria, it also posed as the elder Slavic brother. Subsequently it emerged as the most important representative of the Orthodox religion, of a Russian national church which was to play a major role in the further ideological development of the small Eastern European states.

For the past 150 years Eastern Europe has been forced to become increasingly aware of this lengthening Russian shadow, of a swiftly developing czarist—and later Bolshevik—Russian zone of geographic and political security and interests. First in Pan-Slav nationalism and more recently in Marxist-Leninist Communism, Russia has possessed and skillfully used its political weapons for the weakening of such old rivals as the Habsburg and German empires, and for the eventual penetration and occupation of the entire Eastern European arena. To a large extent both the czars' and Stalin's policies have been guided by a *negative* attitude: a traditional Russian anxiety to prevent any unfriendly or strong political power from establishing itself in Eastern Europe and using it as a convenient springboard for further expansion toward the east. Since 1945 the Soviet government's security designs have clearly included all of the small Danubian-Balkan states which had been exploited in earlier days by other expansionist great powers and had often been built into offensive bases of military and political action.

We now turn to the most recent period of Eastern European history and propose to survey the intricacies of its latest imperial wave—the twenty-odd years of Soviet domination and control.

Major Political Changes Since World War II

The most realistic way of appraising the complicated political scenery of the Eastern European area is to rely on a historically oriented method of double-entry bookkeeping. Thus, we consider the "pros" and "cons" of the Soviet-Eastern European relationships essentially from the twofold perspective of certain factors of cohesion, balanced on the opposite side of the politico-economic ledger by factors of division. The former grouping catalogues the forces which have operated in a *centripetal* direction, binding the individual Eastern European nations to the U.S.S.R. and, on the whole, strengthening the newly won and established colonial position of Soviet Russia. The latter category has exerted *centrifugal* tendencies which have weakened and in the long run undermined the once monopolistic status of the Soviet Union. It is difficult to break down these two large groupings of factors into concise and historically accurate time phases, but for approximately a 12-year period in the post-World War II era (1944–1956) the cohesive factors considerably outweighed the divisive forces, while ever since the climactic revolutionary events of 1956 the areas of disruption have become more evident and characteristic. Thus, for several of the Eastern European nations involved here, the last decade marked the end of a satellite era of abject and total dependence on the U.S.S.R. and ushered in the flowering of truly *polycentric* "New Communisms."

Factors of Cohesion

Keeping in mind this approximate time element, we turn to the centripetal forces linking the Soviet Union to its once-satellite partners in Eastern Europe. These have been partly of an institutional, and partly of a diplomatic or persuasive character.

GEOSTRATEGIC AND INSTITUTIONAL FORCES

Among the geopolitical and military factors the time element has probably been the most basic and unpublicized fact of life militating in favor of closer U.S.S.R.-Eastern European relations. Well over two decades of "colonial rule" have left an indelible impact on these societies and have particularly influenced the lives and educational pursuits of their younger generations. Given another 15 or 20 years of Soviet Communist political patterns, despite the gradual loosening of the colonial bonds, it will be most difficult to shake off and reduce to a minimum the long and corrosive impact of cultural Russification and Communist political ideology. Thus, while obvious and primitive in its impact, the time factor has certainly favored the U.S.S.R. ever since its most recent appearance in Eastern Europe in the 1944–1945 period.

An equally long-term force has been the Soviet use, control, and exploitation of the area's strategic resources. Foremost among these must be the mining of uranium in the favorably located Ore Mountains (on the Czechoslovakian-East German border), the use of Hungarian bauxite, Polish iron and coal, not to omit control over at least 1500 miles of the Danube River, an immensely important means of inland navigation with political and military overtones. Broadly strategic in actual use and potential exploitation also are the industrial capacities of such technologically advanced societies as East Germany, Poland, and Czechoslovakia, as well as the agricultural resources of Hungary, Rumania, and—to a lesser extent—Bulgaria.

The U.S.S.R.'s economic gain from the satellite economies has been actually twofold: direct and bilateral in some areas (particularly where the advanced skills, the higher technological level of knowledge and expertise of individual peoples or groups could be exploited without intermediaries), but indirect and multilateral in several other situations. The latter activity has resulted in a network of complex economic arrangements, in an intensified Soviet effort to promote regionwide integration. Founded in 1949 (and mislabeled as the "Molotov Plan"), the Council of Mutual Economic Assistance (CEMA, also known as

COMECON) tried to organize the various economies of the Eastern European countries into a cohesive and self-sufficient bloc. Since 1955, in particular, COMECON's frantic activities have increasingly reflected the double intention of Soviet leadership, first, to tie Eastern Europe firmly to the U.S.S.R. by skillful exploitation of economic resources and divisions of labor among the individual countries, and second, to keep the satellite economies in fair-to-prosperous shape, thus guaranteeing the passive cooperation of their peoples and hopefully preventing a recurrence of the revolutionary blowups of the 1953–1956 period. CEMA has played an eminently political role in Soviet-bloc relations; as a significant organization in the promotion of unity, it has considerably increased its activities during the past few years after a period of relative inactivity.

Probably even more relevant to our troubled "Cold War" world is the cohesive application of a military integration factor, namely the Warsaw Treaty Organization or Warsaw Pact (WTO). Also founded in 1949, and also goaded into more activity after 1955, WTO has attempted through a multilateral military design to establish and keep secure the Soviet Union's postwar strategic safety zone in Eastern Europe. There is truly nothing mysterious or complicated in this latter-day imitation, and Communist version, of a traditional nineteenth-century Western "sphere of influence" notion. WTO can be considered the Stalinist revival and expression of age-old czarist ambitions to secure the flanks of Russia, to bolster militarily its exposed and vulnerable westernmost boundaries, and to develop an imperial "Cordon Sanitaire" all of its own.

Seen in this context, the Soviets' current military "safety zone" in the Danubian-Balkan area seems to serve an effective double function. In a negative sense, it intends to exclude the Western enemy (NATO, the United States, etc.) from the region by denying its use and control to all non-Communist forces. This significant denial factor is then compounded by a second related positive function, namely the inclusion of the region into aggressive military blueprints by the Warsaw Pact forces. By this we mean the launching of offensives from Eastern European bases, the planning of weapon and food caches at strategic points, the control of satellite airfields and the deployment of highly trained

and battle-ready Soviet divisions in such key countries as East
Germany and Hungary. For about ten years after the end of
World War II Red Army troops were stationed in almost all
of the Eastern European countries. In 1955, these troops were
withdrawn from Rumania, Poland, and Bulgaria, and since then
East Germany and Hungary have served as armed-forces nuclei
for the Soviet military.

The geostrategic picture emerging from this pattern of Soviet
military planning points to a carefully calculated future use of
Eastern Europe as a potential, conventional battleground of sorts.
The Soviet Union's military emphasis is clearly on the centrally
located clearinghouse status of East Germany. The 22 Soviet
divisions, comprising 420,000 Russian troops, stationed in the
DDR also serve to express, indirectly at least, the Soviet military
planners' disgust with satellite troops which, despite the manifold
Warsaw Treaty Organization bonds, have been considered unreliable and probably expendable. In case of a direct "hot war"
in the area, local military establishments are likely to be used
sparingly, with the following restricted alternatives available:
(1) they will be completely ignored by the Soviet military leadership; (2) they will be used cautiously, in small units, for localized
"guerrilla war" purposes; or (3) they will be promptly disarmed
as not only unreliable, but as actually subversive—especially in a
situation which would go counter to the nationalistic expectations
of, say, Polish or Hungarian troops.

Within this limited context, the newly developed people's (or
national) armies have been kept well armed and ready for battle.
Bolstered by Soviet officers in most of the high-ranking positions,
they must be considered important cohesive forces; indeed, the
Warsaw Pact operates as a tightly knit institutional bond between
the U.S.S.R. and its former satellites in Eastern Europe.

Beyond the economic and military forces of cohesion, there
looms the basic political-governmental link. This consists of the
national Communist parties which are, after all, more or less
slavish imitations of the structure of the CPSU, with parallel
administrative procedures and personnel policies. During the
Stalinist period of total, monolithic control (1944–1953), the
U.S.S.R. succeeded first in transplanting and then in proliferating
Soviet Russian governmental, bureaucratic, police repression, and

economic patterns of operation in a wholesale manner, throughout Eastern Europe. Thus, the local replicas of the dominant "body politic" reflect many similarities and instinctive duplications of the Soviet original.

Two political developments might serve to illustrate this point. During the critical "take-over" years of 1944–1948, it was Soviet direction and violent Stalinist impulse that helped to clear the way for the *institutional* establishment of Communism in this area. Stalin's carefully planned "revolutions from above" systematically and ruthlessly destroyed the major, native political forces, such as members of the liberal middle class or of various peasant groups, which might have offered resistance to Communism. The first institutional contacts between the Soviet leaders and the newly established satellites were the series of National Democratic Fronts, Fatherland Fronts, and People's Fronts which served as useful shields for the newly emerging, but still anemic, local Communist parties.

The second linkage developed in later years when Communist hierarchies were clearly and openly in power. The factor of cohesion then asserted itself more effectively on the party leadership-to-party leadership level. Soviet impulses, radiated from Moscow, were promptly received and translated into local action by the Warsaw, Budapest, Bucharest, or Sofia exponents of Stalinism. Until recently a slavish imitation of the Soviet leadership pattern was clearly observable on the satellite scene. For example, when Stalin turned against Tito, native Titoists were arrested, persecuted, and often executed throughout Eastern Europe. When, on the contrary, Stalin's fury eventually turned against the cosmopolitan international Communists (the so-called "Muscovites"), then a long list of Paukers, Slanskys, and Clementises were quickly silenced, if not liquidated, and the pendulum swung back to the national type of Communists. At this point of the leadership dialectic the Gomulkas, Kádárs and Gheorghiu-Dej's were beginning to re-emerge and be placed in positions of power.

Nor did the death of Stalin interrupt this process. After March 5, 1953 local Stalins suddenly faded away throughout Eastern Europe, and the hour struck for "collective leadership." When, in turn, "collective leaders" in the U.S.S.R. slowly began to wither away and yield their places to Nikita Khrushchev, a corresponding narrowing of the spectrum occurred in satellite regimes. One-man leadership, or at most, dual government raised its ugly head from Czechoslovakia to Bulgaria and—in imitation of Khrushchev's rise to power—the "cult of the individual" returned to Eastern Europe despite the conflicting and occasionally disturbing background music of de-Stalinization. Following Khrushchev's political demise of October 1964 the Soviet impulses temporarily lost their pervasive vigor while the various Eastern European regimes adopted a "wait-and-see" attitude toward the colorless Brezhnev-Kosygin team in the U.S.S.R. In the meantime, the principle of qualified one-man leadership prevailed with occasional tactical "splittism" separating the Prime Minister's job from that of the more powerful First Secretary. For example, in July 1965 János Kádár relinquished the Prime Ministry of the Hungarian government to Gyula Kállai. This move did not serve to undermine Kádár's "strong-man" position. Generally speaking, however, the institutional link prevailed with a 10- to 12-month lag. For well over a year after Nikita's removal, the Khrushchev pattern persisted in Eastern Europe with a combination of "cult of personality" and restricted, semitotalitarian powers reposed in one man.

PERSUASIVE AND DIPLOMATIC FACTORS

Extending beyond the more rigid and formal institutional umbrella combining Soviet and East European leadership elites, there is the more tenuous and intangible link between their respective Communist parties. This involves memberships-at-large which enjoy first monopoly position on the home front, and then have political and cultural connections in neighboring countries and with "good Communists" everywhere. Both of these factors are of importance since in a Communist society the Communist party is after all the central organization, and its members must be assured some form of economic security and ideological protection. Although the criteria of what constitutes a "good Communist" are often nebulous in the extreme, it is clear that no Communist regime could permit wholesale attack on devoted party members by those whose party zeal and loyalty are open to question. Such behavior would ultimately undermine the authority of the party itself.

The same informal defensive alliance prevails between the *good* Russian Marxist and the *good* satellite Marxist. Occasionally a major crisis reveals the depth of this area of "persuasive cohesion." In the spring of 1965, a conspiracy was unmasked in Bulgaria involving several high-ranking officials, leading to some arrests and at least one suicide. Party First Secretary Todor Zhivkov, mentioning the plot for the first time in public, gave full expression to Soviet-Bulgarian diplomatic cohesion by stating that:

In the West the reactionaries are now screaming that some plot has been discovered in our country which was aimed at separating us from the Soviet Union, and I do not know what other nonsense. . . . *There is no force on earth which could separate the Bulgarian People's Republic from the Soviet Union.* We have been and will continue to be with the Soviet Union in life and death.

Intraparty links have been strengthened over the years through a number of media which have been of a partly cultural and partly ideological coloring. While many of these policies have originally been used to further a conscious Russification drive among the satellite nations, particularly in the Stalin era, in recent years they have been less obvious and less effective. In historic terms, the following Soviet propaganda weapons have been most useful in Eastern Europe: (a) the compulsory teaching of Russian language and literature from the grade-school level all the way to the Ph.D.; (b) a broad-based and tremendously comprehensive cultural exchange program saturating the satellite countries with an endless flow of "cultural" missions ranging from school teachers through agricultural experts to opera singers and ballet dancers. Not only local universities were utilized in this program, but also a veritable across-the-board network of Soviet Friendship Societies, Institutes, Scientific Academies, operating both as instruments of this Russification drive, as well as the sources of endless streams of propaganda publications in Russian and in the local language; (c) a conscious and systematic play on the Eastern European peoples' justifiable fear of West Germany as the principal Central European warmonger, picturing, by way of a dramatic contrast, the U.S.S.R. as the model of a peaceloving and totally relaxed nation of "friendship and so-cialism." In recent years the fear of a belligerent, revanchist Ger-many has been further escalated to include a hatred of NATO, of the American presence in Europe, and—in general—of an alleged Western predisposition to engage in warmongering and "adventurist" military policies. At any rate, both persuasive and diplomatic policies of the U.S.S.R. have shrewdly built upon the pre-World War II Third Reich and the wartime Nazi image of the "Teutonic conqueror," and have deeply affected Czech and Polish public opinion. Last but not least, the impact of careful transplantation of so many Soviet Russian governmental, bureau-cratic, and economic patterns in the past two decades has ex-pressed itself in the moulding, shaping, and transformation of daily life into a Communist satellite world, operating on the levels of cultural, political, and ideological evolution in a startlingly parallel manner.

Factors of Division

The clusters of "divisive" forces can be described as negatively influencing Soviet-East European relations and, on the whole, working against the Soviet Union's national interests in this area. Thus they tend to weaken and undermine the once unassailable and monopolistic "control position" of the U.S.S.R., ending most of the imperial dreams and designs which the Stalin era had generated. Here we shall be concerned with three major sets of divisive factors: (a) the inadequacy of Communist leadership, (b) the increasing impact of nationalism, and (c) the decentrali-zation and diminution of police terror and violence. The opera-tional result of these forces has been an ideological "erosion," generally weakening the hold of Marxism-Leninism over the political landscape of Eastern Europe.

The inadequacy of the political elite groups has been a long-term characteristic of Balkan-Danubian Communism. It has re-flected two equally important ingredients which combined with and reinforced each other. These are moral weakness and the exploitation of economic privileges which together have frustrated and paralyzed the high postwar expectations of the satellite peoples. These expectations and hopes flowed from the bitter experiences and untold sufferings to which Eastern Europeans were subjected, first under several terrible years of Nazi occupation, and subsequently under the tragedies of World War II. It is difficult to understand from the perspective of 20 years that in 1945 and 1946 even the newly returned Communist leaders (who had spent the war years in Moscow receiving Comintern-style, typically postgraduate Marxist-Leninist indoctrination training), held the promise of ushering in a brave new world of economic and political improvements.

These hopes were short-lived indeed. The weary and war-torn peoples of Eastern Europe soon perceived the justification of that pessimistic remark that the next round will be even worse than the last one. Moral deficiencies were clear and obvious in the personalities of such extreme left-wing Socialists as Jozef Czyrankiewicz, Zdenek Fierlinger, Árpád Szakasits, and Otto Grotewohl who cheerfully led their respective Polish, Czech, Hungarian, and East German Social Democratic parties down the path of betrayal under the broad heading of a "voluntary merger" with the Communists. By 1948 the newly merged and now truly monolithic United Workers' parties accomplished total internal control and a monopoly position in political life. In typically Communist fashion, the former Socialist traitors were at first rewarded with nominally prominent jobs (Prime Minister, President of the Republic, etc.), but were discarded soon afterward as having outlived their usefulness to the Communist cause.[3]

In human terms it was equally disappointing to witness the replacement of those Communist leaders who had departed, either via the purges or through natural death, by even more formidable and disliked new political figures. Klement Gottwald's death in the early spring of 1953 raised Czech hopes which, however, were soon deflated when the even more truculent Antonin Zapotocky followed him in the presidency of the Czech People's Republic. Walter Ulbricht of East Germany and Ana Pauker of Rumania, in turn, represented not only the low point of Stalinism in action, but also projected the other ingredient,

[3] The only major exception has been the ideologically acrobatic figure of Jozef Czyrankiewicz who at this writing still serves as Poland's Prime Minister.

namely economic abuse onto the political stage of Eastern Europe. Marshal Tito and his "New Class" of former partisan leaders have also truly enjoyed the benefits and privileges of high rank in a captive society whose citizens for many years lived on the verge of starvation and in miserable housing. The new elite's exploitation of political power and fabulous standard of living ignored the fact that, with the exception of Tito, they had been originally placed in positions of authority by Soviet bayonets and on Stalin's instructions. In addition they seemed to rub in the point that a Communist dictator could be perfectly content to be unpopular, to govern happily in complete disregard for public opinion, and with a minimum consensus of his disgruntled subjects. While Walter Ulbricht is the towering monument to such massive unpopularity, Ulbricht-style Stalinists (Vulko Chervenkov, Anton Yugov, etc.) have been leaders in Bulgaria and even when illusory promises of "liberalization" appeared for a brief moment in history, they rapidly disappeared under the inevitable pressures of Communist totalitarianism. Such was the case of Wladyslaw Gomulka who held forth a truly revolutionary promise in October 1956 but proved to have feet of clay in the steadily deteriorating and reactionary period following Poland's "finest hour," its exciting popular rebellion.

The aura of economic inequality and deterioration has not been confined to the various elite and subelite groups of Eastern Europe. By the mid-nineteen sixties it has pervaded the masses, creating not only feelings of ideological apathy and indifference, but also a general sense of venality and economic double-dealing. "Blat" (the Communist version of payoff, blackmail, and bribe) is endemic throughout the region, based on the well-articulated battle cry: "Let's work against the State!—Who cares if *they* (the authorities) are gypped," resulting in short working hours, tremendous absenteeism, stealing, and embezzling public funds. These creeping abuses are complete denials in practice of every basic tenet of Marxism-Leninism, and yet the Communist regimes accept them in silence, hoping to achieve by economic concessions an uneasy political truce. This process is particularly obvious in Kádár's Hungary and Gomulka's Poland where the regimes have literally attempted to buy by bribery and leniency at least the passive cooperation of a large sector of their reluctant populations. It must also be admitted that this skillful maneuver has enlarged the circle of those who now possess a vested interest in the maintenance and perpetuation of the Communist system.

The impact of nationalism has been historically an all-pervasive force on the Eastern European political stage. In recent years a significant renaissance of anti-Soviet, and frequently of anti-Communist, nationalism has occurred in two principal and important directions—political and cultural. These two aspects of nationalism have asserted themselves through the related media of expression of the state, religion, and language.

The "state" concept has been a historically deep-seated tradition in this area. It has been embodied in long successions of ruling elites which have possessed too many and too vital national roots to be simply suppressed (forever) by a Russian-dominated Communism. The ruling classes have created the "state," and in turn the "state" has produced the "nation" idea. Whether in its primary political manifestations, or in its more recent secondary economic implications, the individual Eastern European country's nation-concept is bound eventually to turn against Russian control and shake off this latter-day imperial domination as it did the Austro-Hungarian or Turkish overlordships.

This is the context in which religion and language emerge as significant divisive forces. The former has truly shaped the peculiar national identity of each country. It has had a particularly disruptive effect whenever the national group has been a submerged minority with a different religion from the one which ruled it. Thus we have seen Catholic Poles and Hungarians exposed to Orthodox Russians, Protestant East Germans under Orthodox Russians, Orthodox Rumanians in close contact with Hungarian Catholics. This characteristic substructure of "religious Balkanization" has then been immensely complicated by the superstructure of Communism, Sovietization, and Russian Orthodox predominance. Each major religion has gradually been forced to assume a posture, a policy line of its own vis-à-vis Soviet Communism. The broad spectrum of behavior patterns ranges from the heroic resistance of Cardinals Stepinac, Mindszenty, and Wyszynski (respectively in Yugoslavia, Hungary, and Poland), which can only be described as an open collision course between Communism and Catholicism, through the Jewish religion (on the whole, determined and skillful opposition complicated by pressures to make possible the mass exodus of remaining Jewish groups to Israel), to Protestantism (mixed behavior, with a genuine willingness to seek accommodation with Communism in such countries as Hungary, but with a satisfactory record in East Germany where both Lutheran and Calvinist ministers have shown exceptional determination and resistance to the Ulbricht regime in the face of a nearly hopeless local situation) all the way to the various *national* Orthodox churches (Rumania, Bulgaria) which have cooperated completely with their Communist governments as religious servants of a secular master. It is important to stress that nationally oriented churches have not been able to offer the resistance to Communism that truly international religious institutions were capable of providing. International Communism appeared most vulnerable when opposed by Catholicism or the forces of Zionism. Although religious instruction is now either suppressed or minimized in these countries on the national level, the churches—as international institutions—have been unwilling to yield ground to the ideological onslaught of Marxism-Leninism. Hence their significance as divisive and/or disruptive elements in the life of this former satellite zone.

The linguistic factor closely parallels the religious one as Greeks, Serbs, Croats, Slovenians, Bulgars, Magyars, *and Russians* today increasingly oppose each other in the Balkan-Danubian area. This linguistic differentiation, in turn, helps strengthen a Polish, Hungarian, or Rumanian national identity. Specifically, in recent years the Soviets' cultural drive toward Russification has been effectively decelerated with the closing of language schools and institutes, the downgrading of Soviet Friendship and Cultural Societies, the minimizing of Russian language instruction, and even the restrictions imposed in the broad field of Soviet-sponsored cultural exchange programs. Such a systematic de-Russification process has been most vigorously conducted in the non-Slavic linguistic cultural areas, as in Hungary and Rumania, but its residual impact has also been observable in such uneasy (and anti-Soviet) "neutral" borderlands as Finland and Austria. Bulgaria, Slavic and pro-Russian, finds itself at the other end of the scale, with Czechoslovakia and Poland occupying an in-between position.

Changing patterns of police terror and violence have certainly contributed to the strengthening and assertion of Eastern Europe's *centrifugal* political tendencies. The key fact has been a gradual diminution and decentralization of the terror and repression aspects of life under these Communist regimes. In this context the *New Course*, following Stalin's death in March 1953 brought about major and qualitative changes throughout the area. Ten to fifteen years later these slowly evolving patterns have begun to produce a different, and more relaxed, ideological environment and social atmosphere.[4]

One aspect of this complicated problem has been an increased emphasis on "socialist legality" in recent years. While it would be an exaggeration to talk in terms of the Communist regimes' observance of civil (human) rights, legal and court procedures are being far more carefully and meticulously handled than under Stalinism or in the immediate post-Stalinist (1953–1956) period. Various People's Courts, Komsomol (youth movement) courts and others now interpret "socialist law" in a less arbitrary and offensive manner. Within narrowly prescribed political limits, the practical application of legal principles has improved to the point where it can stand public scrutiny. By normal Western standards, of course, there is still an immense and often incomprehensible dichotomy between the theory of jurisprudence and its daily, administrative interpretation.

While *basic* coercion and violence patterns may not have altered in the past decade, the *visual* differences between the old, Stalinist police state era and today's post-Khrushchev period are indeed immense. The all-pervasive secret police apparatus has been de-emphasized and, following the Soviet pattern, reorganized, broken up into several administrative subgroupings and deprived of its more obvious repressive functions. Vigilance seems to have replaced open terror and brutal repression as police surveillance and innocuous city jails have gradually re-

---

[4] Albania, Bulgaria, and East Germany (the DDR) must immediately be excepted from this generalization; they have neither relaxed police terror, nor have they created a happier (or more acceptable) national atmosphere.

placed mass arrest, slave labor, and the concentration camp. The image of the secret police has been carefully transformed (especially in Poland and Hungary) so that they are no longer presented as organs of open persecution and brutality, but as agencies of prevention and "persuasive coercion"—occasionally referred to as "coercion with sugar coating." Each of the people's democracies has desperately tried to conceal, or even eliminate, the old manipulators of the purges and the handlers of the guillotine, impressing upon its captive society that the executioners' places have now been taken by friends and helpers of the populace. "Prevention instead of repression" has been promoted into a new theory, that of "social prophylaxis," in which police and security organs are primarily called upon to render cooperation and assistance to the various comrades' courts. In a presumably enlightened and restrained dictatorship a machinery "capable of coercing" is supposed to have replaced the bloody, unmitigated and active police terror so characteristic of the Stalinist system. Thus decentralized *potential* terror has gradually replaced direct mass application of violence: "administrative coercion," as a Soviet writer recently observed, "has yielded to an even greater extent to other forms of economic, political and moral action."

While the pattern has been more violent in such countries as the DDR, Albania, or Bulgaria (where one high official was forced to commit suicide in connection with an antigovernment conspiracy in the spring of 1965), the mass purges, the dreadful "voluntary confession," and the farcical but frightening show trials of the 1940s and 1950s have been conspicuously missing from the Eastern European political landscape of the 1960s.

Future Expectations for Eastern Europe

For the past few years the Soviet Union's former Eastern European satellites as well as Tito's Yugoslavia have been caught in two gigantic power struggles: the Sino-Soviet dispute and the Soviet-American Cold War. Despite their own quiescent attitudes, they have been embroiled in a "double-pincer" type of world political situation. In view of this potentially disastrous position their obvious and justifiable fear is that they will become the atomic battlefields of the near future, trapped—as so often in the past—by their hopeless buffer location between struggling giants. Khrushchev's "peaceful coexistence" theory has elicited immediate endorsement and genuine approval by the peoples of the Danubian-Balkan region. Khrushchev's thesis has been vastly preferred to the bloodthirsty Maoist assumption that almost all forms of war are both inevitable and desirable. After the Hitler and Stalin eras popular emotions of vengeance and mass malevolence are unimaginable; they have been replaced long ago by suspicion, fear and the deep-seated desire to be left alone. To this extent then Eastern Europeans fervently hope that the Soviet-promulgated doctrine of peaceful coexistence will prove to be ideologically durable and practical—in short, that it will be more than a purely tactical device of international Communism, but will eventually blossom into a serious strategic theory. "We must accept it," they keep stressing, because most of the other alternatives are "too dreadful to contemplate." Khrushchev's political demise in October 1964 has not affected this fervent popular hope for continued coexistence as a *permanent* line of Communist foreign policy.

Other important future attitudes of Eastern Europeans must also be stated here briefly: their increasing indifference to ideology combined with trends of economic unreliability and political instability as far as the Soviet Union is concerned. All three of these "mood-patterns" imply a growing spirit of defiance and independence among the area's future ruling elites. Gomulka's, Tito's, and Kádár's heirs will be much more difficult to control and keep in line ideologically than the current crop of aging Muscovites and run-down ex-Stalinists. Clearly, the once ambitious integration and annexation plans of the U.S.S.R. will be increasingly frustrated, contradicted, and deflated by indigenous future leaderships in the Danubian-Balkan region. As a great catalytic force, the phenomenon of *polycentrism* (by which we mean differing patterns of Communism adapted to the national conditions of individual countries) will further accelerate all these latent tendencies and speed up changes both in the U.S.S.R. and in its increasingly complex relations with the former satellites. The current search for autonomy will continue unabated, and the Eastern European peoples will be able to shore up their national positions vis-à-vis the declining power and hegemony of the Soviet Union with a growing measure of effectiveness.

At the same time the outer limits of such *centrifugal* polycentrism remain clear and observable in Eastern Europe. Unhappily for this vulnerable area, the goals of the U.S.S.R. have an aspect of permanence and constancy for the ex-satellites. While operational techniques and concrete policies may change and fluctuate, these changes—to use Marxist categories—are bound to be more quantitative than qualitative. There are set and tangible boundaries beyond which the existing and future leaderships of Eastern Europe's Communist societies will be incapable of progressing. Although short-term policies of "liberalization" and "humanization" are being widely heralded as harbingers of major and triumphant political transitions, in ideological terms the French axiom, "Plus ça change, plus c'est la même chose!" startlingly applies to a truly long-range perspective of Eastern European politics.

CHAPTER TWO

Poland

The General Setting

PERHAPS THE most striking characteristic of the thousand-year history of Poland has been the constant change of its borders, the Polish state shifting on the map of Europe from west to east and back again. In order to understand its present political problems, it is necessary to give at least a brief account of the primary conditioning factor of postwar Communist Poland, namely its new position on the European continent. Of equal significance is the background of Polish Communism examined in terms of Poland's historical relationship to Russia.

Poland on the Map of Europe

The results of World War II radically changed the external circumstances of Polish national existence. The Polish state—which in 1952 formally adopted the name of the Polish People's Republic—is by 20 percent smaller than its prewar predecessor. In the east, it lost 46.5 percent of its former area to the Soviet Union, but in the west it gained the major part of the former German province of East Prussia, the entire area of eastern Germany up to the rivers Oder and Western Neisse, as well as the city and environs of Szczecin on the western bank of the Oder. The new western border was determined by the July 1945 Potsdam Agreement of the three Great Powers which placed the territories detached from Germany "under the administration of the Polish state," reserving "the final delimitation" of the border to the future peace conference. While not recognized *de jure* by a number of Western powers, including the United States, the

23

Oder-Neisse line, which is regarded by the Polish and Communist-bloc governments as final, became a *de facto* international boundary.

Thus, while its center remained the same, the "new" Poland was moved approximately 130 miles westward, at the same time acquiring considerably shorter borders and a much longer seacoast with three major ports on the Baltic. The acquisition of the so-called Western Territories greatly increased the industrial potential of Poland which gained the major part of the great Silesian coal basin and other natural resources, as well as a highly developed industrial establishment which provided a solid foundation for changing the country into a modern industrialized state. With its 121,130 square miles (about the same size as New Mexico) Poland is the largest and definitely the most important state of Eastern Europe.

However significant, the geographical changes were more than overshadowed by the revolution which took place in the ethnographic, social, and economic structure of Polish society. For the first time in its modern history Poland became homogeneously Polish and Roman Catholic. In 1964 its population reached around 31 million and is constantly growing, its natural increase being among the highest on the European continent. Having achieved in the postwar period a sounder balance between industry and agriculture, the government embarked on a process of further industrialization. In its course, Poland progressively changed from a predominantly agricultural to an industrial society. The percentage of people depending for their livelihood on agriculture fell from 60 in 1931 to 38.7 in 1960; correspondingly the number of those dependent on industry rose by 1960 to well over 25 percent of the entire population. A direct consequence of this development was a sharp decline in the rural population which by 1962 represented only 51.9 percent of the nation as compared with 72.6 in 1931.

Background of Polish Communism

In their approach to the emergence of socialism, both Marx and Engels had nothing but scorn for the Russians and the Slavs of Austria-Hungary. Yet this general rejection of the Slavs had one exception, namely, the Poles. As a nation, they hardly fulfilled the Marxian recipe for a society prepared for a social revolution. The bulk of the population were peasants settled on land suffering from relative overpopulation and thus producing a special class of the so-called "rural semi-proletariat" characteristic of underdeveloped agrarian societies. The Poles did not have a sufficiently strong middle class; they were prevented from embarking on the course of bourgeois constitutionalism; and last but not least, their proletariat was small, had little organization, and practically no class consciousness.

The reasons for Marx's interest in the Poles, whom he set apart from the rest of the Slavs, were similar to those of the German liberals of 1848. Throughout the nineteenth century, the Poles were one of the most revolutionary nations, their rebelliousness being directed in the first place against Czarist despotism, generally regarded as the main enemy of all progress. As a result, they were supported not only by the German liberals—who regarded Young Poland as a sister of Young Germany—but also by Marx and Engels.

When in the last two decades of the nineteenth century organized socialism appeared in Poland, it was characterized by extraordinary heterodoxy of both form and substance. Those who conceived of socialism in terms of Polish patriotism were fiercely opposed by the protagonists of extreme internationalism who went so far as to deny the utility of an independent Polish nation. In the nineties this dualism, which in Poland was more fundamental than anywhere else, found its expression in the strife between the patriotic and militantly anti-Russian Socialist party, and the strictly Marxian and highly internationalist Social Democratic party of the Kingdom of Poland and Lithuania. Most of the time the Socialists retained the upper hand, mainly because of their appeal to Polish traditional nationalism. Only after the 1905 revolution—when the initial course of events in Russia seemed to justify their policies—did the Social Democrats, strengthened by left-wing Socialists and working hand in hand with their Russian comrades, seize the initiative.

The failure of constitutionalism, however, dealt a serious blow to the cause of socialism and particularly to the Social Democrats who lost the little contact they had with the masses and turned into a party of highly sophisticated and theorizing intellectuals. Despite their opposition to the "social patriots" in the Polish Socialist party, the representatives of Polish Marxism did not see eye to eye with Lenin, the foremost leader of the Socialist Left. Particularly significant were the many differences separating him from Rosa Luxemburg who, not without justification, regarded herself as a more uncompromising Marxist.

It was not surprising that Luxemburg soon found the circumstances of the Polish socialist movement too narrow for her lofty ideas and personal ambition. By the end of the century she acquired German citizenship, becoming a leading figure of the leftist faction of the German Social Democracy. She continued to wield a tremendous influence on developments within the Polish workers' movement, especially when, on December 16, 1918, the Communist Workers' party of Poland was founded. The new party found itself in conflict with the right-wing Socialists whose leader, Jozef Pilsudski, suddenly emerged as the most important personality of postwar Poland. With an unusual lack of psychological insight the Polish Communist leaders formulated their program in such a manner as to offend the innermost feelings of the Polish people. Following the "Luxemburgist" tradition, they displayed complete disregard for the newly won Polish independence; also, their dogmatic insistence on the collectivization of land could not endear the party to the peasants. Indeed, within less than one year the Communist party willingly accepted the status of illegality, preferring it to any action which might imply recognition of the "semi-feudal" Polish state.

Its attempt at organization of councils of workers' delegates and of Red Guards being unsuccessful, the party more and more began to rely on Soviet aid. This further alienated it from the Polish nation, which began to regard it as a foreign agent. It was in this role that during the 1920–1921 Soviet-Polish War the Polish Communists proceeded to the organization of a Provisional Revolutionary Council in the city of Bialostok. This abortive attempt destroyed the last chances of support for the party among the Polish part of the population, whose revulsion against Communism became identified with the centuries-old hostility between the Poles and the Russians. The internal life of the party, whose congresses had to meet on Russian soil, was characterized by constant squabbles, factionalism, and ideological conflicts. Within the Comintern it earned for itself the reputation of the *enfant terrible* of international Communism, suffering from two basic shortcomings which, especially in the period of Stalin, came to be regarded as the most dangerous deviations, namely those of "left-wing sectarianism" and "bourgeois nationalism."

Thus it was not surprising that the bloodbath into which the Soviet Union was thrown after the murder of Kirov soon affected prominent members of the Polish Communist party. During the Great Purge of 1937–1938 almost the entire leadership of the party, including men who were "invited" to Moscow from the Spanish battlefield, were summarily dealt with by the NKVD, some being physically liquidated, others sent to various forced labor camps. At the beginning of 1938 the party was dissolved by the Comintern because of its contamination by "agents of Polish fascism."

The 1939 attitude of the Kremlin toward Poland all but destroyed the last remnants of Communism in that country. Deprived of leadership and disillusioned in their Marxian faith, the few Communists who remained under German occupation succumbed to ideological confusion. Thus they took no part in the anti-Nazi resistance, its main burden being borne with great gallantry by the Polish Home Army, operating under the command of the exiled government in London. The confusion was aggravated by the behavior of the Kremlin which acted as if the Polish problem had been solved once and for all.

It was only after the Nazi attack against Russia that Stalin was forced to recognize the continued existence of Poland. Soon it became clear, however, that his understanding of a "strong and independent" Poland, to be established after the war, was entirely different from that of the London government-in-exile. When he realized that it would not accept his dictates, Stalin returned to the ideological approach, proceeding in January 1942 to the revival of the Polish Communist party. Its new name, the Polish Workers' party (henceforth referred to as PWP), could not easily improve the tarnished record of Communism. It was for this reason that the party took great pains to present itself as a spokesman for Polish nationalism and partisan of national unity. This to an even greater extent was true of the Union of Polish Patriots which was founded in March 1943 as a counter-weight of the London government.

As the Red Army advanced westward, the still very small group of Communists and their supporters continued to gain ground, especially after the May 1943 breaking off of diplomatic relations with the London government. Yet the average Pole retained his loyalty to his representatives in exile and to the underground Home Army. The people generally could not recognize the differences between the more nationalistic and conciliatory Communists and those who were fully subservient to Moscow. Indeed, when a member of the former "native group," Wladyslaw Gomulka, was elected the PWP Secretary General, the Communist party's unpopularity among the people remained unchanged.

At the end of 1943, the PWP created a National Council to act as a *de facto* government. In July 1944 the Council fused with the Patriots' Union, creating a Polish Committee of National Liberation which was given the name of Lublin Committee, after the Polish city in which it was established. There, the so-called July Manifesto was issued. This was a proclamation to the entire Polish nation, which carefully avoided anything that might hurt its national feelings and promised to rebuild the country on the basis of the "broad principles" of the 1921 democratic constitution. The tragic failure of the August 1944 Warsaw uprising, which clearly demonstrated the impotence of the London government, represented an important landmark in the Communist surge to power. Only at the end of the year was Warsaw taken by the Red Army. It was followed closely by the Lublin Committee which organized itself into the provisional government of Poland.

Whatever the intentions of the Western powers might have been, the decision reached at Yalta greatly enhanced the power and prestige of the Polish Communists. The government which they dominated was recognized as the sovereign power in Poland. The stipulation that this government be "reorganized on a broader democratic basis with the inclusion of democratic leaders from Poland and from Poles abroad," and that free elections be held as soon as possible, could hardly prevent the Sovietization of postwar Poland.

From Gomulka to Gomulka—Four Stages of Communist Poland

The political fortunes of Wladyslaw Gomulka, the third Secretary General of the Polish Workers' party, were closely associated with the postwar history of Poland, reflecting the four stages of its dramatic development. It was Gomulka who, after 1945, secured an absolute monopoly of power for the PWP, mercilessly crushing all its opponents. His 1948 elimination from party leadership inaugurated the period of Stalinism. The third stage was that of the "Thaw" which followed the death of the Soviet dictator and was characterized by a gradual return to some of Gomulka's ideas and practices. Finally, his October 1956 return to power started the fourth period of Polish Communism in which Gomulka again became the uncontested leader of the party and country.

POLISH COMMUNISM—1945–1954

While it was at the mercy of the Soviet Union, Poland only gradually assumed the characteristics of a Communist state. Its post-1945 development can be divided into two periods. The first, as noted above, started with the June 1945 formation of the Provisional Government of National Unity and ended at the time of the June 1948 purge of Gomulka. The subsequent second period of Stalinism lasted until the middle of 1954, when the repercussions of the death of the Soviet dictator began to affect the political atmosphere of Poland.

From the very beginning the Yalta idea that the Polish government could be broadened so as to include representatives of genuinely democratic political parties was doomed to failure. The only real opposition to the Communists came from the Polish Peasant party and its leader, Stanislaw Mikolajczyk. While First Vice-Premier and Minister of Agriculture, his position in the cabinet was that of isolation; he was faced with overwhelming odds which neither he nor anyone else would have been able to cope with. Even what should have been his greatest strength, namely his uncompromising stand against foreign intervention, was used with great skill against him and his party. Such intransigence, the Communists hinted, would have been an open challenge to Moscow which would, in such a case, incorporate Poland outright into the Soviet Union. In addition, the Communists blunted the arguments of their opponents by continued insistence on a special Polish way to the establishment of socialism, which would respect small and medium private property and require neither collectivization nor the creation of the dictatorship of the proletariat. The attack against the Catholic Church, the formidable spiritual opponent of Communism, was pursued with great caution, creating an impression that only its temporal activities were to be curtailed.

Yet the PWP would have had no chance of success, had it not been for absolute support from the Soviet Union, whose army was in firm control of Poland. Only thus was it possible for the Communists to retain all important levers of power in the government, adding to them the economically significant Ministry of Recovered Territories, headed by Gomulka, the PWP Secretary General and Vice-Premier of the government.

Whatever the program of the Communists might have been, in one respect at least, from the very beginning the regime's conduct blatantly belied its promises. Gomulka might have not spoken of the dictatorship of the proletariat, but nonetheless he was bent on the destruction of any political force which would be genuinely independent of the PWP. Mikolajczyk's party found itself opposed not only by the Communists but also by their socialist allies, as well as by a bogus Peasant party, set up under Communist sponsorship, and by the Democratic and Christian Labor parties, equally dominated by the PWP. After a cleverly devised referendum, rigged to embarrass the Polish Peasant party and create the impression of overwhelming support for the government, the regime proceeded to organize elections to demonstrate the impotence of the peasant opposition. In keeping with the order to win the election even before it was held, the Communists unfolded a wave of terror against the Polish Peasant party and its leaders. The responsibility for the acts of violence, as well as for the subsequent electoral fraud, must be ascribed to all PWP leaders, including Gomulka who, as early as July 1945 referred to Mikolajczyk as "a symbol of all anti-democratic elements, . . . the enemy of democracy and of the Soviet Union."

After the election, whose result proved to be a foregone conclusion, Poland quickly assumed the forms of a one-party totalitarian state. Pressing their victory to its logical conclusion, the Communists subjected the remnants of the Peasant party to systematic persecution, forcing its leaders, including Mikolajczyk, to escape to the West.

It was not surprising that in the "electoral" campaign the Communists appealed to the patriotic sentiments of the Polish people. The same Communist tactics were pursued as in the other Eastern European countries, nationalism having been abandoned immediately after victory was achieved. Gomulka, however, refused to accept the Stalinist version of proletarian internationalism, following what he regarded as an independent Polish road to socialism. He continued his resistance to collectivization, doubted the utility of the Cominform, and favored conciliation with Yugoslavia. While inadmissible from the point of view of the Russian dictator, these heresies were dwarfed by Gomulka's dangerous spirit of independence of judgment and action which predestined him to become the Polish victim of the Stalin-inspired wave of purges and trials in Eastern Europe. At the September 1948 meeting of the Central Committee of the party, Gomulka's colleagues, who until recently had supported his "special road to Communism" policies, turned against him and charged him with "rightist-nationalist" deviation.

It was only after much resistance that the Polish Communist leader accepted his guilt. Yet his recantation and its external setting were unique in the history of international Communism. The atmosphere of the meeting was more one of tacit resignation than of vindictive hatred. Threats were mingled with appeals and cajolery. Also, Gomulka's recantation was by no means in accord with the Stalinist recipe. Having pleaded guilty and admitted his "errors," the demoted leader of the PWP almost defiantly exclaimed, in reference to the Polish countryside, that "there must be some elements of a Polish road to socialism."

Even before Gomulka's final liquidation the fusion of the Socialist and Polish Workers' parties took place. The Unification Congress of December 1948 resulted in the foundation of the United Polish Workers' party (hereinafter referred to as the UPWP). While three socialist leaders, including Jozef Cyrankiewicz, were included in its 11-member Politbureau, they had no influence on its policies. The Ideological Declaration adopted at the Congress rejected the concept of a special Polish road to socialism and conformed entirely to the Stalinist interpretation of people's democracy as a different brand of the dictatorship of the proletariat.

Gomulka's fall was consummated only in November 1949 when he and his main accomplices lost all their party and government positions and were forbidden to participate in all party work. By then the party and the entire country were in the firm grip of Stalinism, which gradually penetrated into all spheres of public life. That Gomulka, who in 1951 was put under house arrest, escaped the tragic fate of Slánský, Rajk, or Kostov, can perhaps be best explained by the fact that his deviationism was originally shared by the majority of those who acted as his judges.

After Gomulka's elimination, the party changed its nature, assuming more and more the characteristics of its Soviet counterpart. Gomulka's role as the leading Communist was taken over by Boleslaw Bierut, the President of the Republic. This veteran had spent several years in Russia, which enabled him to read the mind of the Soviet dictator better than any other Polish Communist. While becoming the center of a personality cult similar to Stalin's, his position was definitely weaker than that of the other leaders of the Eastern European Communist parties. He shared his power with two other representatives of Polish Stalinism—the Deputy Premier, Jakub Berman, often referred to as the "gray eminence" of the regime, and Hilary Minc, an outstanding economist, who after 1949 held the position of Chairman of the State Planning Commission, dutifully emulating the Soviet example. The standing of Jozef Cyrankiewicz, the former socialist leader who greatly contributed to the liquidation of his own party, was of relatively minor significance, since he was overshadowed by the older members of the Politbureau. On the other hand, another relatively new member of that body, Stanislaw Radkiewicz, the Moscow-trained Minister of Public Security, became one of the most dreaded persons in Poland.

Under the new leadership the UPWP infiltrated into all governmental organs, dismissing the few non-Communists still remaining in influential positions. It took over direction of all nonparty organizations, changing them into tools of its policies. Above all, the party became the sole director of Polish economy. The Six-Year Plan inaugurated in 1950 emphasized the production of capital goods at the expense of consumer goods and pressed down the already pitiably low standard of living. Industrial workers were put into the straitjacket of Soviet discipline and methods, such as increased work quotas or "norms," longer working hours, lower wages, and other aspects of socialist competition.

Perhaps most characteristic of the period of Stalinism was the vicious campaign conducted by the regime against the two basic elements of Polish national life—the peasantry and the Roman Catholic Church. It was in the realm of agriculture that the party leadership encountered bitter peasant opposition which found expression in nonfulfilment of deliveries to the government, wholesale slaughter of cattle, and overconsumption. While forced to make a number of concessions, caused by the alarming decrease in total agricultural production, the party made no radical changes in its policy aiming at the "socialization" of the countryside. By 1953 the Six-Year Plan exceeded its goal in industry but in agriculture it remained 12 percent below its target.

The resistance of the Polish peasantry was basically instinctive. Compared to it, the opposition of the Roman Catholic Church was based on a solid organization and discipline combined with the political experience of the Catholic hierarchy. It was not surprising that the Communist government tried to avoid a head-on clash with so powerful an adversary, preferring to pursue a policy of "peaceful" coexistence. The victory of Stalinism, however, upset the rather precarious balance of power between the two basically incompatible antagonists. The onslaught against the church started with an aggressive campaign of atheism which was accompanied by constant interference with the religious instruction of children, aiming at the very heart of the Catholic position. Responding to this challenge, the Vatican issued, in July 1949 a decree excommunicating all Catholics who were members of the party or its willing tools. After this "provocation," the government took a whole sequence of measures seriously affecting the continued existence of the church. In this struggle the church found a fearless leader in the person of the new Polish Primate, Archbishop and later Cardinal, Stefan Wyszynski.

Realizing the danger of serious disturbances, the Polish Communists negotiated in April 1950 an agreement—modus vivendi —with the Polish Episcopate. As was to be expected, both parties made important concessions, but the fact that the Pope retained his spiritual authority was regarded as an important Roman Catholic gain. But soon it became obvious that the regime regarded the agreement as a mere maneuver, refusing to live up to its terms. In the decree of April 1953 the government, in direct violation of the 1950 agreement, usurped control over matters of ecclesiastical jurisdiction, reserving for itself the right to remove priests engaged in "anti-state" activities. The decree provided a basis for an all-out campaign against the church. A number of bishops were arrested, the circulation of the Catholic press greatly restricted, and the teaching of religion gradually eliminated from the schools. The struggle reached its climax in October 1953 when Cardinal Wyszynski was placed under arrest. Despite outward appearances, however, the regime proved unable to break the backbone of the church organization and, above all, to detach the Catholic clergy from its flocks.

Another distressing aspect of Stalinism was its attempt to dominate the intellectual and artistic life of Poland. Increased pressure on writers to conform to the required "socialist realism" and attempts at introducing rigid controls over all forms of artistic life subjected the representatives of Polish science and culture to constant humiliation and frequent persecution.

It was in this period that a consolidation of Soviet control over the life of the UPWP and the state took place. While the Kremlin reserved for itself the final decision on all major issues, the regime enjoyed considerable leeway in deciding on the tactics to be used in implementing policy. Of the different types of control, most important by far were those exercised over the Polish armed forces and organs of public security. The former were achieved through the appointment of Konstanty Rokossovsky, a Russified Pole, to the office of the Minister of National

Defense and his choice as a member of the party Politbureau. Even more pronounced was the Soviet influence in the security forces headed by Radkiewicz, the Soviet-trained protagonist of Stalinist ruthlessness.

Curiously enough, the practices of Stalinist terror survived by more than one year the personality with whom they were associated. The reason for this phenomenon must be sought in the strength and character of the UPWP. From a small political faction it had developed into a large elitist party. The monopoly of power, as well as their privileged position, prevented not only the leaders but also a considerable part of the rank and file of the party membership from realizing the extent of their isolation from the masses of the Polish nation.

POLAND AFTER STALIN

The existence of a gap between the party and the people was clearly revealed at the Second UPWP Congress in March 1954. Of the 1128 delegates, only 272 were workers and 108 were peasants, while well over 600 were party functionaries, state officials, and members of the intelligentsia, all holding the most important and best paid positions in the Polish state. It was not surprising that this most privileged "class" of the system was unprepared to make more significant concessions to the concept of the "New Course." Following the Soviet example, the "cult of the individual" was no doubt condemned and the principle of "collective leadership" accepted. As a result, the First Secretary of the party, Bierut, gave up his post of Prime Minister, being replaced by Jozef Cyrankiewicz. But apart from these external changes, only general promises of greater emphasis on the production of consumer goods and of more support for agriculture were the utmost limits to which the Polish Communist leaders were prepared to go.

Soon after the congress, however, all the accumulated injustices of the past decade filled the minds of the people and pushed the party into a defensive position. Believing that it might control the growing pressure for liberalization, the party leadership gave way to the reform movement. At the same time, it admitted past mistakes and promised to avoid them in the future. There followed a general debate in which, at first, the outstanding representatives of the Polish literary and artistic life participated. They attacked the senseless enforcement of "socialist realism"; but later the entire life of Polish society—its dreariness, hypocrisy, and harshness—was subjected to scathing criticism. The writers found enthusiastic supporters among young intellectuals and students whose Warsaw weekly, *Po prostu*, became the most effective and valiant fighter against Stalinism. Last but not least, the more courageous party members, who did not succumb to the demoralization characteristic of the period of Stalinism, declared themselves in favor of the reform movement. Finally, the UPWP leadership allowed the reopening of the discussion of the "Polish road to socialism."

The Twentieth CPSU Congress of February 1956 dispelled all doubts which might have still existed about the acceptability of a more independent policy of the Eastern European regimes and Communist parties. The most important result of the congress, Khrushchev's condemnation of Stalin, was to have much more significance in Poland than in the other countries of the area. As has been pointed out, ". . . for most Poles Stalinism and Communism were one and the same thing."[1] Thus not only the late dictator but also the whole system he represented were subjected to direct criticism. The fact that the congress declared the 1938 dissolution of the Polish Communist party and the liquidation of its leaders to have been based on false evidence tended to underline the failure of the Communist experiment. The death of Bierut, less than a month after the CPSU congress, and his replacement by Edward Ochab, a reformed Stalinist, paved the way for further changes in the organization and practices of the state and party. One of his first acts was the public announcement of the release of Gomulka (in reality he had been set free at the end of 1954) and his two associates, Spychalski and General Komar.

One after another, there followed new and more intensive expressions of a revival of political life. It was recognized that the *Sejm*—the traditional Polish parliament—which for years appeared to be nothing but a body of yes-men, should assume deliberative,

[1]M. K. Dziewanowski, *Communist Party of Poland, An Outline of History* (Cambridge: Harvard University Press, 1959), p. 258.

controlling, and even legislative functions. Radkiewicz was excluded both from the cabinet and the Politbureau, and repressive measures were taken against his former subordinates in the state security apparatus. In the beginning of May he was followed by Jacob Berman, one of the main representatives of Polish Stalinism. If not the officers, then at least the enlisted men of the wartime Home Army *(Armya krajowa)*, who until recently had been regarded as traitors, were fully rehabilitated. A new wave of more sophisticated and daring criticism developed among the writers, journalists, and in the ranks of the enthusiastic members of the young intelligentsia whose discussion clubs pursued a systematic political education of their members.

Yet, had they been restricted only to the members of the educated classes, the liberalization efforts would have had only a limited effect on the Polish nation. That this did not happen was due to the June 1956 strike and revolt of the Poznan workers. While protesting against low wages, shocking housing conditions, and other economic privations, these workers also demonstrated for more freedom.

At the meeting of the UPWP Central Committee soon after the Poznan uprising the whole issue came under careful scrutiny. Diehard Stalinists, led by Zenon Nowak, chose this conference for their counterattack, using the insurrection as a convenient pretext for demanding a return to ideological orthodoxy and political repression. Following the policy of their Soviet protectors, they attributed the Poznan events primarily to a conspiracy of foreign agents. After some hesitation, Ochab and Cyrankiewicz, who became the leaders of the reform faction, rejected this pat interpretation, admitting the fundamental justice of the workers' complaints and promising remedy. It was at this meeting that Gomulka, Spychalski, and Kliszko were formally rehabilitated and three new members selected for the Politbureau, all of them in favor of fundamental changes. It was significant for the internal conditions in the UPWP that both factions—the Stalinists (named the Natolin group after their meeting place in the outskirts of Warsaw) and the reform Pulawska faction (its headquarters were on Warsaw's Pulawska Street)—made an attempt to gain Gomulka for their side. Even after he decided to join forces with the latter, the contest remained in the balance.

Developments, however, favored the reformers, especially when Ochab, entirely abandoning his Stalinist past, threw his weight to their side.

The second half of 1956 was perhaps the most lively in the post-1945 history of Poland. Rightly or wrongly, the personality of Gomulka—the victim of Stalinism—became the symbol of the democratization movement. While drawing its strength largely from the non-Communist public, the reform faction operated within the framework of the party, which seemed unable to keep pace with the popular demands. The *Sejm* gained further importance and political independence; leading economists declared collectivization to be an obstacle to agricultural improvement; and meetings asking for further democratization continued to increase in number. Even more important was the emergence of workers' councils which were spontaneously elected by the workers, acting independently of the official trade unions and the government and claiming the right to participate in running individual enterprises. All these reforms—demonstrating the failure and collapse of the Stalinist economic policies—caused the resignation of the chief planner, Hilary Minc, the most significant opponent of Gomulka.

It was at this moment that the stage was set for the final showdown between the orthodox and reformist factions within the UPWP. The main reason for the success of the latter must be sought in the support it received from the great majority of the nation which—perhaps imprudently but definitely sincerely— believed in the possibility of major and far-reaching changes that could secure for Poland internal freedom and external independence.

THE OCTOBER 1956 REVOLT

The dramatic developments at the ninth plenary session of the Central Committee of the UPWP, which started on October nineteenth and lasted for three days, seemed to confirm the optimism of the Polish people. The fact that the leaders of the liberalizing faction disregarded the demands and threats of Khrushchev and other leading members of the CPSU, who arrived in Warsaw in order to prevent the expulsion of prominent pro-Soviet leaders from the Politbureau of the Polish Communist party, gave special satisfaction to the public. There were many factors which caused the Soviet leader to change his mind. Of these, three seemed to have been decisive. In the first place, the Polish "rebels" were not defenseless. Secondly, the Soviet leaders realized that disturbances in Poland might serve as a spark which would ignite the fires of smouldering rebellion in other parts of Eastern Europe. Last but not least, Khrushchev found what was more than a face-saving device in the realization that the new leadership of Poland, however insistent on internal independence, was composed of sincere and convinced Communists who recognized the necessity of a close Soviet-Polish alliance.

Thus within three days, Poland went through a bloodless revolution which reached its main goal on October 21st when a new Politbureau was elected. In it, the main representatives of Stalinist orthodoxy were missing; on the other hand, Gomulka assumed the leadership of the party, being elected its First Secretary. The majority of the people regarded his return as a victory of both Polish nationalism and the cause of further liberalization. The memory of his postwar militant Communism seemed to have been entirely wiped out by his 1948 revolt against Stalinism and subsequent imprisonment which earned him the admiration of the nation.

Gomulka's triumph opened a new phase in the history of postwar Poland. In its wake came a number of significant changes in the party, government, and nonparty organizations. The decrease of Soviet influence was demonstrated by the replacement of the Defense Minister, Constantin Rokossovsky, by Gomulka's associate, General Spychalski, and the dismissal of over 30 Russian high officers who acted as "advisors" in the Polish army. Gomulka insisted on the democratization of the party and the entire public life of the country. Having suggested that inefficient "producers cooperatives" be dissolved, the new leader encouraged a development which in less than three months brought about the total collapse of Polish collectivization. The promise of support for the newly created workers' councils raised the hopes of industrial workers for full participation in the management of individual enterprises.

More significant—because of their moral and national implications—were two other measures taken by the Gomulka regime. The release of Cardinal-Primate, Stefan Wyszynski, and of other members of the Catholic hierarchy from arrest, and the subsequent conclusion of a modus vivendi between the state 'and church were regarded as the most tangible results of the October revolt. Especially were the reintroduction of religious instruction in schools and the reduction of governmental control over church appointments generally acclaimed as indications of a genuine change of heart on the part of the UPWP. The second step which increased the prestige of Gomulka's regime concerned the new relationship of Poland to the Soviet Union. The leader of the party proudly proclaimed the universal validity of the principle of different roads to socialism, adding that "the model of socialism can also vary." While he emphasized the feeling of friendship of the Polish people for the Soviet Union, he sought its basis in the recognition of the "principles of equality and independence." Indicative of the continued close association between the two parties and states was the November 1956 military and economic agreement which formally respected the sovereignty of Poland.

THE AFTERMATH OF THE OCTOBER REVOLT

The general enthusiasm for the new regime prevented the public from noticing a few significant facts, whose importance was realized only when reflected against Gomulka's subsequent policies. As early as the first days of the "glorious" October period, the new leader of Polish Communism insisted on the party's monopoly of power, warned against "hesitant" elements in the ranks of the intelligentsia, and clearly dissociated himself from the most advanced members of the liberal faction. Instead of giving support to the liberals, Gomulka diplomatically assumed the position of the center, opposing both the dogmatism of the Natolin group and the extremist tendencies of the reformers.

Soon after the January 1957 elections, which resulted in a vote of confidence in Gomulka, a gradual retreat from the 1956 policies of liberalization started. While continuing their attacks against the Stalinist dogmatists, Gomulka and his faction stepped up their onslaught against the liberals, now termed "revisionists" and declared to be the greatest danger for the party and the regime.

Also, the workers' councils, another achievement of the Polish October, were strictly subordinated to the party, deprived of all political power, and expressly denied the right of ownership of the individual factories in which they operated. In October 1957 the mainstay of Communist liberalism, the weekly *Po prostu*, was banned because of its "nihilistic and deviationist tendencies."

A large number of causes and factors combined first to arrest and then to reverse the trend toward liberalization which gained Poland the sympathy and respect of the free world.

One of the key issues was the behavior of the intellectuals who, in the opinion of the party leaders, abandoned the tenets of Marxism-Leninism and succumbed to pseudoliberalism, in reality serving the interests of the bourgeoisie. Their conviction was greatly strengthened by the defection in the spring of 1958 of Colonel Pawel Monat to the United States. Having served as military attaché in Peking and Washington, he possessed confidential military and intelligence information that was highly embarrassing to the Polish government. The fact that Monat was a product of the October 1956 upheaval reaffirmed Gomulka's mistrust of the revisionist intellectuals and caused him to harden both the political and the cultural policies of his regime. Thus, beginning with 1958, the Polish intellectuals were forced into a defensive position. The changed atmosphere made itself felt in the meetings of the organizations of Polish writers, journalists, and scientists who were urged by the representatives of the party to pay more attention to the interests of the Communist regime. While used more sparingly than in other Communist societies, "administrative" measures were applied several times against those who exceeded the limits prescribed by the party. The passive resistance of the intellectuals against the ever-increasing pressure was broken in March 1964 when 34 leaders of Polish cultural and scientific life submitted a letter of protest to Premier Cyrankiewicz. In it, they criticized the cultural policies of the government, protesting particularly against the tightening of censorship practices and insisting on the preservation of the constitutionally guaranteed freedom of expression. The regime responded by repressive actions against some of the signers of the protest, changing its attitude only because of the unfavorable publicity abroad. Later in 1964, one of the signers, Melchior Wankiewicz, an outstanding author and a naturalized American who returned to Poland in 1958, was sentenced by a Warsaw court for slandering the Polish state, to 18 months of imprisonment.[2] While the charges on which he was convicted had nothing to do with the March protest, his case provided further evidence of the increased tempo of the whittling away of the 1956 freedoms.

Also the attempt at far-reaching economic reforms, made after the return of Gomulka, failed to bring about the expected results. The "Polish Economic Model," prepared in 1957 by a new organ, the Economic Council, aimed at a drastic reorganization of the administration and management of the national economy. However, a number of factors combined to prevent the Council from putting the major part of its reforms into effect. Influenced by the 1958 Monat incident and using the economic crisis of that year as a pretext, Gomulka accepted the advice of those who favored a return to conservative economic practices. In theory, Polish economists continued to discuss and develop the economic model as envisaged by the Council, but in practice traditional views of centralized administrative direction prevailed. The Council gradually lost all its influence and in 1963 was officially abolished. At the same time, the workers' councils were deprived of their role as organs of workers' self-government. They were merged with the party committees and trade union works' councils of the individual enterprises into so-called Workers' Self-Government Conferences which, in practice, came entirely under the control of the management and the party.

The return to orthodox policies failed to save Poland from the problem of the rapidly growing population. The necessity to create new jobs for hundreds of thousands of new workers was made more difficult by economic mismanagement resulting in what the regime termed "overemployment" and "overstaffing," the solution of which was sought in mass dismissals of workers and officials. In the beginning of the sixties, the country was swept by a whole series of strikes (which, again, were declared illegal) and other indications of labor unrest. It was not surprising that the 1964 and 1965 meetings of the party organs were almost entirely devoted to the economy. Most recently, some of the formerly rejected proposals of the economic revisionists, particularly those relating to the decentralization and democratization

[2] The Polish government, however, did not dare to put the sentence into effect.

of national economy, were gradually rediscovered and accepted by the party and government.

Another area in which a progressive withdrawal from the October 1956 ideals took place was that of church-state relations. At first, there was mutual toleration and even harmony. This reconciliation, however, was by no means complete. The Gomulka government took no action against Piasecki, the self-styled leader of the pro-Communist *Pax* movement. Also, the largest church welfare organization, *Caritas*, which in 1950 was placed under state control, was not returned. Equally significant was the continuation of the so-called "Patriot Priests" movement, willingly collaborating with the regime.

After the 1958 tightening of controls, the approach to religion hardened. The Communist government used its powers to the full, not shrinking from violations of the 1956 modus vivendi with the Roman Catholic Church. The conflict centered around a number of problems, of which religious education and taxation of church property were the most important.

Fearful of church influence over the youth, the government first introduced far-reaching limitations on religious education in schools. Then such education was removed from public schools altogether, and finally an oppressive and troublesome system of controls was introduced over its exercise in churches and other religious buildings. Beginning with 1959, a new fiscal policy was initiated, subjecting the income of the clergy, as well as churches and a whole variety of religious and church institutions, to full taxation. The fact that the taxes were not always exacted, or were arbitrarily fixed, tended to act as a thinly veiled act of blackmail destined to keep the church in line, representing "a kind of Sword of Damocles, which, though normally suspended in mid-air, might descend on selected victims at any time."[3]

Despite this ever increasing pressure, the Polish Episcopate headed by Cardinal Wyszynski refused to be cowed into submission. Characteristic of his defiance was his statement made after the 1961 elections. Speaking of what he called "inner" freedom, he declared:

. . . a political system can build streets and factories, but it cannot administer in the same way human consciences. There exist moral

[3] Richard Hiscocks, *Poland Bridge for an Abys?* (London: Oxford University Press, 1963), p. 302.

values which have nothing to do with political systems, and that exist independently of regimes and pressures. . . .

The tacit recognition of the fundamental truth of Wyszynski's words and the realization of their special validity in Poland prevented the Communist regime from doing away with all the post-1956 privileges of Polish Catholicism.

The most significant departure from the spirit of the Polish October was the dramatic transformation which took place within the UPWP. No doubt the external circumstances of Polish national existence—particularly the country's geographical position and the apparent necessity of Soviet aid for the defense of its western territories—impeded further extension of the liberalization trend. Yet the 1957 reversal of the policies of liberalization cannot be explained by external factors alone. Its reason must be sought also in the personality of the Polish leader himself. His intellectual background, his mentality of a party functionary, as well as his essentially Communist outlook, prevented him from understanding the abstract ideas of freedom propagated by the "liberals" and the "revisionists." It was only in order "to save Polish Communism from its own excesses" that Gomulka made use of these unwanted allies. Nor did he entirely associate himself with the "Pulawska" group of prewar Communists, but made a bid for the support of some of his former enemies of the dogmatic "Natolin" group, striking a balance between the two factions. While substantially weakened at the Second UPWP Congress, the dogmatists continued to play a relatively important role. After the Monat affair, however, Gomulka proceeded, in October 1959 and after, to a radical shake-up of the party and government, appointing former Stalinists to more important functions and forcing the last representatives of the liberalizing wing of the UPWP to resign.

By the end of 1962 the dormant political group of those who were members of the Communist resistance against German occupation—usually referred to as the "Partisan" group—began to emerge as an influential factor in Polish national life. By inclination they stood nearer to the Stalinists, being in favor of more energetic antichurch policies, more stringent controls over the intellectuals, and an authoritarian approach to the building of Polish Communism. At the Third UPWP Congress, held in

June 1964, Gomulka managed to uphold his position of leadership and secure the unity of the party, but only after having made significant concessions to the more radical factions. At the end of this same year the Partisans scored further important gains. As a result, the 12-member Politbureau—while still firmly in the hands of the pro-Gomulka group—at present includes two "hardliners" with definitely Stalinist pasts and one representative of the Partisan group. What was perhaps most important was the appointment of the leader of this faction, F. Moczar, to the office of the Ministry of the Interior.

There is no doubt that some gains of the initial Gomulka period have remained. After some hesitation the idea of the Soviet-type collectives was definitely abandoned. The Church, while under constant harassment, has been able to uphold its independence and is much better off than the Churches of the other East Central European states. Finally, Polish Communism has secured a relatively high degree of independence and respect in return for the recognition of Soviet leadership. Apart from these three characteristics, there is little that distinguishes the Gomulka regime from that of the other Communist states of the area. The spirit of optimism of the "Polish October" is gone; Gomulka lost much, if not all, of his glamor as an indomitable fighter against oppressive Stalinism, and a general *malaise* took hold of Polish society which simply cannot accept the fact that "a better and freer life," has been dissipated and replaced by the rigors of an autocratic and at times aggressive regime.

Polish Political and Governmental System

THE UPWP—ITS STRUCTURE AND LEADERSHIP

While relatively significant in the international Communist movement, the Polish party has never achieved popularity in its own country. Both its leadership and its rank and file have been painfully conscious of the fact that the overwhelming majority of the people regard them as a foreign element in the national life. Thus, when the events of 1943 brought about the creation of the new Polish Workers' party, the chances of its success among the masses were negligible. As in the past, it was closely associated with Russia, for which the Poles had feelings of continued hostility. Attempts to "Polonize" the party, such as the adoption of a new name, which left out the word "Communist," and the recruitment of allies from among the members of the radical fringes of the socialist and peasant movements, did little to change the opinion of an average Pole.

Even the leaders of the party, and above all its third Secretary General, Wladyslaw Gomulka, knew that without Russian aid and the use of fellow-traveling opportunists they could never assume a decisive position in the nation. Compared to the majority of Eastern European Communist parties, the PWP, which at the beginning of 1945 had only 20,000 members, was ill-equipped for taking control over the country. It was in sore need of party cadres and lacked reliable trained personnel to perform even the most essential governmental functions.

The re-establishment of the external governmental framework was much easier than the building of the PWP. Despite the intensive recruitment campaign, for a long time the party remained smaller than the Socialists. In December 1948, although substantially weakened, the Socialists brought into the new United Polish Workers' party administrative and organizational talent, enabling it better to fulfill its role of leadership of the state. At the same time, the party membership swelled to over 1,500,000.

The new party displayed two striking defects of which it has been unable to rid itself to the present day. The first was the lack of internal unity that resulted in the continued purges, intrigues, and factionalism. This caused an immense turnover in party membership, which steadily declined after 1948, sinking after Gomulka's verification campaign to less than 1,100,000 in March 1959. It took the UPWP almost 16 years before it managed to exceed its 1948 size by 68,000 members. In reality, however, the party is still considerably weaker than it was at the time of its founding, having dropped from 6.1 to 5 percent of the greatly increased Polish population.

Equally serious is the second perennial defect of the UPWP, namely, the "incorrect" social composition of its membership. Instead of consisting predominantly of workers and peasants, the party's backbone is the intelligentsia. Another shortcoming of the party, which partly explains its slow growth, is its inability to attract young people. This is particularly true of the university students for whom the "conflict of generations" is nothing but a convenient pretext for not joining the ranks.

In the period of Stalinism the party apparatus grew out of all proportion to its size, soon succumbing to rigid bureaucratization. As in other states of Eastern Europe, the party bureaucracy developed into a privileged class separated from the nation both by its beliefs and behavior, and by the comforts of life which it enjoyed. The leadership of the UPWP, however, was not sufficiently cohesive or conformist to be able to maintain unity under the attack to which it was exposed after the Twentieth CPSU Congress. It was this lack of solidarity, as well as "the spark of independence, sometimes carefully camouflaged by outward servility,"[4] that provided the impetus to the movement which brought Gomulka back to power. In his first speech the reinstated leader of Polish Communism promised a far-reaching democratization of the party, particularly insisting on the introduction of "adequate control by Party bodies over the Party apparatus." Viewed from the vantage point of an almost ten-year development, Gomulka's efforts to infuse more responsibility into the life of the party bureaucracy remained largely unsuccessful. While many of the excesses of the past were eliminated, the mentality of the party "bosses" did not change.

There is little that would distinguish the UPWP organizational structure from that of other Communist parties. The party is divided into five tiers organized on the basis of a combination of territorial and functional principles. The former corresponds to the administrative divisions of the country; the latter, which is determined by the place of employment of the party members, is especially important on the lowest organizational level—in the primary party units. These may be of three types: functional, when they are composed of members working in factories, mines, governmental agencies, etc.; village, when they serve the population of rural areas; and territorial, for the urban population not organized in production units. The territorial village organizations assume special importance in view of the fact that the Agricultural Circles, described as Poland's substitute for collective farming, cannot be used for strictly party purposes.

The central organs of the party fulfill the same tasks as their

[4] Dziewanowski, *op. cit.*, p. 256.

counterparts in other Communist societies. This is particularly true of the party congresses which since 1943 have met altogether five times—in 1945, 1948, 1954, 1959, and 1964. The rubber-stamp nature of these allegedly supreme party gatherings explains why internal factionalism, which is characteristic of the UPWP, did not make itself felt at any of the congresses. The same cannot be said of the Central Committee in which the first steps leading to the "glorious" October were taken, setting an example to the still divided Politbureau. The decisive role, however, of the Central Committee was closely associated with the short-lived period of Communist "liberalism." The abandonment of the 1956 policies was accompanied by a decrease in the influence of the Central Committee as a truly independent body, its importance being derived from the hard core of its members holding important positions in the party and government. Even so, membership in this body is sufficiently significant to serve as an indication of the relative strength of the individual party factions.

The uncontested master of the country is the 12-member Political Bureau of the Central Committee. Controlled by Wladyslaw Gomulka, it is predominantly composed of his most intimate associates—men like Marian Spychalski or Zenon Kliszko—who shared his fate during the Stalinist persecution; those who combined with him in the 1956 internal revolt, such as Edward Ochab; and the less influential former socialists, Cyrankiewicz and Rapacki. The lack of unity which characterized the past history of Polish Communism underlined the importance of the party apparatus as a cohesive force within the UPWP. While in the central and regional secretariats of the party close adherents of Gomulka predominate, within the broader framework of the apparatus, including the subordinate party level, adherents of different groups, and especially the Stalinist one, can be found. Yet it is the personality and the great political skill of Gomulka which represent perhaps the most powerful unifying factor of the Polish Communist movement. He has long ceased to be a mere symbol—as he was in 1956—and has become an energetic and resourceful leader insisting on internal discipline and absolute political monopoly for the party whose interest, in his mind, is and must be the sole criterion of all issues and actions.

The effectiveness of Gomulka's leadership is greatly enhanced by the fact that the majority of his subleaders in the Politbureau and the Central Committee secretariat possess a number of almost identical characteristics, such as those of age, class background, educational standards, and most importantly, political career and experience. It is from this point of view that the 1964 admission of two former Stalinists and one representative of the Partisan group into the Political Bureau should be viewed. These changes could not have taken place without the approval of Gomulka whose control over the party remains supreme. Despite its consolidation, however, the UPWP has been unable to gain popularity among the people.

Perhaps the most eloquent expression of the difficulties of Polish Communism has been its attempt to create a genuine mass youth movement. Despite its more than two million members, the pre-1956 Union of Polish Youth came to be regarded as the personification of the evils of Stalinism. It was not surprising that this monopolistic organization fell apart when the edifice of Polish Stalinism disintegrated. Young people, especially those gathered around the weekly *Po prostu* and those associated in the numerous youth clubs throughout the country, became the most energetic supporters of the liberalization movement. Failing to grasp the realities of the situation, at first they called for absolute associational freedom, accepting only grudgingly the "advice" of the party leaders that there would be only two youth organizations—the Union of Socialist Youth in the cities and industrial centers, and the Rural Youth Union in the Polish countryside. While considered quasipolitical, both unions were declared to be socialist organizations engaged "under the leadership of the UPWP" in the struggle against the hostile forces of capitalism and in the concrete tasks of building socialism.

The new associations, whose close subordination to the party was highly reminiscent of the detested Union of Polish Youth, caused great disappointment in the ranks of young people who hoped for more autonomous, ideologically inclusive, and more imaginative youth groups. To this day the two unions have failed to achieve a membership comparable to that of the pre-1956 organization.

Nor can the regime draw any consolation from the fact that

the Polish Students' Union has been able to incorporate almost 80 percent of all students. Membership can be regarded as compulsory, having become the main test of the sociopolitical attitude which is decisive for the granting of scholarships. In December 1962 a high party functionary severely criticized the behavior of the students, many of whom have been unable to understand "that only conformity of personal efforts with national objectives can open the way for the development of their talents and abilities."

As pointed out by Zbigniew Jordan, the main characteristic of Polish youth, whose hopes for a new and better order remain unfulfilled, is the "ideology of withdrawal" expressed by loss of interest in public affairs and internal emigration which can be found in all modern autocratic societies. Even more evident is this new ideology in the youngest generation which has nothing but scorn for the hypocritical world of the adults.

NON-COMMUNIST "PARTIES" AND NON-PARTY ORGANIZATIONS

The aura of "pluralism" in the otherwise streamlined political system of Poland is provided by a huge number of political and social organizations which, it is held, represent the interests of different groups of the population. Despite their political importance, none of these organizations—including the non-Communist parties—can be regarded as pursuing independent policies of their own. In an overwhelmingly non-Communist country, they serve as an indispensable instrument by which the regime transmits its policies to the masses, propagandizes for their acceptance, and controls their execution. Organizationally these groups follow a pattern similar to that of the UPWP, their hierarchical structure being based on the territorial divisions of the country with national headquarters located in the state's capital. The most important political and social associations are grouped in the so-called Front of National Unity and its central, regional, and local committees. Designed to symbolize the idea of national solidarity, its main purpose is to serve the regime's electoral organization. The Front prepares one single electoral platform, selects the condidates, and lends its name to the single list which is submitted to the electorate.

Whatever the size, significance, and aims of the individual members of the National Unity Front may be, their *raison d'être* from the Communist point of view is always the same—to act as auxiliaries of the Communist party. This is also true of the two non-Communist political parties—the United Peasant party and the Democratic party. As early as the end of 1956 Gomulka rejected the concept of genuine opposition parties and emphasized that "freedom for all political parties also means freedom for the bourgeois parties." The post-1958 retreat from the liberalization policies gradually reduced the non-Communist parties to absolute subservience to the Communist regime.

Yet, even to this day, the size and scope of activities of the Polish non-Communist parties are definitely much larger than those of their counterparts in the other Eastern European states. For in Poland, the existence of more than one party is a necessity stemming from the overall weakness of the UPWP which alone would be unable to provide for the smooth functioning of the complex structure of a Communist society. Of particular importance is the aid which it receives from the United Peasant party whose 322,000 members organized in 23,000 circles are an important political factor. Of similar, though much smaller, significance is the Democratic party which represents the members of the intelligentsia, artisans, and small businessmen. Despite their relatively large representation in the *Sejm*, Council of State, and in the central and local organs of governments, the two non-Communist groups cannot be regarded as parties in the Western sense of the term. Having no choice but to support the UPWP's effort in the building of socialism, they provide no real alternative to the voter.

Apart from political parties and youth organizations, the National Unity Front includes a number of mass associations. Of these the most important and definitely most numerous are the trade unions with a membership of almost 7 million from a labor force of over 8 million. However, they have little in common with a true workers' union, being controlled by the government and pursuing policies determined by the UPWP leadership. There are many other associations, such as the huge Women's League, the Polish-Soviet Friendship Society, the Union of Fighters for Freedom and Democracy, and a host of social and professional groups which, although not directly affiliated with the Front, must be regarded as auxiliaries of the government in the execution both of its long-range programs and immediate tasks.

A special type of professional organizations are the peasant Agricultural Circles which after 1959 became the main vehicle of the regime's agricultural policies. The aim of these centers, which are portrayed as the continuation of the traditional prewar farmers cooperatives, has been described as follows:

> The Agricultural Circle is a voluntary, universal, socio-economic peasant organization rallying the peasants for work on development and improvement of agricultural production through the coordination of individual efforts by mutual aid and collaboration.

At first destined to serve as a transition to collective farming, this new approach to organizing agriculture has assumed all the characteristics of a permanent approach to the "socialization of the countryside." Even so, the acceptance by the Polish farmers of the Agricultural Circles has been less than enthusiastic. By the end of 1963 only about one-fifth of the farmers were members and approximately one-third of all villages had no Agricultural Circles.

Our listing of major social organizations did not include the Catholic Church, potentially the most powerful group speaking on behalf of the majority of the Poles. For the Catholic hierarchy has consistently refused to accept the ideological leadership of the UPWP. The tenuous balance of power between these two mighty competitors bears witness to the political significance of Polish Catholicism of which the Warsaw regime is so painfully aware. As in other Eastern European states, the regime has attempted to weaken, or at least to neutralize, the influence of the church. The support which it granted to the *Pax* and the Christian Social Associations, not to speak of the abortive attempts to organize pro-Communist "Patriot Priests," ended in dismal failure. In its endeavor to establish at least some degree of contact with the Catholic masses, the regime recognized a group of Catholic intellectuals known as *Znak* (Sign). Despite its at times critical attitude toward the regime's policies, *Znak* was admitted into the National Unity Front and granted parliamentary representation. Its policies are based on a peculiar blend of unreserved Catholicism and anti-Marxism with a firm belief in the necessity of practical cooperation and even accommodation between the Communists and Catholics. One might wonder why the Communist regime tolerates a handful of men who have the courage to oppose and even publicly criticize certain of its policies, at the same time claiming to speak for "millions of people in Poland" and expressing their views and demands to the UPWP. The answer to this question can be hardly unequivocal. It may be a tacit recognition of the relevancy of the Catholic point of view in an overwhelmingly Catholic country. It may, on the other hand, be an ingenious maneuver of the party to blunt Catholic opposition. Whatever the real answer may be, *Znak* represents a unique phenomenon in the Communist world and, as pointed out by one observer, "may well be likened to a barometer, registering the direction of political pressures in Gomulka's Poland."[5]

CONSTITUTION AND GOVERNMENT

For almost seven years after "liberation," the formal political basis of the Polish Republic was a series of documents whose mutual relationship was unclear and open to different interpretations. Pro-Soviet leaders insisted on the continued validity of the liberal-democratic constitution of March 1921 and used it as a weapon against the "reactionary" government in London. Once in power, however, they lost most of their interest in this democratic document. Thus, in the famous Manifesto of July 21 1944, the two revolutionary organs—the National Council of the Homeland and the Committee of National Liberation—were enjoined to act only "on the basis" of the 1921 constitution whose "fundamental principles" were declared to remain in force until the adoption of a new constitutional charter. These principles were never spelled out, the organs of Communist revolution being free to take measures conflicting with the fundamental assumptions of the constitution. This was particularly true of the decree relating to the creation and organization on all administrative levels of a net of National Councils and conferring on the highly unrepresentative and essentially self-

[5] Adam Bromke, "The 'Znak' Group in Poland," *East Europe*, Vol. 11, No. 2 (February, 1962), p. 15.

appointed National Council of the Homeland the standing of the traditional national parliament—the *Sejm*; of similar significance was the decree establishing within this body a Soviet-type presidium. Also the legislative measures introducing land reform and the nationalization of key industries, enacted in 1944 and 1946, lacked constitutional sanction. The same could be said of a number of other decrees, not only in the realm of criminal but even of private law. Thus the so-called "Little Criminal Code" of November 1946 added new offenses and increased penalties for existing ones, all in order to provide adequate protection for state and public property. Equally important from the political point of view was the new regulation of family law which dissociated marriage from all confessional ties, passed as early as September 1945. Last but not least, a whole series of decrees, the first going back to July 1944 created different police and state security organs.

After the "election" of January 1947 Poland's Constituent *Sejm* proceeded to a number of legislative measures seemingly introducing order into the legal system and returning to some of the Polish constitutional traditions. The provisional "little constitution" of February 19, 1947, re-established the traditional office of the President of the Republic, determined the powers of the legislature, provided for a Supreme Auditing Board, and declared the principle of the independence of the courts. At the same time, however, this same document included provisions indicating continued development toward Soviet constitutional patterns. It adopted, at least in part, the Communist concept of the unity of powers. This trend was best illustrated by the powers and organization of the newly created State Council which was nothing but a modified Soviet Presidium headed by the President of the Republic. While it did not act as a collective head of state, this new body combined both legislative and executive functions. The most serious shortcoming of the "little constitution," however, was the absence of a bill of rights; it was omitted at the insistence of the Communists who refused to accept a traditional Western democratic list of the rights and duties of citizens. Instead, the *Sejm* adopted a mere declaration which—while unanimously voted—was not legally binding.

The constitution did not prevent further introduction of Soviet institutions and administrative practices, representing little more than a "decorative fig-leaf on Poland's developing totalitarium structure."[6] While some of its "alterations" were in change of emphasis, others were outright extraconstitutional. Thus the State Council arrogated for itself the power to issue executive orders (not mentioned in the constitution), becoming the most important organ of government, especially in matters of local administration. Within the cabinet a new institution emerged—the Presidium of the Council of Ministers—based on the Soviet example. Perhaps most important was the law of March 1950 regulating the greatly increased powers of the National Councils. The executive bodies—the presidia—of the National Councils were subjected to the control of their own council and to that of the presidia of the next higher level of local government, and through them to the organs of the central government. During the almost five and one-half years of the "provisional constitution," a large number of legislative measures were taken, adapting the legal, economic, and cultural life of Poland to the Soviet model.

The uncertainty and vagueness of the constitutional system was perfectly suited to a policy of gradual Sovietization. Thus the Constitution of the Polish People's Republic of July 22, 1952, by which the country finally acquired the status of a "People's Democracy," was fundamentally a summary of the achievements of the regime. While basically similar to the other People's Democratic constitutions, it represented evident progress in emulating the Soviet example. Both the preamble and the first article clearly express the class nature of the People's Republic. In it the power belongs not to the people, but to the "working people of town and country." The role of the state is to secure the interests, as well as the material and cultural growth, of the working people, at the same time carrying on a relentless struggle against "those classes of society which live by exploiting the workers and farmers."

The tripartite system of economy, characteristic of all people's democracies, has been blurred by the omission of the concept of private property. The state recognizes and protects three types of ownership: state property, especially socialized industry; individual property of land and other means of production belonging

[6] Dziewanowski, *op. cit.*, p. 229.

to farmers, draftsmen, and persons engaged in domestic handi-crafts; and, finally, personal property. As in the entire Eastern European area, ownership of land in production cooperatives—the Polish version of the Soviet collectives—remains at least nom-inally in the hands of the individual cooperative members. The fact that protection of the individual property of the peasants is not declared to be unlimited but is "recognized and protected on the basis of existing legislation" seems to confirm the assump-tion that, at the time of its promulgation, the constitution envis-aged possible compulsory collectivization. This danger has been averted since the 1956 collapse of the collective farms and the new emphasis on Agricultural Circles.

The 1952 constitution is based on the concept of a unified and centralized state power which includes not only the legislative, but also the controlling and executive functions. The totality of this power is vested in the unicameral *Sejm* which, theoretically speaking, is the focus of all governmental activity. Its powers, while similar to those of other parliaments, include the passage of national economic plans and the election of the members of the 15-member Council of State. Unlike its provisional predeces-sor, the new Council of State is endowed with powers practically identical with those of the Soviet Presidium. It is an executive organ, serving as the collective head of state and controlling the local People's Councils; it has the right to issue decrees with the force of law and to legislate during the intervals between sessions of the *Sejm*; finally it exercises judicial powers, being responsible for universally binding interpretation of laws.

In Poland, as in other Communist systems, the most impor-tant function of the greatly expanded government is the direc-tion of national economy, particularly the preparation of eco-nomic plans and the supervision of their execution. The com-petence of the Council of Ministers, the supreme executive and administrative authority, is rather broad and includes powers of a definitely legislative nature. In its relation to the *Sejm*, the position of the Premier and his government seems to be the same as in all parliamentary systems.

Also in the organization of local government the 1952 con-stitution follows the example of the Russian Soviets. In keeping with the principle of unified state power, there is, theoretically speaking, no distinction between the central and local organs of government. The latter are represented by the formerly revolutionary National Councils which are organized territorially on four different levels—provinces, counties, municipalities, and urban and rural communes. Under the supreme control of the Council of State, each exercises all functions of government within its own jurisdiction. The executive organs of the National Councils are the locally elected presidia whose officials act on behalf of both the local and the central government.

There is little that would distinguish Poland's basic law on the administration of justice from that of other Communist societies. The judges, who are both lay and professional, lack the usual guarantees of independence in the exercise of their function, being assimilated into the civil service. They are denied not only the right of judicial review but also forbidden to question the validity of governmental decrees and ordinances. Last but not least, the list of fundamental rights and duties of citizens is almost an exact copy of the list in the Soviet constitution; it includes far-reaching economic rights as well as a general indication of the means by which the state is to provide for implementing them.

The main purpose of the Polish constitution is to provide as broad a framework as possible for the transformation of society —the elimination of the exploiting classes, the combatting of bourgeois-capitalist practices, and the positive construction of socialism. Thus, like other Communist basic laws, that of Poland fails to give even a remotely accurate picture of the governmental and political organization of the country. The actual bearer of sovereign power within the Polish state, the UPWP, and the principle of democratic centralism which guides all party and state activities, are not even mentioned. And yet it is the party which decides on the composition, organization, and work of all governmental organs. The legislative committees of the *Sejm*, which include non-Communist deputies, might have been able, in the period following October 1956, "to make a positive contribution to government" and even force the party to make meaningful "concessions"; but the parliament as such has been unable to rid itself of the deadening effect of Communist conformity. The same is true of other constitutional organs whose members, with the exception of those who hold important party positions, are experts and not politicians. They are limited at best to decision-making, the actual shaping of policies being the prerogative of the Communist party.

Typical of the unreality of the 1952 constitution are its vague provisions relating to the principles of electoral law. The pre-1956 totalitarian type of voting, introduced by the constitution, became evident only from the provisions of the electoral law which adopted the Soviet type of voting practices. While nominated by "mass social organizations of the working people," the candidates ran on the single list of the National Front with only one candidate for each seat in the *Sejm*. The National Front was dominated by the UPWP which unilaterally decided also on the nomination of "reliable" Peasant party, Democratic party, as well as non-party, candidates.

The situation changed after the October 1956 revolt. While Gomulka's promise "to enable people to elect not merely to vote" remained unfulfilled, Poland introduced an electoral system unique in the Soviet bloc. It retained the single National Front ticket but the candidates appearing on the ballots in the individual districts were allowed to exceed by two-thirds the number of seats to be filled. Voters were permitted to express their preference for certain candidates by deleting names of others from the ballot. In the January 1957 election there were 750 candidates of whom only one-half ran as members of the UPWP, the rest being divided between the two non-Communist parties and nonparty candidates. In view of the fact that only 459 candidates could be elected, there seemed to exist at least a theoretical possibility of a Communist defeat. That this did not happen was due to the popularity of Gomulka, who managed to secure the support even of the Catholic Church, and to a number of other technical reasons which rendered a Communist defeat practically impossible.

In the two subsequent elections, in 1961 and May 1965, the UPWP could no longer rely on the popularity of its leader. The 1961 change of the electoral law in favor of the Communist party alone can hardly explain the surprising "stability" of Polish political life. The almost identical results of the 1961 and 1965 elections give credence to a suspicion that the distribution of seats originated rather in a quota agreement than in a genuine electoral contest. The nature of the election is best revealed by the fact that a large part, if not the majority, of voters make no

use of the facilities for secret balloting. The Poles themselves
have realized the artificiality of their elections, referring to them
as "consent elections" organized for the purpose of registering
approval with the Communist party policies.

The inclusion of Poland in the Soviet bloc gave rise to a legal
development which to this day has not been entirely terminated.
This, of course, does not mean that the Warsaw regime lacked
energy in its endeavor to secure the legal foundations of its new
economic and social order. There is no dearth of new laws
relating to the organization of public security, the administration
of justice, and those necessary for the establishment of the socialist state. Also, the regime adopted uncompromisingly the traditional Communist approach to law, subordinating it to the general line and immediate needs of the UPWP. Speaking at the
Third Party Congress, Wladyslaw Gomulka referred to the
"struggle for the establishment of socialist justice and legality"
and the necessity of a "further adjustment of the existing legislation to the needs of the Polish state."

Gomulka's words bear witness to a unique characteristic of the
legislation of People's Poland. Despite their insistence on the
necessity of change, the Polish legislators proceeded with great
caution in the replacement of the prewar statutes and regulations. More than any other state of Eastern Europe, Poland
endeavored to maintain some degree of continuity with the past.
As a result, the building of socialist law took place only gradually, large segments of the prewar legal system being retained.
This is still true of certain parts of the Criminal Code and the
Code of Criminal Procedure, as well as a host of other politically
less important statutes. The 1960 Code of Administrative Procedure, while entirely new, has retained a number of characteristics of the old law. The same can be said of the 1964 Civil
Code which in many respects shows traces of conservative legal
thinking.

Facing the Future

With a grave risk of oversimplification one may venture the
following diagnosis of the future political development of the
Polish People's Republic.

1. There are overriding external political circumstances which determine the policies of the Warsaw regime. The Polish Communists suffer from political schizophrenia which causes them to pursue a strictly pro-Soviet course, while at the same time they gravitate toward their traditional Western associations. Polish nationalism is as strong as ever; but its effect on Polish behavior cannot but underline the duality of the political orientation of the country. While less conspicuous, anti-Russianism has not disappeared, but its weight is increasingly counterbalanced by recognition of Russian military strength as a shield against German endeavors to regain territories lost after World War II.

Another factor which tends to underline Polish dependence on the Soviet Union is of an economic nature. For some of its main resources—particularly iron ore and oil—the new industrialized Poland is largely dependent on its great eastern neighbor.

2. While the atmosphere of the "Polish October" is gone, a return to the crude methods of Stalinist oppression is no longer a possibility. The effect of the post-1958 "recompression" is, above all, of a psychological nature, creating a feeling of despair and hopelessness, especially among the youth. This sentiment is further aggravated by more frequent recourse to "administrative and organizational measures" by which the Communists are trying to bring the fundamentally hostile population into line with their policies. For the forces of anti-Communism—particularly the Catholic Church and the peasantry—have not given up their opposition. Yet only resort to a policy of outright violence could change the fundamentally cautious and realistic policy of the Polish people, bringing about the repetition of the 1956 events.

3. Gomulka has been able to mould the UPWP into a more potent instrument of power than it was in the past. However, the two main defects of Polish Communism have not been eliminated. The UPWP still suffers from an incorrect social structure, since almost 50 percent of its members are members of the intelligentsia. More significant is the continuation of the internal feud within the party, clearly expressed by the sudden decrease in the power of the Interior Minister, Mieczyslaw Moczar, one of the leaders of the Partisan group. The transfer of the military security forces from his Ministry to that of the Ministry of National Defence was a serious weakening of his political

position. It is clear that more than ever the future stability of the Polish Communist regime depends on the continued leadership and vitality of the First Party Secretary, Wladyslaw Gomulka.

BIBLIOGRAPHICAL NOTE

Books mentioned in this short selective list are divided into four broad categories, dealing with the postwar Sovietization of Poland, the political and social transformation during the period of Stalinism, the October 1956 revolt, and finally books describing the political and social aspects of the regime of Wladyslaw Gomulka. The first category is represented by Arthur Bliss Lane's *I Saw Poland Betrayed* (Indianapolis: Bobbs-Merrill, 1948), concerned with the effects of the catastrophe that befell Poland in the closing days of the war and after, and Stanislaw's Mikolajczyk's *The Pattern of Soviet Domination* (London: Sampson Low, Marston, 1948), describing his unsuccessful attempt to prevent the Sovietization of his country. Of special interest is Stefan Korbonski's *Warsaw in Chains* (New York: Macmillan, 1959). It reflects the views of those Polish Peasant party members who spent the war years in Poland.

There are three works which provide a good analysis of the changes and internal convulsions in the six years of Stalinism. Particularly important is the excellent study by Adam B. Ulam, *Titoism and the Cominform* (Cambridge: Harvard University Press, 1952), partly devoted to the discussion of the 1948–1949 demotion and humiliation of Wladyslaw Gomulka. Another outstanding volume is by Czeslaw Milosz, *The Captive Mind* (New York: Knopf, 1955), analyzing the complex process which brought a part of the Polish intelligentsia into the service of Stalinism. A more methodical consideration of the political and constitutional system of the pre-1956 period can be found in *Poland*, edited by Oscar Halecki (New York: Praeger, 1957).

There is a large number of publications examining the 1956 "glorious October" revolt. Flora Lewis analyzes the internal development which led to Gomulka's reinstatement in *A Case History of Hope: The Story of Poland's Peaceful Revolution* (Garden City: Doubleday, 1958). S. L. Schneiderman's *The Warsaw Heresy* (New York: Horizon Press, 1959), and Frank Gibney's *Frozen Revolution* (New York: Farrar, Straus & Cudahy, 1959) note the changes which began to appear in Gomulka's policy of national conciliation.

Publications providing surveys of the post-1944 developments, as well as discussions of the most recent phase of the Gomulka regime include Richard E. Staar's *Poland 1944–1962: The Sovietization of a Captive People* (New Orleans: Louisiana State University Press, 1962), and Richard Hiscocks' *Poland: Bridge for an Abyss?* (London: Oxford University Press, 1963). Another important source for understanding the past and present policies of Communist Poland is Marian K. Dziewanowski's *The Communist Party of Poland: An Outline of History* (Cambridge: Harvard University Press, 1959). Andrzej Korbonski's *Politics of Socialist Agriculture in Poland: 1945–1960* (New York: Columbia University Press, 1965) analyzes the changes in the agricultural policies of the Communist regime.

Among the more valuable recent articles are John M. Montias' "Communist Rule in Eastern Europe," *Foreign Affairs* (January, 1965), and K. A. Jelenski's "Poland," in Walter Laqueur and Leopold Labedz's *Polycentrism* (New York: Praeger, 1962). The most important periodicals carrying articles on the countries covered in this book are: *The American Slavic and East European Journal, Current History, East Europe, The Polish Review, The Slavic Review, Survey, World Politics, Problems of Communism,* and *The Hungarian Quarterly.*

CHAPTER THREE

Czechoslovakia

The General Setting

AMONG THE many factors influencing the emergence and nature of Communist Czechoslovakia, two played a decisive role. One was the geopolitical position of the country in the center of Europe; the other was the highly developed social and economic system of prewar Czechoslovakia which made it the most suitable testing ground for the teachings of Karl Marx.

GEOPOLITICAL POSITION

By its size and number of inhabitants the Czechoslovak Socialist Republic (CSSR) ranks among the smaller Eastern European states, its territory comprising 49,354 square miles, or little more than the size of North Carolina. It consists of the two western Czech provinces—Bohemia and Moravia-Silesia—and Slovakia, which forms the eastern part of the country. The province of Ruthenia, which belonged to prewar Czechoslovakia, was ceded to the Soviet Union in June 1945. As of December 1964, the Republic had well over 14 million people; more than 9 million (65.9 percent) are Czechs and roughly 4 million (28.6 percent) Slovaks, the rest being divided among the four national minority groups of which the Hungarians in southern Slovakia are the most numerous (3.8 percent). Following the Potsdam Agreement the once large German minority has been reduced by transfer, mainly to West Germany, to less than 150,000. The most significant aspect of the population movement between the 1950 and the March 1961 official census has been the much greater vitality of the Slovaks than that of the Czechs. The natural increase of the former amounted to 18.4 percent, whereas that of the latter only to 8.2 percent.

Czechoslovakia inherited from the past a relatively well balanced and highly developed economy, having acquired the largest part of the industry of the former Austro-Hungarian empire. After its inclusion in the Soviet political and economic orbit in 1948, its planned economy continued the process of further industrialization, paying little attention to agricultural production. By 1960 around 52 percent of the population was employed in industry, building, and transport, whereas only 26 percent worked in agriculture and forestry. As a result the economy lost its former equilibrium, developing a number of fundamental imbalances. The striking increase in industrial output was vitiated by an almost catastrophic decline in agricultural production which was aggravated by the collectivization drive along the lines of the Soviet model. The second imbalance consisted in the lopsided stress on the output of producer goods. This was done at the expense of consumer goods, including those which in the past had represented the bulk of Czechoslovak exports and had secured for the country the hard currencies necessary to maintain its rather high standard of living. This development was accompanied by a gradual foreign trade reorientation, Czechoslovakia becoming one of the most important suppliers of heavy industrial goods in the Communist orbit. Apart from its unprofitable deliveries to certain developing countries, within the framework of the Communist foreign aid program, Czechoslovakia lost almost all of its remunerative Western and overseas economic contacts.

More important than its industrial potential was Czechoslovakia's strategic position of a wedge driven from the western borders of Russia to a distance of almost 500 miles into the heart of the European continent. In the atmosphere of a peaceful and cooperative Europe it was predestined—as believed by many Western observers—to play the role of a bridge between the East and the West. The postwar aggressiveness of Stalinist Russia, which aimed at the Sovietization of the European continent, demonstrated the unrealistic nature of the Czechoslovak attempt to live in peace both with the Soviet Union and the Western powers. Thus, instead of serving as a bridge between the two worlds, Czechoslovakia was changed into a Soviet Communist bridgehead into Western Europe.

That this was the use that Stalin was determined to make of Czechoslovakia was clearly demonstrated by the February 1948 *coup d'état* which ended the tragic postwar period of Czechoslovak democracy. The aim of this fundamentally violent action was more than to assert the revolutionary character of the Communist party, to prevent an election in which it was certain to suffer serious losses, or to satisfy the radicalism of its more extreme wing. For Stalin, who ordered the Communist seizure of power, the main purpose of the establishment of the dictatorship of the proletariat in Czechoslovakia was to protect and secure an important outpost for the Soviet Union and international Communism in the center of Europe.

MARXISM-LENINISM ON TRIAL

In 1918, when the Czechoslovak Republic came into being, there was a marked difference between its eastern and western provinces. Slovakia was almost entirely agricultural and less developed from the sociological point of view. The western part of the Republic had features typical of the European West—a large and specialized industrial establishment, intensive and relatively mechanized agriculture, and an advanced degree of urbanization.

Hand in hand with industrialization, which started as early as the first decades of the nineteenth century, came the process of social and political differentiation which in the Czech lands developed along patterns very similar to those of Western Europe. At the end of the seventies Marxian socialism penetrated into the area, reaching its zenith with the emergence of a strong Social Democratic party in the 1907 election. During the post-1918 twenty years of independence Slovakia was also exposed to the influence of Western political thought and practice so that by 1938 the entire country had developed both sociologically and politically into a Western type of society.

Thus the classical Marxian pattern of economic and social development, which was absent in 1917 Russia, and to a greater or lesser extent in practically all the states which after 1945 came under the sway of Soviet Communism, was present in Czechoslovakia. Having distorted some of the basic tenets of Marxism, Lenin claimed that Russia was ripe for a socialist revolution; but he recognized the supremacy of the Western proletariat—particularly that of Germany—declaring it to be better equipped for the creation of a socialist society. But not until 1945 was Communism to prevail within the sphere of Western civilization. When this happened, conditions which accompanied the Nazi defeat and the general feeling of hatred against the Germans prevented East Germany from being considered for the role which, in the early years of the Bolshevik revolution, Lenin had assigned to the German nation. Thus Czechoslovakia was the first country which seemed to provide a propitious workshop for testing the economic and political tenets of Marxism. The existence of large-scale industry and masses of class-conscious proletarians was accompanied by experience in modern constitutionalism of which the middle class was the main representative. All this pointed to the possibility of a more independent and imaginative approach to the building of socialism than in the agricultural and sociologically more backward countries of Eastern Europe.

Compared with other Communist parties of this area, the party of Czechoslovakia (henceforth referred to as CPCS) had a number of definite advantages. As in practically all democratic countries of the West, it was allowed to operate legally. Absence of persecution, while detrimental to the revolutionary spirit of the party, proved extremely beneficial from the point of view of its size and internal organization. In the last parliamentary election of 1935 the CPCS, which included all the nationalities of the Republic, received 10.3 percent of all votes. After 1945, during the period of Soviet occupation, it was the most influential participant in the postwar government; as a result of the May 1946 election, in which the party received almost 38 percent of the popular vote, its Chairman, Klement Gottwald, became Prime Minister. When the Communists seized power, they seemed to lack the main disadvantages that stood in the way of other Eastern European Communist parties. The CPCS leadership had almost three years of practical governmental experience; it could make use of the majority of the civil servants who had no choice but to work for the new regime; above all, it had at its disposal numerous, well-trained cadres capable of putting into effect the individual stages of progressive communization.

Whatever the economic, sociological, and political conditions of its previous existence might have been, the CPCS failed as an original interpreter of scientific socialism. During the more than 16 years of its rule, it developed no new theoretical concepts or formulations, nor did it contribute to the practical application of Marxist doctrine. Its leadership proved incapable of independent thinking, soon establishing for their country the unenviable record of having the most slavish imitation of the political patterns and governmental forms of the Soviet Union. It was no accident that until the second half of 1962 Prague had one of the largest and ugliest statues of Stalin; rather the statue was symbolic of the character of Czechoslovak Communism.

From Gottwald to Novotný

There are two highlights in the development of Communist Czechoslovakia—the 1948 seizure of power, and the adoption of the July 1960 constitution by which Czechoslovakia became the second European state to have achieved the more advanced stage of social development, namely that of socialism. The history of this period is largely connected with the personalities of the three Presidents, Klement Gottwald, Antonín Zápotocký, and Antonín Novotný. While by no means independent agents, and receiving direct orders from the CPCS and its representatives on all major issues, their leadership is associated with different phases of the economic and political development of the country.

POLICIES OF STALINISM—TOEING THE MOSCOW LINE

Having within six fatal days in February 1948 achieved an absolute monopoly of power, the CPCS proceeded with great determination to lay the foundations of a "socialist" society. On this at times tortuous path it was to be guided by the shining example of the Soviet Union. The first months of the new regime were marked by the repressive activities of the Action Committees which were created for the avowed purpose of putting into effect the Communist revolution. It was in this period that the first thorough purge of the administrative apparatus took place and that all existing institutions and organizations were changed into agencies of the Communist government. The tragic and mysterious death of the Foreign Minister, Jan Masaryk, the resignation and subsequent death of President Edward Beneš—all within less than six months—marked the end of an era that had been closely associated with these two names. The democratic and tolerant leadership of the prewar republic was replaced by men who approached their task from the point of view of the doctrine of class struggle.

Unlike other European Communist parties, including some of the smallest and least important ones, the Czechoslovak party possessed no outstanding political figures. Its history was marked by indecision, internal strife, and above all, lack of revolutionary spirit. This last shortcoming was characteristic even of Klement Gottwald, the leader of the radical wing, who did little to infuse a spirit of militant bolshevism into the party policies. Whatever may be said of his initial postwar intentions—and there is reason to believe that he envisaged an evolutionary development toward socialism—he lacked both the will and strength of character to oppose the dictates of the Kremlin.

In his 1948 surge to power Gottwald was accompanied by two men who, at least on the surface of things, differed in their general approach and political tactics. Rudolf Slánský, a prewar close associate of Gottwald, was a taciturn, calculating, and highly doctrinaire individual whose ambition was matched only by that of Gottwald. He was second to none in his emulation of Stalin, being generally regarded as one of the symbols of subservience to Moscow. When Gottwald became Party Chairman, Slánský succeeded him as Secretary General, clearly using his position to the detriment of his predecessor. Antonín Zápotocký seemed to be made of different stuff than his two colleagues. He displayed qualities rarely found among Communist leaders—a good sense of humor, understanding for the man in the street, and at times even a degree of humility. He ranked third in the hierarchy, his actual power stemming from his chairmanship of the powerful Revolutionary Trade Union Movement which played a decisive role in the 1948 coup. After Gottwald's elevation to the presidency, Zápotocký became Prime Minister. It was in this period that he proved that his "human" qualities were more apparent than real.

The picture of Communist leadership would remain incomplete without mentioning at least the most important subleaders. In Czechoslovakia, perhaps more than in other Communist countries, a distinction could be drawn between fanatical demagogues, such as the Propaganda Minister, Václav Kopecký, or the Slovak Communist party leader, Viliam Siroký, and the more suave and sophisticated men like Jaromír Dolanský (First Deputy Premier) or Vlado Clementis, the highly cultured successor of Jan Masaryk in the office of the Foreign Minister.

The 1948 victory—accompanied as it was by the sharing of spoils—helped to bring about a temporary halt to internal party feuds. For some time it seemed as if the Communist leaders themselves failed to see the true meaning of the revolutionary process they had instigated. Thus the first Moscow-ordered revision of membership in the autumn of 1948 was generally welcomed as purging the party of the hundreds of thousands of opportunists who had decided to jump on the bandwagon. Only in the spring of 1949 did the full impact of Stalinism make itself felt, finding its expression in the revival of old rivalries, such as that between Gottwald and Slánský, and in the complete surrender of the Communist moderates who became mere cogs in the Stalinist totalitarian setup. This explains the silence, and therefore complicity, of such men as Dolanský and Clementis in the wholesale imprisonment of innocent people and in the death penalties meted out to the group headed by Milada Horáková, accused of high treason. The second purge, closely following the March 1950 dismissal of Clementis, took place in an atmosphere of terror. When it ended, in February 1961, a number of outstanding party members, such as Clementis, Šling, Švermová, and others, were behind bars awaiting trial. At the end of the year they were joined by Rudolf Slánský, until then the second most powerful Czechoslovak Communist.

It is difficult, if not impossible, to fathom all the causes of the November 1952 spectacular trial which sent Rudolf Slánský, Vlado Clementis and nine other men to the gallows. No doubt the trial was only a part of the methodical bloodletting in the entire Communist orbit, ordered by Stalin and his cohorts. But only the MVD and the Czechoslovak secret police records could reveal what criteria were employed in selecting the culprits, determining what their crimes were, and in deciding on punishments to be meted out. No doubt certain facts seemed to prejudge the general direction of the purge. There was tension between Gottwald and Slánský; Clementis displayed "embarrassing" tendencies toward Slovak patriotism; the leading positions of some of the victims in the country's economy made them liable to charges of economic sabotage. Yet the horrendous and absolutely unbelievable charges levelled against the accused, the dramatic staging of the trial, the abject confessions, and the Vishinsky type of prosecution—all this was clear-cut evidence of Soviet masterminding of the entire proceedings.

Sweeping through the highest party circles and exacting the lives and freedom of thousands of people, the purge was a traumatic experience for the CPCS and the entire nation. Gottwald would have welcomed demotion and punishment for his opponents; what happened, however, went far beyond his expectations and set an ominous precedent for himself and all those who survived. Thus, stricken with panic and fearful for its life, the entire party leadership soiled its hands, becoming closely associated with Stalin and his crimes. One might add that the purging of one group of leaders paved the path to success for those who managed to survive. It was no accident that after the demotion of Slánský, the star of Antonín Novotný, his subordinate and a typical *apparatchik* began to rise. By the end of 1953 Novotný, the man destined to become the third leader of Communist Czechoslovakia, was both member of the Organizational Secretariat and the party's Central Committee Presidium.

Of equal significance was the influence of the trial on the entire nation. Having created an atmosphere of witch-hunting, it changed the country into a paradise for informers, and gave the final seal to the cult of Stalin and his Czech apprentice, Klement Gottwald. The events of 1952 had a deadening effect on the population and accelerated the development toward totalitarian uniformity. Delivering the party into the hands of the *apparatchiki*, the trial emphasized the existence of a rift between the party and the rest of society. These facts explain why the opportunity, created by the almost simultaneous deaths of Stalin and Gottwald, for gradual liberalization of the system, remained unused. The new President, Zápotocký, assisted, if not actively then at least passively, in the draconic and Stalinist destruction of the anti-Communist elements and then of the Slánský-Clementis group. Having sold himself entirely to the system which brought him to power, he lost whatever moral fibre he might have possessed. Moreover, he no longer controlled the party apparatus which came into the hands of the new First Secretary, Antonín Novotný, one of the main artisans of the 1952 purge. Novotný found a faithful follower in Viliam Široký, the new Premier, whose rise to prominence was closely associated with the application of Stalinist methods in his native Slovakia.

Surprisingly enough, the fall of Stalin tended to work in favor of the continuation of his heritage in Czechoslovakia. It lent additional importance to the principle of internal unity which alone, the Communist leaders realized, could save them from disaster. The strong and highly disciplined group of secretaries and other beneficiaries of the regime closed ranks, accepting with gratification the new principle of collective leadership. It was, however, the consciousness of collective guilt, rather than political or personal loyalty, that became the foundation of the strength of the post-Stalin CPCS. The country's tragedy lay in the lack of a Communist dissenter, all the leading party members being almost insolubly bound together by the weight of their responsibility.

At first the effects of the post-Stalin "Thaw" remained almost unnoticeable in Czechoslovakia. Indeed, the regime felt strong enough to admit its financial bankruptcy by proceeding, in June 1953, to a financial reform which resulted in wholesale impoverishment of the major part of the nation. The fact that at least in certain parts of the country, namely in the industrial center of Pilsen, violent anti-Communist riots occurred, was a tribute to the perseverance of the democratic opposition which dared to revolt against a totalitarian regime whose determination and vitality remained unimpaired. No doubt the atmosphere of the "Thaw" also forced the government to a number of reforms which, however, were limited to what was regarded as absolutely necessary. Thus, for some time more emphasis was laid on the production of consumer goods, concessions were made to independent peasants, and the trend toward collectivization was mildly reversed. Believing these new "reforms" to be only a temporary deviation, the Communist leaders refused to risk a policy of genuine concessions which, in the past, had almost inevitably sounded the death knell for tyrannical regimes.

Much more significant for the CPCS were the repercussions of Khrushchev's violent attack against Stalin in 1956. Far from succumbing to panic, the CPCS leadership maintained its customary unity, proceeding to what might be described as a mild but well-organized retreat. Having conceded mistakes committed by the Soviet dictator, Novotný laid the emphasis on Stalin's "positive role" in Communist history. In discussing Gottwald's role as Stalin's Prague representative, Novotný obliquely condemned the "cult of the individual," but at the same time pointed his accusing finger against the entire Central Committee. Then, almost as if on second thought, he dismissed from all government and party functions A. Čepická, Minister of National Defense and Gottwald's son-in-law. This arbitrarily picked victim was the only "Stalinist" to lose his position before the developments of the early sixties.

Even this partial admission of guilt—accompanied as it was by some relaxation of terror—revived the forces of opposition, especially among young intellectuals. The Second Writers Congress and the traditional student May festivities (Majales) took place in an atmosphere of rebellion against the Communist stranglehold over the cultural life of the country.

Alarmed over the possible consequences of more lenient and conciliatory measures, the Communist leaders decided to reverse the gears of the liberalization process and return to a policy of threats, intimidation, and repression. Paying lip service to the slogans against the cult of the individual, the party gradually assumed its old Stalinist form and substance, emphasizing that any opposition from any quarter would be mercilessly broken. As a result, the Polish "October" and the Hungarian revolt left the CPCS well prepared for any emergency, relying in the last analysis on Soviet bayonets. Indeed, the Hungarian events strengthened Novotný's belief in the correctness of his orthodox and dogmatist stand. Thus the years 1956–1960 saw a progressive stiffening of the party line and the reintroduction of the practices of Stalinism. When President Zápotocký died, in November 1957, he was succeeded by the colorless First Secretary of the party who—like Gottwald—managed to keep in his own hands the top party and state posts. Under his guidance Czechoslovakia gained the reputation of being one of the most dogmatic and uncompromising Communist regimes of Eastern Europe.

Despite its absolute power, Czechoslovak neo-Stalinism was engaged in a constant struggle against revisionism, liberalism, and even "utopian" socialism—vices to which a large part of the intelligentsia, including some who belonged to the CPCS, had a tendency to succumb. Special attention was paid to Slovakia which gradually emerged as a center not only of revisionism but also of "bourgeois nationalism." An interminable succession of well advertized trials for espionage, treason, antistate activity, and sabotage lent reality to the regime's threats, serving at the same time as an instrument of relentless class warfare against the remnants of the bourgeois-capitalist system.

It was in this climate of fear that Czechoslovakia made giant strides on its path toward "Socialism." By the end of the fifties independent enterprises in services, small trade, and small-scale building were liquidated, their former owners being branded as class enemies. Also, the legal and practically the entire medical profession were socialized. The transfer of privately owned apartment houses to the state completed the suppression of the "exploiter elements" in the cities. In the countryside "voluntary" collectivization was pursued with great energy, being accompanied by a merciless struggle against the "village exploiter," the *kulak*. The termination of collectivization, together with the final liquidation of the antagonistic classes, became the coveted goal; its attainment would signal the advent of socialism. This stage was reached in April 1960, when the party published the draft of a new constitution in which it was stated that Czechoslovakia had reached the stage of full-fledged socialism. The draft was submitted to the people for nationwide discussion, approved by a specially convened party conference at the beginning of July, and finally "unanimously" passed by the newly elected National Assembly, on July 11, 1960.

THE COMMUNIST PARTY AND NONPARTY ORGANIZATIONS

After February 1948 the CPCS in many respects still differed from its model, the CPSU. In the past it had operated within the framework of a democratic system of government, competing with other political parties and endeavoring to increase its membership. Instead of weeding out unreliable members, who had found their way into the party in the turbulent postwar years, the Czechoslovak Communists continued their campaign of indiscriminate recruiting. By October 1948 the CPCS had around two and one-half million members, becoming one of the largest Communist parties outside the Soviet Union. Despite a whole series of subsequent purges which decreased the total membership by approximately one million, to this day it serves in the entire Communist world as a typical example of the application of the non-Leninist concept of a large party.

While subservient followers of Stalinist Russia, the Czechoslovak Communist leaders entered the period of Stalinism with a party based at least in part on a Leninist organizational pattern. Indicative of this fact was the existence on all party levels of a dichotomy of power which was divided between the still-existing Party Chairmen and Party Secretaries. Above all, the power of the National Chairman was in no way comparable with that of the CPSU Secretary General. Despite his chairmanship of the 22-member Presidium of the Central Committee (the rather odd counterpart of the Soviet Politbureau), his position within that body was only that of *primus inter pares*. Another deviation from the Stalinist organizational pattern was the existence of the primary party units which were exclusively based on the local residence of the individual members.

The elimination of these deviations from the Soviet model served not only the purposes of Stalinist uniformity but also expressed the individual phases of the intraparty struggle which flared up soon after the February victory. Gottwald merged the function of the Secretary General with that of the Party Chairman, thus depriving his rival, Slánský, of the main source of his power. Instead, he set up two new party bodies—the Political and Organizational Secretariats—both under his personal control. Finally, the Commission of Party Control was created to act as a watchdog over party loyalty. The abolition of the Party Chairmen save on the primary units level and the disappearance of the Central Committee Presidium, removed the last remnants of the "democratic" past of Czechoslovak Communism. Soon after that came the establishment of primary units in the individual factories and places of employment, territorial organization being allowed to continue only as a temporary measure on the village level.

When, in 1954, the Political Secretariat was renamed the Political Bureau and the old Presidium abolished, the organization of the CPCS became identical to that of the Soviet Communist party. The party structure was similar to a ladder wide at the bottom and narrow at the top. But the external facade of the CPCS was as deceiving as that of its Soviet counterpart. The highest representative organ, the Party Congress, which between 1948 and 1960 met only three times (1949, 1954, 1958), proved to be nothing but a glorified rubber stamp. The meetings of the much less important Party Conferences are hardly worth mentioning, despite the fact that the last one of 1960 approved the new socialist constitution. The Central Committee of the party, theoretically elected by the Congress, lost practically all significance. Especially after the 1949–1954 purges it was reduced to an assembly of men not daring to express any other opinion than that dictated by the party leadership. This, as in the U.S.S.R., was vested first in the Central Committee Presidium and later in the Political Bureau which acted as the real and only policy-makers within the party and country. While theoretically elected, the members were self-appointed, their election being a mere formality. The Politbureau worked hand in hand with its Secretariat, composed of the First Secretary (until 1952 Secretary General) and up to four Deputy Secretaries. The Secretariat was divided into two kinds of sections, those responsible for party affairs and those dealing with the individual branches of government. After the affair of Slánský, who tried to use his office as a stepping-stone to supreme power, the Secretariat lost much of its importance, the new Secretary, Gottwald, deriving his power mainly from the traditional prestige of the President of the Republic. After his death, the secretaryship was bestowed on Antonín Novotný, the lackluster star on the Communist political horizon. While extremely important for the implementation of Politbureau policies, the Secretariat never regained its former significance.

On the intermediate level of the party ladder were the regional, district, and city organs, their structure being basically the same as that of the central party apparatus. From the point of view of political power they were organized hierarchically and on the basis of democratic centralism which emphasized the binding nature of the decisions of the higher party organs. The main political task of these intermediate organs was to serve as a connecting link between the central apparatus of the party and its grass roots on the lowest and widest rung of the ladder. The main aim of the primary party units was to provide as close a relationship as possible between the popular masses and the leading organs of the party. Their many diverse tasks, ranging from purely party functions to ostensibly nonpartisan activities, could be best summed up as the mobilization of the broad masses for the fulfillment of the economic, political, and cultural programs of the party and government.

The goal of this elaborate apparatus was to create a highly disciplined and ideologically conscious elite capable of leading the rest of the nation toward "socialism." To achieve this goal, the 1952 Party Statutes insisted on two contradictory principles, one emphasizing uniformity of judgment and ideological monolithism, the other referring to the traditional Communist slogans, such as intraparty democracy, businesslike discussion, etc. As in the Soviet Union, the obvious contradiction was resolved by applying the principle of democratic centralism and by the delivery of the party and the entire country into the hands of political secretaries, which was as complete in Czechoslovakia as in the Soviet Union. Typical of the CPCS emulation of the Russian example was the cult of criticism and self-criticism which developed into a senseless ritual, having no relationship to the actual behavior of party members.

A discussion of the party organization would be incomplete

without reference to the Communist party of Slovakia (CPS). The Communists encouraged it at the end of the war, principally to strengthen their position in the first National Front coalition government. After the 1948 seizure of power, however, the two parties were reunited, the CPS being granted nominal autonomy within the framework of the CPCS. In reality, the Slovak party organs, both in theory and practice, were nothing but tools of the central party organization.

After the 1948 coup, the Communists initiated two bodies responsible for the organization of youth. Relatively more successful were the Soviet-type Pioneers for children—an organization introduced into all schools and regarded as compulsory. The same could not be said of the far more important Union of Czechoslovak Youth which, although dominated by the party, was not a part of it. The activities of its some 1,100,000 members were guided and supervised by the party which visualized the organization as a huge reservoir from which it could recruit more class-conscious and ideologically better trained members. From the very beginning, however, the Union created difficulties to which the party failed to find a satisfactory solution. Indeed, the history of the youth movement has been that of progressive alienation from a society which managed to destroy the old values but was unable to replace them by new ones, creating in the minds of young men and women a spiritual vacuum and a sense of desperation.

By the end of the fifties the CPCS leadership realized the failure of its youth movement. There was little increase in the number of members and many local organizations remained only on paper, with only about five percent of the total membership belonging to the party. Instead, Czech and Slovak youth sought self-expression in turning to the West. American jazz, dances, films, and literature—in fact everything which had a Western label—fired their imagination. While essentially nonpolitical, this had political repercussions because it dealt a final blow to Communist attempts to create a Czechoslovak version of the "Homo Sovieticus."

While it assumed an absolute monopoly of power, the CPCS decided to retain at least formally the grouping of political forces which it had used so successfully in its surge to power.

After the 1948 coup the so-called Regenerated National Front of Czechs and Slovaks was created, being composed not only of different mass organizations but also of non-Communist "political parties."

Having fused with the Social Democrats, the Communists permitted the shadow existence of four such parties which, however, were reduced to absolute political insignificance. Thus there existed the external paraphernalia of the Czechoslovak Socialist party, the People's party, the miniscule Slovak Freedom party, and finally the successor of the former Slovak Democratic party, the Slovak Renaissance party. The outstanding characteristic of these parties was their subservience to the regime. Their participation in the National Front turned this body into a very useful tool of Communist policies. It was on the basis of the single ticket of the National Front that the first plebiscitary election of May 1948 and all subsequent elections took place. On this ticket invariably a small number of carefully selected representatives of the "non-Communist parties" were included. Also in the government, which formally continued to be based on the National Front, a few non-Communist fellow travelers were allowed to sit. Apart from lending to the essentially illegitimate regime at least a vestige of respectability, the National Front played the role of another of the famous "transmission belts" used by the party for controlling the non-Communist majority.

But far more important than the quasipolitical parties were the different social organizations which even under the Communist regime were allowed to exist within the framework of the National Front. Their role and functions, however, were perverted so as to serve the needs of the state. Thus some of the existing "non-party" organizations belonged to major weapons of Communist revolution, becoming important intermediaries between the government and the people. This was particularly true of the so-called Revolutionary Trade Union Movement which, in February 1948 helped to bring about the Communist seizure of power. Since then it has lost the last vestige of whatever independence it might have possessed. Instead of serving the interests of the workers, it became a faithful servant of their employer, the all-powerful Communist state. As in the U.S.S.R., the use of the trade unions was further increased by their administration of certain functions, such as the operation of medical care, social insurance, the family allowances system, as well as arbitration of disputes between individual workers and management.

While the trade unions acted as "a school of Communism" in the factories, the same role in the countryside was entrusted to the Unified Agricultural Cooperatives, the Czechoslovak version of Soviet collectives. From modest beginnings in 1949, they developed into a merciless instrument of class struggle. After the liquidation of the "village rich," the middle and small peasants were forced "voluntarily" to hand over their land to the cooperative farms. These farms provided the CPCS with an effective method of control over a part of the population whose individualism presented a potential source of discontent and resistance. The influence of the average cooperative member over the administration of the farm was negligible, his main function being to approve of policies dictated from above. As in the Soviet collectives, so in the Czechoslovak agricultural cooperatives, the "internal democracy" was "merely another variant of the technique of mobilized participation and assent which the modern totalitarian state utilizes to maintain the fiction of unanimity."[1]

Of similar significance were the organizations exclusively serving the purpose of indoctrination, such as the huge Union of Czechoslovak-Soviet Friendship, or the more select Society for the Dissemination of Political and Scientific Knowledge. Practically all fields of human endeavor, both artistic and intellectual, were put into the straitjacket of Communist-controlled organizations, such as the unions of Czechoslovak composers, artists, architects, journalists, and writers. It was this last which in the post-Stalin period became a source of constant trouble for the party and its leaders.

On the other hand, a number of other organizations, such as the "Gymnastic Association *Sokol*," were dissolved because of their incompatibility with the new regime. While in an entirely different category, the churches, and especially the Roman Catholic Church, were exposed to systematic persecution. By the start of the fifties, the primate of Czechoslovakia, Archbishop Josef Beran, having refused to surrender his ecclesiastical rights, was deprived of his position and deported to an unknown place.

[1] Merle Fainsod, *How Russia Is Ruled* (Cambridge: Harvard University Press, 1953), p. 459.

The Moravian archbishop and a number of bishops suffered a similar fate, many of them being tried and condemned to long terms of imprisonment. The State Office of Church Affairs took over control of the Catholic Church and together with the Communist-sponsored "Catholic Action" undertook the task of destroying the fabric of church organization. Despite the external success of these endeavors, Archbishop Beran "became a martyr and quasi-saint in the eyes of many non-Communists."

LAW AND GOVERNMENTAL STRUCTURE

Strangely enough, the first constitution of Communist Czechoslovakia of May 9, 1948, was marked by a high degree of moderation. It retained many principles and institutions characteristic of Western constitutional traditions, combining them with rules expressing the theory and practice of the new order.

Of special interest was the continuation of the office of the President of the Republic, the time-honored institution of Western constitutionalism, which greatly added to the self-confidence of its Communist holder. It was less in its actual form than in its potentialities that the new fundamental law violated some of the most basic principles of modern constitutionalism. While it introduced the familiar concept of tripartite economy (state, cooperative, and private), it stressed state property which could be extended by further nationalization which, it was expressly stated, could not be limited by law. The effectiveness of its Bill of Rights more often than not was vitiated by far-reaching limitations and exclusions. The new administrative system of People's Committees, which served as a powerful weapon of Communism in its early postwar period, was confirmed and declared to be the expression of genuine self-government. The Committees were entrusted with all aspects of public administration, including criminal jurisdiction. Lip service was paid to the principle of "effective decentralization," but in reality the People's Committees—which existed on the communal, city, district, and regional levels of the territorial organization—were subordinated to higher executive organs.

Perhaps most significant were the provisions relating to Slovak autonomy, which were to honor the promises made to the

Slovaks at the end of World War II and after. Although the constitution confirmed the existence of a separate Slovak nation possessing equal rights with the Czechs, the Republic was declared to be a unitary state of two Slavic nations. The idea of broad autonomous powers was abandoned in favor of strict centralism. The powers of the Slovak National Council, as the organ of legislative power, and those of the Board of Commissioners, who were to serve as the Slovak executive, were greatly curtailed in comparison with what they had been between 1945 and 1948. Yet this meager grant of autonomous rights was glibly described as recognition of "the national individuality of the Slovak nation."

Despite its Western veneer, the constitution—being based on the Marxist-Leninist interpretation of history—was a document ideally suited for progressive Sovietization. Its true significance is to be sought in the Declaration, an introductory but also integral part of the document. This Declaration spoke disparagingly of the prewar "bourgeois-democratic" system, extolled the Soviet Union and the absolute validity of its example, and foreshadowed the establishment of a new social and political order —socialism. The political atmosphere in which it operated precluded any other concept of socialism than that existing in Stalinist Russia.

The scope of this study does not permit even a general survey of the most important legislative enactments passed under the 1948 constitution. It soon became clear, however, that the new legislation would become a vehicle of cruel and merciless class struggle. There were basically three categories of statutes used to carry out this purpose: (1) those passed in order to abolish the last vestiges of the liberal democratic past; (2) those aimed at the establishment of a totalitarian police state; and (3) those which were destined to openly serve the process of social and economic revolution which, in Communist doctrine, leads to the crushing of antagonistic classes and gradually achieves classlessness, the prerequisite for the building of socialism.

Most important in the first category were the electoral laws, the reorganization of the People's Committees as organs of local government, and the revamping of the entire judicial system which was strictly subordinated to the government and through it to the CPCS. Of similar significance were the statutes reorganizing public prosecution, which assumed a key position in the administration of justice.

Typical of the second category of laws were those passed in order to catch up as quickly as possible with the almost total control over things and men, including men's minds, characteristic of the last years of Stalinism in Russia. Here one should mention the act establishing forced labor camps, the introduction of administrative criminal justice, and statutes reorganizing the police forces, as well as those aspects of criminal law and procedure which were destined to serve the interests of the all-powerful state.

While practically all of the new legislation was an integral part of the "grandiose progress" toward a classless society, of special significance were the numerous statutes relating to the social and economic foundations of the national life. These included a series of measures bringing about complete socialization of industry, trade, and services, as well as acts forcing the peasants "voluntarily" to enter into the Unified Agricultural Cooperatives. In addition, this category of laws included statutes of an outright vindictive and absolutely ruthless nature, openly directed against whole groups of the population who were branded as "enemies of the people" or "anti-social elements" and, as such, subjected to morally humiliating and materially destructive sanctions.

Following principles established by Lenin, the party retained supreme control over all governmental activities, the governmental organization assuming the function of the "transmission belt" of Communist theory and practice. While turned into an effective instrument of Communist rule, the existing framework of government remained fundamentally unchanged. Yet the old structure was given an entirely new content and, as time passed, changes took place which made it imperative to introduce new mechanisms to serve the needs of the new order.

This was particularly true of the main representative organ of liberal democracy, the parliament. The National Assembly was declared to be supreme in the legislative area, but in practice it became a powerless tool of the CPCS, faithfully executing its orders and serving its purposes. This new role was also expressed in the manner in which the parliament was elected. In keeping with the first 1948 electoral law, the voters retained, in theory if not in practice, some degree of choice. As was to be expected, however, this choice remained unused, the May 1948 election becoming a plebiscite in which, rather surprisingly, almost 20 percent of the voters, either directly or indirectly (by abstaining), expressed themselves against the single National Front list. The two other elections in the period preceding the establishment of socialism, those of 1954 and 1960, were conducted on the basis of a new electoral system which entirely eliminated the element of choice. The nomination of candidates to be put on the single list of the National Front was entrusted to this Communist-dominated body itself, which was responsible for their registration with the electoral commissions. As a matter of course, only one candidate was registered and submitted for the approval of the electorate.

In its actual operation the National Assembly was marked by the briefness of its sessions, lack of discussion, and the almost embarrassing unanimity of its decisions. At best the deputies acted as local propagandists for the regime and its policies.

The most important institutions of executive power—the presidency, the premiership, and the cabinet—were distributed among the Communist leaders in keeping with their rank within the party. In contrast to other Communist systems, the office of the President retained its primary political significance, being reserved to the actual leader of the CPCS. Second in rank was the Premier, whose office has been reserved for a Slovak since 1953. While theoretically equal, the individual members of the cabinet were dominated by those who belonged to the Political Bureau of the party. Despite the increased scope of its functions, caused by the nationalization of the entire industrial establishment, the cabinet lost much of its pre-1948 importance. Its members, unless they held important party functions, were relegated to the position of mere administrators.

The broad and rather vague administrative functions of local self-government were entrusted to the People's Committees which at least theoretically were endowed with dual competence —to act as representative organs and to participate in actual administration. In their actual operation, these "people's organs" had no more independence than their model, the Russian Soviets.

With the exception of the lowest administrative level, the influence of the lay representative element was replaced by that of the highly bureaucratized class of professional administrators appointed in keeping with the wishes of the party. The local executive organs had dual responsibility—one to the district People's Committee, the other to the corresponding executive organ of the higher People's Committee and, in the last analysis, to the central government. It was the latter type of responsibility that became the backbone of the entire public administration system.

At the beginning of 1960 a new organizational pattern of local government was adopted, creating new administrative divisions in keeping with the general economic requirements of the country. As a result the number of regions was reduced to 10 and that of districts to 108.

In order to fulfill its guiding role, the party developed a number of policies and agencies to carry them out. Of these perhaps most important was the Leninist principle of democratic centralism. Other means of control were no less formidable. In all government agencies there was the watchful eye of the primary party units; the Ministry of State Control became domesticated to such a degree as to be continued even after the abolition of its Soviet model; there were the financial and planning controls within the framework of the Uniform Economic Plan. Last but not least, there were the police operating on all levels.

Czechoslovakia in the Stage of Socialism

It was perhaps logical that the first European society (next to the Soviet Union) to reach the advanced stage of "socialism" was Czechoslovakia—a country whose Communism was characterized by an absolute lack of independence and originality, being nothing but a faithful replica of the Soviet Union's. Fittingly enough, this "giant step" toward the construction of a mature socialist society took place under the leadership of Antonín Novotný, the drabbest and intellectually most unimaginative of the Communist leaders of Eastern Europe. In fact, the only distinction possessed by Novotný and his second-rate subleaders was their close association with the period of Stalinism and its reign of terror. As in the past, the consciousness of this profane association continued to act as the most powerful element of unity and a hidden but unmistakable "guide to action" of Czechoslovak Communist leadership. This subconscious feeling of guilt was to a large degree transmitted to the carefully picked party functionaries who were groomed to assume positions of leadership in the future.

In 1960, however, Novotný and his chief supporters seemed little aware of the fundamental weaknesses of the society which they had helped to create. While somewhat ruffled, the ship of state managed to steer successfully through the turbulent sea of the Hungarian and Polish revolts and to make only insignificant concessions to the spirit engendered by the Twentieth CPSU Congress. Indeed, on the surface it appeared as if under "neo-Stalinism" Czechoslovakia would be able to achieve socialism without a catastrophic lowering of the standard of living. Yet, at the beginning of 1960 there was little to justify this assumption. As Edward Taborsky has pointed out, the economic policies of Communism "delayed rather than accelerated the country's progress to higher living standards." The few successes, such as a more equitable distribution of the generally decreased wealth and the establishment of an all-embracing system of social security, at best could be regarded as relative.

All this the Communist leaders refused to admit, pointing with great pride to the immensely increased industrial production, while they carefully swept under the carpet the ever-increasing signs of catastrophe in agriculture. Thus the advent of "socialism" was greeted with a sycophantic chorus of praise, extolling Czechoslovakia as a state in which exploitation of man by man has been eliminated once and for all. This momentous fact was to be formally expressed in the July 11, 1960, constitution which changed the People's Democratic Republic into the Czechoslovak Socialist Republic (CSSR).

THE 1960 SOCIALIST CONSTITUTION

The new basic law is a well drafted and rather concise document which is marked by three fundamental characteristics.

In the first place it emulates to a much greater extent than its 1948 predecessor the contemporary Soviet constitution. This is particularly true with regard to the position of the CPCS, to which the constitution grants the position of "the leading force in society and the state." Of equal significance is the abolition of the principle of the separation of powers, which is reflected in the new status of the National Assembly as the supreme organ of state power, and in the entirely Sovietized reformulation of the rights and duties of citizens.

Secondly, the new constitution conceives of the CSSR within the general context of the international development toward socialism and Communism. Its drafters went beyond the legal and political framework of their Russian model, taking account of "the most recent developments within the socialist states." The constitution declares that the construction of mature socialism and the transition to Communism will take place hand in hand with the Soviet Union and other socialist countries. It refers to the necessity of close economic cooperation with the U.S.S.R. and other socialist states, to be based on the "international socialist division of work." In addition to tracing the basic political and economic orientation of Czechoslovak foreign policy, the new fundamental law introduced in a somewhat inconclusive manner another novelty of contemporary Communist constitutionalism, namely, the idea of the withering away of the state. It deals with social organizations "to which certain tasks of state organs are to be gradually transferred." There are two other innovations which deserve to be mentioned. The constitution speaks several times of Marxism-Leninism, declaring it to be the guiding principle of the cultural and intellectual life of society; equally interesting is the inclusion of the concept of democratic centralism to be applied in all state and social organs.

The third point to be noted is the attempt of the constitution to make use of Czechoslovak social, political, and economic traditions. This aim, however, was accomplished only in part and largely with regard to the purely formal aspects of the constitution. The preservation of the presidency, however, is definitely more than a mere formality. As previously emphasized, the CPCS leaders did not fail to appreciate the prestige of having an office located in the majestic Hradcany castle and associated with the names of the founders of independent Czechoslovakia. Another Czechoslovak specialty was the continuation of the National Front, an institution connected with the immediately postwar bourgeois parliamentarism. While not mentioned in the constitution or in the amended electoral laws, the National Front still includes—in addition to its leading core, the Communist party—the remnants of the four pre-1948 "political" parties. There is still another aspect of the Czechoslovak constitution which is worth mentioning. It has no provision on the ownership of cooperative land and the private plots of cooperative members. This deviation, however, seems to have been caused by an overdose of zeal, anticipating future changes in the U.S.S.R. Foreshadowing the early emergence of a "single socialist ownership" (as forecast by Khrushchev at the CPSU Twenty-First Congress), the Czechoslovak Communists prepared for this development by avoiding the issue of land ownership when they wrote their constitution.

Last but not least, the 1960 basic norm further curtailed what remained of the autonomous rights of the Slovaks. The Slovak National Council was retained but its legislative powers were strictly limited. The old type of Commissioners, who served as an organ of executive power, were replaced by new Commissioners selected from the 16-member Presidium of the National Council. Their competence was restricted to matters falling within the curtailed jurisdiction of the National Council or to those economic and cultural tasks allotted to them by the central government.

Implementing the new constitution, which reflected the existing social and legal system, required only a few legislative enactments. Noteworthy was the replacement of the outdated Civil Code and Code of Civil Procedure by new statutes more in accord with the principles of the socialist constitution. Of similar significance were the new Penal Code and the Code of Criminal Procedure, the former introducing "the degree of danger to society" as a decisive criterion of criminal responsibility. A large number of offenses were removed from the jurisdiction of courts and transferred to Local People's Courts, People's Committees, and various commissions which were empowered to mete out punishments aiming at the re-education of the culprit. The Local People's Courts were to represent "the development of socialist statehood into Communist self-administration," providing for direct participation of the people in the judicial process.

Perhaps the most striking feature of the new Czechoslovak constitution was its ability to combine polished form and good legislative technique with the most advanced political, social, and economic aims of Communism. It is not without irony that soon after its promulgation the material conditions it was designed to reflect proved unworthy of its lofty tone and high-sounding phrases.

STALINISM UNDER ATTACK

In the middle of 1960 signs of economic decline began to appear. As long as the natural richness of the country remained unexhausted, there existed an illusion of at least relative prosperity, and the Communists could shamelessly attribute the country's most favorable position in the Soviet bloc to the alleged effectiveness of their policies and of the socialist system. But beginning with 1961 the country started its astounding descent down the ladder of economic prosperity. It was then that the party leaders were forced to give up their inept attempts to cover up the catastrophic decrease in agricultural performance and openly admit the existence of a "food problem." Even more vexing were the unexpected difficulties besetting the industrial establishment which prided itself on being the most advanced of the entire Soviet orbit.

Thus agricultural production, having stagnated for a number of years, took a downward plunge, and industry began to suffer from serious shortcomings, such as bureaucratization and bad organization, bad quality of products, and a general slowing down of industrial growth. As a result, the Five-Year Plan for 1961–1965 had to be abandoned, as well as its successor, the more ambitious Seven-Year Plan for 1964–1970. Instead, stopgap one-year plans were adopted with little hope of being fulfilled. The growth of national income fell to less than one percent both in 1962 and 1963. Industrial production and productivity of 1963 were lower than those of 1962 and, above all, agricultural production showed no signs of improvement, falling below the 1936

level. In their frantic endeavor to find a quick remedy to the
ever-growing misery, the regime declared the partial economic
decentralization, instituted in 1958 and modelled after Khrushchev's reforms, to be responsible for the 1961–1962 slump and
returned to centralizing measures supervised by the party.

As was to be expected, economic difficulties were soon accompanied by difficulties of a political nature. The main characteristics of the progressive intraparty crisis were described, perhaps
unwittingly but definitely accurately, by the Communist ideol-
ogist, Vladimír Koucký. Criticizing the shortcomings of the
contemporary Czechoslovak theater, he referred to the rather
odd and inadmissible treatment accorded the younger generation which was dramatized as "suffering from the sins committed
by their fathers who succeeded in thoroughly disgusting the
young people with socialism."

Koucký's analysis was perfectly fitted to the psychology of
Novotny and his henchmen who realized that genuine de-Stalinization, called for by the younger generation, was bound to reveal
their complicity in Stalin's crimes and thus undermine the very
foundations of their political position. While most of the victims
of the 1949–1954 purges had long been secretly released, Novotný
stubbornly clung to the notion of the fundamental guilt of
Slánský and his partners. Only the developments of the Twenty-
Second CPSU Congress forced him to take a more radical stand
on the de-Stalinization issue. Announcing, in November 1961
that the monstrous 18,000-ton Stalin monument would be removed, he emphasized that in the period between 1948 and 1953,
when he was not "a member of the higher party membership,"
Slánský made a deal with the security apparatus aiming at putting the party and state under his own control. Not he—Novotný
—but the Stalinist "security machinery, which Slánský started
moving," was responsible for his own downfall. Realizing the
weakness of his arguments, Novotný found it necessary to return
to the case of Klement Gottwald, accusing him of passivity
which enabled Slánský to carry on his disruptive activities. Having thus spread the burden of guilt, Novotný announced that the
body of Gottwald would be removed from the Vitkov mausoleum
and be buried "in the same manner as those of other leading
fighters of the Party."

The political significance of de-Stalinization was emphasized by the affair of Rudolf Barák, a high party and state official who, in February, 1962, was arrested for embezzlement of state funds and later condemned to 15 years of prison. While the case of this former Minister of the Interior is still obscure, there is reason to believe that his fall was due to personal rivalry with Antonín Novotný. In his endeavor to replace Novotný and become the "supreme" ruler of Czechoslovakia, Barák decided to make use of evidence which he had acquired in 1956 as chairman of a special commission charged with revising the 1949–1954 trials and purges. At the June 1956 CPCS Conference two contradictory statements on the work of this commission were made. One was by Novotný, who declared that there was no reason for the rehabilitation of Slánský and his partners; the other was by Barák, who spoke of "crude violations of socialist legality" and promised to provide the party with the "historical truth." The report of this commission was never published, Novotný and his fellow Stalinists being able to push through their own point of view. The situation changed after the 1961 CPSU Congress re-emphasized further de-Stalinization. There is reason to assume that Barák, who at the time of the great purges was not even a Central Committee member, made an attempt to use Novotný's Stalinist past as an argument for his removal, going perhaps so far as to inform the CPSU leadership of this serious handicap of the Czechoslovak leader.

Dissension in the party leadership, of which the Barák affair was a definite manifestation, encouraged malcontents within the party to attack the shortcomings and failures of the regime. The inability of the government to cope with the food shortage, its policy of exporting huge quantities of products sorely needed at home, and, above all, the economic aid to developing countries, particularly Cuba, aroused indignation and public criticism.

Yet the long-delayed Twelfth Party Congress, which finally met in December, 1962, turned out to be a well staged performance in the best traditions of Czechoslovak neo-Stalinism. Novotný himself assumed the role of a de-Stalinizer. Mentioning the few persons who had been rehabilitated, he "wisely" observed that some of the victims of the 1949–1954 purges, while innocent of certain offenses for which they had been unjustly sentenced, were nevertheless guilty of other crimes with which they were not even charged. The "last" stage of de-Stalinization would be modest, he announced, pointing out that this task had been assigned to a new commission which was busily at work examining the merits of the individual cases. Novotný's arguments were supported by his close partners, Bacílek and Hendrych, who emphasized the wisdom of Novotný's 1961 approach to the cases of Rudolf Slánský and the Stalinism of Gottwald so that it was "not necessary to change anything in regard to the guilt of Slánský and a few others."

The congress found no new solution to the many shortcomings of the regime and the ideological confusion in the party ranks. The party, which adopted new statutes modelled after their 1961 CPSU counterpart, underwent no significant changes, especially in its leadership which remained under the firm control of Novotný. As compared with 1958, its membership rose by around 247,000, reaching the figure of over 1,588,000 full-fledged members and over 92,000 candidates, organized into 46,209 basic organizations.

The apparent victory of neo-Stalinism, however, proved to be short-lived. The investigation of the rehabilitation commission, created by the Twelfth Congress, proved to be less "modest" than anticipated by the CPCS leader. Even before the publication of its report, Josef Urválek, whose successful prosecution in the Slánský trial earned him the lofty office of President of the Czechoslovak Supreme Court, submitted his resignation "for health reasons" in March of 1963. The removal of Karol Bacílek from all high party functions, which was announced in May, was not accompanied by any such explanation. It is clear that he was forced to retire into more obscure party positions because of his role as Minister of National Security during the period of the great purges.

It is difficult to assess the actual motivation of Novotný's sudden deference to the principle of de-Stalinization. However aggravating the discoveries of the rehabilitation commission might have been, they alone would hardly have compelled the Communist leadership to drop one of its most trusted members. It may well be that Novotný acted under pressure from Khrushchev who advised gradual de-Stalinization to improve the position of the highly unpopular Czechoslovak government. There emerged, however, another powerful factor which greatly increased the overall pressure on the harassed Communist leadership. It was the revival of a well coordinated action of Slovak and Czech intellectuals, especially those organized in the Union of Slovak Writers, the Union of Czechoslovak Writers, and the Union of Slovak Journalists. Holding conferences in the months of April and May, they returned to the belligerent spirit of 1956, expressing their dissatisfaction with the government and clamoring for more freedom and final liquidation of the ignominious consequences of the cult of the individual.

This tendency was clearly evident at the Czechoslovak Writers' Congress, which removed from its presidium a number of Stalinists; but the laurels in the de-Stalinization movement went to the Slovaks. In an impassioned address to his fellow writers, the poet Laco Novomeský, jailed in 1945 and only recently readmitted to the Writers' Union, referred to the hanged Slovak leader, Vlado Clementis, as "our common friend and comrade" and demanded absolute rehabilitation of all those who were unjustly punished. Even more spectacular were the proceedings at the Congress of the Slovak Journalists' Union, at which the Czechoslovak Prime Minister, Viliam Široký, was accused of being responsible for the execution of Clementis and the jailing of a number of outstanding representatives of Slovak national life.

If similar statements had been made 10 years ago, they would have had fatal consequences for the speaker. The atmosphere of 1963, however, prevented Novotný from taking radical steps. Realizing that the attack was directed against the entire Stalinist leadership of the party, he and his associates made frantic but unsuccessful attempts to save the political skin of their partner. Their case was hardly improved by the publication, in August 1963, of the final report of the rehabilitation commission which reviewed 481 cases, acquitting or granting full or partial amnesty to all but 70 victims of the purges. Slánský and a few others, while legally rehabilitated, were refused posthumous readmission to the party because of "gross violations of party statutes and principles." The commission's report, as well as the increased pressure from the intellectual critics of the regime, contributed to Novotný's surrender. Like a captain of a ship overladen with cargo, he proceeded to drop some of his ballast. At the end of September, the Central Committee of the CPCS relieved the Prime Minister, Viliam Široký, and the Vice-Premier, Jaromír Dolanský, as well as a number of less important Stalinists, of all their party and governmental functions. The new cabinet was headed by Jozef Lenart, a representative of the younger generation who had received a part of his training in Moscow.

However bitter and humiliating, Novotný's defeat was by no means decisive. All the leading figures of the period of the "cult of the individual" were removed from positions of control, but the main culprit, Novotný himself, remained at the helm of the party and state. Moreover the new team of subleaders, which he appointed, consisted of men who owed their positions to him and were prepared to defend his dogmatist views against incipient revisionism. The CPCS Central Committee session of December 1963 revealed the determination of the regenerated but unreformed party leadership to hold the line in matters of ideology. Koucký, the theoretician of the party, condemned both dogmatism and the cult of personality. His main criticism, however, was directed against the revisionist rebels among the intellectuals. His task was made more difficult by the fact that the party critics were no longer defenseless, having at their disposal a number of literary and general cultural periodicals, such as the Prague *Literární noviny, Plamen,* and above all the Slovak *Kulturný život* which had developed into one of the most outspoken and liberal Communist periodicals of Eastern Europe.

The party leadership, being pressed into a defensive position, could no longer rely on demagogic slogans bolstered by the everpresent threat of political and judicial sanctions. In their duel with the conservatives the revisionists insisted on further deStalinization, a "humanistic" approach to the building of socialism, and independence of thinking and literary creation. They indignantly rejected attempts by the party hacks to limit their criticism to the cultural sphere and to deny them the right to deal with all aspects of public life.

The public discussion which started in 1963 was carried on within the ranks of the party, but soon it resulted in a certain degree of liberalization of the policies of the regime, from which the entire nation derived considerable profit. In October 1963

Archbishop Beran and a number of other Roman Catholic bishops were released from confinement but not allowed to perform their ecclesiastical functions. Another liberalization measure was the sudden opening of the country to foreign tourists and the adoption of a rather generous approach to the problem of travel of Czechoslovak citizens to Western countries, including the United States (provided that the cost of their journey would be paid from abroad). No doubt the attempt to attract tourists was motivated by the desire to secure the sorely needed hard currencies, but the cumulative effect of the two policies provided for unheard of opportunities for contacts with the West. Equally important was the return of the Czechs and Slovaks into the orbit of Western intellectual life, which was accompanied by occasional criticism of the intellectual performance of the Soviet Union. At times such criticism found its way into the pages of general cultural periodicals. Last but not least, opinions were expressed that suggested an objective and therefore more favorable attitude toward Thomas Masaryk, the founder of modern Czechoslovakia, who until then had been depicted as an enemy of the working class and servant of the Western bourgeoisie. Another event, approved in the highest party circles, was the final change in the attitude toward Yugoslavia and its socialist system, which no longer was regarded as revisionist but, on the contrary, as a genuine and successful example of the construction of socialism. It was no accident that the mid-1964 decision of the government to authorize a partial return to private enterprise in certain services took place after the return of the party secretary Koucký from Belgrade. His visit was followed by one by Novotný, who in his speeches extolled the achievements of the "new and socialist Yugoslavia," emphasizing that the past differences between the two countries had been entirely overcome.

The ideological critics of the regime were joined, by the middle of 1963, by a group of young economists who began to press for fundamental revisionist reforms. Voices were raised rejecting the sterile and dogmatic approach to economic theory and practice, and resulting in a "cult of the plan" and in a senseless imitation of unsuitable Soviet practices. At the same time, Czechoslovak economic science, which for the last 14 years had been stagnant, came forward with new and daring ideas. The party was urged to recognize the significance of the economic achievements of the capitalist world, admit that even under socialism the law of supply and demand cannot be disregarded, and cease to approach socialization of industry and collectivization of agriculture as a fetish but to consider them as mere means for the achievement of prosperity. Step by step, the new generation of economists gained ground, at times against stubborn opposition of the orthodox party economists. By the middle of 1964 the need for basic changes was generally recognized, the main problem being the nature and scope of such future reforms.

Most radical and successful was the challenge of the Slovak revisionists grouped around the review *Kulturný život*. Against them the party leadership did not dare to take repressive measures, fearing the consequences of a further aggravation of the rather delicate Czecho-Slovak relationship. On the contrary, in May 1964 the CPCS made, at least theoretically, an important concession to the cause of Slovak autonomy. By a joint Czech and Slovak Communist party resolution the Slovak National Council was empowered to regulate by special legislation all problems requiring special handling in Slovakia. Also, it was decided to return to the old system of Slovak commissioners as organs of executive power (as they had existed before the 1960 constitution), and to considerably increase their number.

It would be wrong, however, to overestimate the influence of the revisionists and the scope of liberalization. While the party leadership was no longer able to completely silence its critics, its response continued to be a mixture of threats and concessions. Above all, it maintained full control over all political organs within the country. This was best illustrated by the June 1964 election which was conducted on the basis of a new electoral law spelling out more clearly that there should be more candidates than seats to be filled. This method, it was understood, was to enable the voter to exercise at least a limited choice. When the election took place, however, there were only 300 candidates for the same number of seats to be filled in the National Assembly, and from among the approximate quarter-million of deputies elected on the different levels of People's Committees the right of choice was exercised only in a very few cases on the lowest communal level. The only positive aspect of the election was the replacement of almost half of the members of the representative organs, the number of "new" persons elected in Slovakia amounting to 70 percent. Equally positive was the insistence on the increased role of the National Assembly. Yet these two indications of "liberalization" were more than outweighed by the behavior of the new parliament, which continued its work with the customary short sessions and "unanimous" decisions. That the party had not given up its right to interfere was demonstrated by a number of "administrative" actions aimed at curbing the rebellious intellectuals and revisionist tendencies.

OUTLOOK FOR THE FUTURE

There is no doubt that Czechoslovakia has gone through a number of significant changes. Ideologically, the last two years have seen the emergence of a strong revisionist movement. Toward the end of 1964 this was shown by the CPCS Central Committee's adoption of a new economic model in which Czechoslovakia presented itself as perhaps the most advanced protagonist of economic revisionism. Through its emphasis on decentralization in direction and investment, the introduction of purely economic criteria into planning and decision-making, and, above all, through the limited adoption of a "free" price system within the three-pronged concept of price-fixing, Czechoslovakia went a long way toward the recognition of traditional economic concepts. On the other hand, even this model—in order to be successful—will require full cooperation on the part of the party apparatus (which has not yet been entirely convinced of its wisdom) and of the population.

That the future development of Czechoslovakia is still in balance has been demonstrated by the rather unexpected "unanimous" election of Antonín Novotný to the office of the President of the Republic. Thus the chief Stalinist, surrounded by a rather large group of sycophantic party dogmatists, is still in charge. That Novotný has suddenly assumed the role of the "chief de-Stalinizer" can hardly conceal the fact that the main characteristic of the period of the personality cult, namely the combination of party and state leadership in the same hands, has not been abolished. The attitude of the party leadership to the revisionist intellectuals occasionally appeared to be one of tolerance, while at other times it was one of contemptuous aloofness. The party could well afford such magnanimity, as the workers, who also had reasons for dissatisfaction, remained silent and gave practically no support to the sophisticated arguments of the intellectuals. The group to which the revisionists might have appealed, namely the middle class, was no longer in existence, having been destroyed by the ruthless class struggle of the fifties.

Last but not least, Novotný managed to weather the dangers stemming from the sudden removal of his close friend and supporter, Nikita Khrushchev. However intimate his relation to the deposed Soviet leader might have been, it was matched by his equally close association with Brezhnev who, on the occasion of the December 1963 extension of the Soviet-Czechoslovak Treaty, praised Novotný as "our close friend," "a loyal son of the Czechoslovak people," and "an indefatigable fighter for Communism."

However, the election of Novotný did not stem either the tide of criticism of the Communist regime or the continued public pressures for further liberalization. Thus, after his February 1965 appointment to the college of Cardinals, the Czechoslovak Primate, Josef Beran, was allowed—on the basis of an agreement between the government and the Vatican—to leave the country for Rome. His office was filled by his own appointee, Dr. František Tomášek, acting as Apostolic Administrator.

As a movement, the still huge Czechoslovak Communist Party has lost its *élan* and its leadership has been further pressed into the defensive. It continues to exist as a rigid "apparatus" of the "New Class," clinging to power and extolling values which every one, including the great majority of the Party rank and file, now regards as having failed. In the course of the past two to three years, preparations for a fundamental overhaul of the entire economic system have again demonstrated the wastefulness and inadequacy of the Czechoslovak economy under Communism. In December 1965 the CPCS leadership made a surprisingly sincere statement, admitting publicly the bankruptcy of its centralized economy; the Communist Party had "committed catastrophic errors which cost the country billions of Crowns."

The fulfillment of the modest 1964 plan did little to dispel the creeping doubts about the profitability of economic relations with the Soviet Union. Evidence of disharmony came to the surface when the Soviet Union failed to meet Czechoslovak demands for deliveries of grain and refused to support the claims of Czech industry in the deliberations of the Council for Mutual Economic Assistance.

The gradual disappearance of the rigid dictatorship of the past has been illustrated by the mounting attack of the writers against the government, resulting in the rehabilitation of certain non-Communist literary figures. On the whole, the orthodox Czech Communist leadership has been unable to defend itself against the renewed onslaught of the opposition forces; it has been bogged down by the insignificance of its own representatives but has been unwilling to abolish the erroneous practices of the past, not daring to admit the fallacy of its dogmatic Marxist-Leninist assumptions.

BIBLIOGRAPHICAL NOTE

Books

Following is a short list of books on the political and governmental development of postwar Czechoslovakia. William Diamond's *Czechoslovakia Between East and West* (London: Stevens, 1947) is a good, though rather overly optimistic, discussion of the first two years of the political evolution of the country under Communism. The literature dealing with Communist policies before and during the 1948 *coup d'état* is more numerous. The following three books deserve to be mentioned: Josef Korbel's *The Communist Subversion of Czechoslovakia 1938–1948* (Princeton: Princeton University Press, 1959) provides a brief but useful analysis of Czechoslovak Communism and the tactics it employed in the struggle for power; Josef Josten's *Oh, My Country* (London: Latimer House, 1949) is a discussion of the February 1948 defeat of the Czechoslovak democrats; Hubert Ripka's *Czechoslovakia Enslaved* (New York: Macmillan, 1950) is a biographical account of the post-1945 development and especially the seizure of power, as seen through the eyes of a democratic member of the government. The first account of conditions in Stalinist Czechoslovakia is that of Dana Adams Schmidt in his *Anatomy of a Satellite* (Boston: Little, Brown, 1952). Constitutional and political aspects of the first 12 years of Communist rule are examined in the excellent analytical study by Edward Taborsky *Communism in Czechoslovakia 1948–1960* (Princeton: Princeton University Press, 1961). Also the volume edited by Vratislav Busek and Nicholas Spulber, *Czechoslovakia* (New York: Praeger, 1957), includes a discussion of the governmental and political system of the country. Illuminating is the book by Vladimir Reisky de Dubnic, *Communist Propaganda Methods: A Case Study on Czechoslovakia* (New York: Praeger, 1960). An interesting sociological analysis of the working of the Communist political system can be found in I. Gadourek's *The Political Control of Czechoslovakia* (Leiden: Kroese, 1953).

Monographs and Articles

Different aspects of the Czechoslovak political and constitutional system have been examined in a number of excellent monographs written by Pavel Korbel, editor of *East Europe*. Typical of his studies are the following publications of the National Committee for a Free Europe: *National Committees in Czechoslovakia* (New York: 1954), and *Parliamentary Elections* (New York: 1952). Korbel and V. Vagassky's *Purges in the Communist Party of Czechoslovakia* (New York: 1952), and *The Supreme Organs of the Communist Party of Czechoslovakia* (New York: 1952) are excellent analyses of the Communist party at the height of Stalinism. Ladislav Feierabend's study, *Agricultural Cooperatives in Czechoslovakia* (New York: Mid-European Studies Center, 1952), gives an account of the collectivization process in Czechoslovakia. Of the more recent articles on the political development of the country the following three should be mentioned: Victor A. Velen's "Czech Stalinists Die Hard," in *Foreign Affairs*, Vol. 42, No. 2 (January, 1964); Edward Taborsky's "Czechoslovakia: Out of Stalinism?" in *Problems of Communism*, Vol. XIII, No. 3 (May–June, 1964); and H. Gordon Skilling, "Czechoslovakia," in *The Communist States at the Crossroads*, edited by Adam Bromke (New York: Praeger, 1965), pp. 87–105.

CHAPTER FOUR

East Germany

The General Setting

EAST GERMANY occupies a unique position in the Communist
bloc. Even the semantics of the East German position reveal
its confused legal and geopolitical status. The term DDR or
GDR, denoting the existence of a German Democratic Republic
is misleading and implies Western recognition. The West German Federal Republic's characterization of this satellite as the
SBZ, Soviet Occupation Zone, or as Middle Germany (*Mittel-
deutschland*) is more accurate, but too clumsy for regular use.
This chapter will employ the "East Germany" term with occasional reference to the DDR. To understand the implications of
the DDR problem, the following pertinent questions ought to be
raised. Is this "satellite" a German state? What brand of Communism does it represent? What are its relations with the Bonn
government, the Western and democratic Federal Republic?
What is its position vis-à-vis the two feuding headquarters of
world Communism, Moscow and Peking, and—last but not least
—what are the ties binding it to such varied East European capital cities as Budapest, Bucharest, Prague, or Warsaw, each of
which is now searching for more suitable patterns of national
Communism? In briefest summary, East Germany can be described as an incomplete and utterly non-self-sufficient sector
carved out of wartime Germany and irrationally established as a
mock state-entity which has been neither German, nor democratic, and certainly not a republic. In view of its basic political
and geographic instability it has also been referred to as the "Albania of the North" in the once homogeneous and monolithic
European empire of the Soviet Union.

The 1945 version of the Soviet occupation zone of Germany

includes five former provinces of the German Reich (Mecklen-burg, Saxony, Thuringia, Saxony-Anhalt and Brandenburg) in their entirety and parts of two others (Pomerania and Silesia). It borders on the Baltic Sea in the north, Poland in the east, Czechoslovakia in the south, and the West German Federal Republic in the west. Of all the unnatural and artificially carved-out border situations, the 1000-mile long zonal boundary separating the two Germanies seems to be the least tenable. Indeed, the phrase "bleeding border" has accurately portrayed the human hardships involved, while the term "Iron Curtain" describes the administrative and ideological irrationalities of separating East from West in Germany.

The present East German regime has been anxious to delete the traces of historic unity and tradition from its territory. In its administrative reform of July 23, 1952, it dissolved the his-torically established earlier provinces and reorganized them in-stead into 14 administrative districts. Most recent unofficial esti-mates placed the population of the DDR at approximately 16.5 million. The population density varies sharply from district to district. Of the few major urban concentrations, the following are noteworthy: Leipzig with about 590,000 inhabitants, Dres-den (490,000), Magdeburg (260,000), Rostock (158,000), and Pots-dam (115,000).

Professor Richard Lowenthal observed in a recent article in Der Monat that: "In the increasingly rusty chain which holds together the Soviet Union's colonial empire in Eastern Europe, the Soviet Zone regime (DDR) is the weakest link." Although this value judgment accurately pictures the power position of the DDR in relation to the once-dominant colonial overlord, it cannot encompass the more complicated ideological profile of East Germany on the spectrum of Eastern European politics in the 1960s.

In terms of such specific political classifications within the Communist bloc of Europe, the DDR clearly belongs to that small (and dwindling) category of East European countries which have obediently adopted Marxist theories and then pro-ceeded to apply them in the most rigorous, and increasingly obsolescent, Stalinist manner. At the present time, only Czecho-slovakia and Bulgaria could be ranked with the DDR among those who pursue not only a "Russian" Soviet orientation, but—in view of the belligerence, toughness, and indiscriminate harshness of both tone and content—an almost "Chinese" (Maoist) line in the ideological alignment of world Communism. The observer of this complex scene must then contrast this trio of countries with the majority of the European ex-satellites which has offered challenging deviations and numerous variations on the pattern, producing the Yugoslav, Albanian, Polish, and even Hungarian "roads to socialism." Needless to say that the DDR's few intellectual dissenters, who timidly advocated a specific "East German road to socialism" a few years ago, have been effectively quieted by the Ulbricht regime by long-term prison sentences. The strident Stalinist (or Maoist) line has never changed in its ideological wavelength ever since the launching of this hybrid German-Russian satellite on October 7, 1949.

In order to appreciate the contemporary development of East Germany, we must first view the two main stages of its political evolution and place Ulbricht's DDR into its constitutional context.

Constitutional Development

STAGE ONE: THE "PEOPLE'S DEMOCRATIC" PHASE (1945–1952)

The "people's democratic" phase, in East Germany's case, consisted essentially of two related features, an armed revolutionary seizure of power, and a subsequent, speedily executed, total centralization of power in a new dictatorship of the proletariat. In theory, furthermore, this "People's Democracy" was portrayed as a full satellite state completely dependent on the U.S.S.R. even while supposedly developing in the direction of a more "advanced" Soviet Socialist republic. Walter Ulbricht's obedient theoreticians also stressed the Stalinist principles of an intensified class struggle, the iron monopoly of the working class, and complete subordination to Soviet-imposed political and labor discipline.

In practical terms this phase saw the emergence first of two major political parties, the KPD and SPD. The former utilized the name *(Kommunistische Partei Deutschlands)* and organizational framework of Germany's traditional pre-World War II Communist party, infusing it, however, with the newly imported Soviet-German agents who appeared in Berlin as early as May 1945 in the wake of the conquering Red Army. The latter used the well-known name of the German Socialist party *(Sozialistische Partei Deutschlands)*. In April 1946 a forced merger, arbitrarily dictated by the Soviet occupation authorities, united the two groups into a new, monolithic workers' party, the SED or Socialist Unity party *(Sozialistische Einheitspartei Deutschlands)*. Displaying political characteristics fully as rigid and bureaucratic as its Soviet counterpart, the SED guaranteed that the Communists would seize all positions of power in the new "state" and inevitably reduced other political forces or groups to mere obedient figureheads. By means of this tightly centralized new *United* party, SED leaders were quickly placed into all top-level positions: Wilhelm Pieck, a veteran Comintern agent and life-long Stalinist, became the first President of the DDR while the former Socialist (SPD) leader, Otto Grotewohl, was rewarded for skillfully steering his own party into the Communist fold with the office of Prime Minister. Walter Ulbricht actually held the central power and authority, formally established as First Secretary of the SED.

The other principal buttress of this hybrid "people's democracy" was the constitution approved by its one-chamber (mock) Parliament in March 1949 and formally passed by a German People's Congress in May 1949. Imitating both the format and the content of other satellite constitutions, this document stressed the *transitional* nature of the first phase with ominous frequency while looking forward to the "completion" or "full construction" of a truly German Democratic Republic. The usual civil rights provisions are cautiously hedged by such characteristic Communist pronouncements as "The economic life of the country must live up to the expectations of socialist legality" (Article 19). The impression is created throughout this document that the broadly formulated and glittering constitutional principles are bound to be limited or even negated in practice by those "concrete conditions under which the proletarian revolution must triumph." Thus the illusion of democracy is being created here with an imposing array of seemingly popular and mass-based institutions (parliament, elections, cabinets, several political parties, etc.); in reality these formal organs have skillfully concealed the all-pervasive power position of the Communist (SED) party.

STAGE TWO: CONSTRUCTION OF THE "SOCIALIST STATE" (1952 —)

The "people's democracy," as we have seen, is essentially a transitional state form whose evolution toward the next highest phase is theoretically both predetermined and inevitable. At a certain important point the "people's democracy" (or "people's republic") transforms itself into a "socialist republic." This historic goal is accomplished when the most important enemies of Communism (the exploiting classes) have disappeared from the home front, when the new economic and social system has triumphed both in the villages and the cities, and when all (remaining) social groups within the state will be bound by a new "spirit of friendly cooperation."

The true dictatorship phase will at this juncture recede into the background, governmental forms of violence are bound to disappear internally, and *socialism* becomes the principal concern and politico-economic goal of the day. There will be no need for internal organs of repression and the socialist state's entire repressive apparatus will be turned to combatting foreign espionage and subversive activities from abroad. Domestically the fundamental feature of this stage in Communist theory is *the single-party state* built on a classless society. Clearly, other political parties will eventually wither away in such situations. Yet it is important to note that in such countries as Czechoslovakia or the DDR they do not disappear completely, but are retained for purely tactical reasons, as needless and meaningless appendices doomed to ultimate extinction at some later date. In the meantime, a National Front of Democratic Germany still boasts of two "bourgeois" party components, surrounded in turn by further docile functional organs like youth groups, trade unions, and a multiplicity of important mass organizations.[1]

---

[1] These features of domestic politics in the DDR are analyzed in detail below, pages 108–110.

Stage two, the socialist phase of construction, is not the "end of the road" in world Communist evolution. Whatever the ultimate phase, "the transition to a utopian and 'pure' Communism" may imply in Marxist-Leninist doctrine, the concept of the "withering away of the state" seems to be unanimously rejected by East German writers. Their country must remain strong and ever-vigilant since the possibility of armed counterrevolutionary attempts may yet jeopardize the eventual victory of Communism. Thus do the theorists of the Ulbricht clique try to speculate about the prevention of another *popular* revolt on the June 17, 1953 pattern, and feebly rationalize in defense of the DDR's exceedingly slow economic and political progress toward the dim, future phases of socialism and "pure Communism." The centralized and mobilized dictatorship so typical of their country is certainly here to stay, as even the most exuberant predictions have so realistically prophesied.

In actual day-by-day practice, the DDR's leaders have specified 1965 as the target date for the construction of socialism. Since this date was totally unrealistic to begin with, one may surmise that by 1965 the DDR has at most reached the 1.5 or one-and-a-half stage of politico-economic development: having progressed beyond the "people's democracy," it has supposedly entered the "socialist construction" phase, but it is far removed from Communism.

Officially the Second Party Conference of the SED, held from July 9 to 12, 1952, was declared as the changeover point from Phase I to Phase II. Party boss Walter Ulbricht proudly announced here that the "systematic construction" *(planmässiger Aufbau)* of socialism had now begun as a result of the combination of two factors:

1. the successful elimination of "class enemies" and "reactionary groups" which had brought about the political dominance of the workers and peasants; and
2. the acceleration of the agricultural collectivization campaign which, according to Ulbricht, was to be pushed forward to completion by April 1960.

Important legal, political, and administrative reforms were carried out at this Congress. In addition to breaking up the historic

Länder into innocuous districts, a judicial reform measure was passed ignoring the earlier legislative guarantees written into the Constitution of 1949. Shades of the Nazi era's People's Courts were conjured up when, instead of interpreting the law, the new act stated as "the duty of the courts" to provide for "the protection of the social and state order, of the Socialist economy, of political, economic and cultural organizations," and (last and least, at the very end of a long paragraph), "for the protection of the legal rights and interests of the citizens."

A law was also passed significantly altering the executive-legislative relationship in the East German satellite government. It broadened the legislative powers of the Cabinet of Ministers at the expense of the unicameral parliament *(Volkskammer)*. The cabinet (or Council of Ministers) was now authorized to issue decrees which had the force of law provided (in a most nebulous manner) that they were "based on the laws and decisions" of the *Volkskammer*, previously enacted, or received the parliament's approval at a later date.

From 1952 on all major SED (Communist) references piously alluded to the steady process of "constructing socialism." A more realistic approach to the *actual* (and not theoretical) state of development in the political life of East Germany was not sounded until the combined impact of the 1956 Hungarian and Polish revolts visibly tightened the Stalinist grip on the SED leadership. Cutting through the murkiness of the usual Communist phraseology, ranking Politburo member and acting *Volkskammer* president, Hermann Matern, soberly observed at a plenary session of the party's Central Committee in the spring of 1957 that: "Our Republic is *by its nature* essentially a state of the dictatorship of the proletariat." Thus flatly contradicting the fancy semantic lies of the previous five-year period, Matern actually pointed to the naked and exact truth. Instead of approaching the blissful state of "pure Communism," the SED leadership has been engaged in building an entirely different type of state; a totalitarian police dictatorship. Marxist theory and East German practice thus present an interesting further variation on Hegel's familiar methodology: the dialectics of the opposite concept, implying a forceful collision between utopian classifications and the malpractices of a colonial power.

Problems of Political Leadership

COMMUNIST "BLOC-POLITICS" IN EAST GERMANY

The political evolution of the DDR has centered around the relatively brief history of the SED, its Communist party thinly camouflaged by the "Socialist Unity" label. The SED first formally appeared in the Soviet Occupation Zone scene in April, 1946 when it merged into a new party the previously independent Socialists and Communists. Wilhelm Pieck (also President of the DDR, died in 1960) and Otto Grotewohl (first Prime Minister of the Government, died in 1964) were appointed joint party chairmen of the SED and, along with Walter Ulbricht, took a guiding hand in its politics.

Since 1946 the SED has undergone two phases of development. Initially its leaders were anxious to encourage mass membership, and by lowering admission standards enticed large numbers of opportunists, fellow travelers and other "joiners" to become members. The Soviet leaders apparently felt that the difficulties of the crucial transition period from "occupation zone" to "people's democracy" could be bridged, or at least minimized, by a Communist party with swollen membership ranks. At any rate, by May 1947 the SED could boast of 1.8 million members, or about 10 percent of the DDR's population.

As the transformation was gradually accomplished, the need for a party (or movement) based on mass support became less urgent and obvious. Slowly, by means of purges and the dismissal of members, the SED assumed the aspect of a cadre party, that is, a relatively small organization dependent primarily on the skeleton framework of experienced professionals (the "cadres"), rather than on the masses of non-Communist opportunists. By a "cleansing" of membership ranks and by a process of "purification," the party's rolls were reduced to about one million in the early fifties. As the SED contracted into a cadre type of movement, it had to rely increasingly on both the *direct* and *indirect* instruments of control at its disposal. Its direct means have consisted of a firm and tightly organized party apparatus and a more

complex state apparatus based on the organs of justice and
public administration. Among its indirect means of political
control two major kinds of organizations began to emerge: certain non-Communist political parties and various mass organizations.

Four satellite parties have been kept alive in the DDR, and
in the best spirit of Communist-inspired "bloc-politics," forced
into the straitjacket of a National Front (*Nationales Front des
demokratischen Deutschlands*). SED-directed front—or "bloc"
politics imply that these nominally existing "middle-class" parties:
the Christian Democratic Union (CDU, Eastern style), the Liberal Democrats (LDPD), the National Democrats (NDPD), and
the German Peasants' party (DBD) not only participate in an
allegedly multiparty government, but also have blocs of membership seats assigned to them in the *Volkskammer*. All four "parties" are obviously and completely dominated by pro-Communist
leadership and blindly serve not only the SED's permanent party
line, but also its changing day-by-day tactical variations, such as
the all-out efforts aimed at complete agricultural collectivization
or at nationalization of all small businesses (in the 1958–1960
period).

In the DDR the most interesting indigenous forms of political
Sovietization have been the rapidly mushrooming mass organizations. These can be properly described as special political, social,
and economic groups created by the regime for the nonparty
masses. They serve a uniquely useful function as a political control device and have proliferated particularly in countries where
the Communist regimes have been notably unstable, weak, and
basically insecure. In Walter Ulbricht's East Germany they have,
therefore, displayed a wide range and variety in their goals and
activities. They also have regular quotas of seats in the *Volkskammer* and are loosely integrated into the government as semilegisla-
tive and propaganda organs.

Described with typical Teutonic heavy-handedness as "community of interest" organizations, the DDR's mass organizations
include among their membership well over half of the country's
16 or 17 million citizens. Their 25 major types range from the
more inconspicuous Democratic Housewives' Association (DFD)
to the Cultural League (KB) to the more ambitious Free Ger-

Political Structure of the DDR

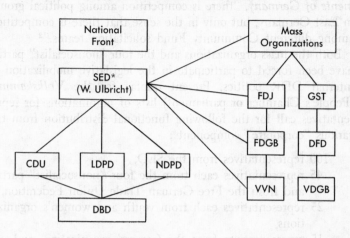

The "Bourgeois" Parties   *The Ruling Communist Party

man Youth Movement (FDJ—with 3 million members), all the way to the immense, involuntary union of artisans and skilled workers of the Free German Trade Union Federation (FDGB—with more than 5 million members). There is, in addition, a Democratic Peasants' Organization (VDGB) and a League of Nazi Victims (VVN). It is also noteworthy that most of these organizations have their own schools based on the widely publicized Marxist-Leninist principle of mass education (*Massenschulung*), for both resident and nonresident students. Their deep-seated educational and propaganda efforts are exploited by the regime to offer the illusion of political choice and of the availability of economic or social alternatives to the non-Communist, urban middle classes. Through the indirectness of this "control" operation, the starkness of Ulbricht's party line has been somewhat blurred in recent years, and its ruthless political objectives camouflaged or diluted without modifying any of the DDR's ultimate goals. The frantic attempts of the "satellite" parties and of the diverse mass organizations have failed to create a sense of political competition or ideological satisfaction among the sullen and indifferent masses of the DDR. "Yes,"

110 EASTERN EUROPEAN GOVERNMENT AND POLITICS

observes Professor Arnold J. Heidenheimer in his *The Governments of Germany*, "there is competition among political groups in East Germany, but only in the sense that there is competition among different Community Fund solicitation teams."[2]

Both the mass organizations and the four "nonsocialist" parties have been forced to participate in the legislative mobilization of internal DDR politics. Present quotas for the *Volkskammer* (People's Chamber or parliament) lists of nominations for representatives call for the following functional distribution from the various "corporate" components:

100 representatives from the SED,
 45 representatives each from the four "nonsocialist" parties and from the Free German Trade Union Federation,
 25 representatives each from youth and women's organizations,
 15 representatives from the farmers' organization, and
 10 representatives from among the "intellectual workers" of the Cultural League.

The SED leadership has complete veto power over all National Front nominees and can make any number of selections on its own. Elections then consist of the obedient ratification of all nominees for parliamentary representation. Turnouts have been large in recent "elections" and the *total* endorsement of the National Front list should not have come as a political surprise. In 1958, 98.9 percent of the voters qualified to participate in the elections showed up and 99.87 percent of those who voted were counted as fully endorsing the list of representatives. In the most recent elections, of October 20, 1963, the Communist-controlled bloc (or Front) received 11,523,481 votes (99.95 percent), taking all 434 *Volkskammer* seats. The non-Communist opposition, on the other hand, received 5764 votes (0.05 percent) with 4614 ballots (0.04 percent) declared invalid. The single-list pattern of these elections has successfully combined the fanaticism of the Nazi-style elections in Adolf Hitler's Third Reich with the meticulous ruthlessness of similar electoral procedures in Stalin's Russia.

[2] Arnold J. Heidenheimer, *The Governments of Germany* (New York: Crowell), 1961, p. 179.

CULT OF PERSONALITY, DE-STALINIZATION, RE-STALINIZATION, AND
PURGES IN EAST GERMANY.

If any adjectives could properly describe the essential characteristics of East Germany's political development, the two most
appropriate ones would be "contradictory" and "negative."

The term contradictory is truly justified since Walter Ulbricht's regime has succeeded in combining great institutional
insecurity with Stalinist ruthlessness and toughness. Within the
framework of this system basic political weakness has never been
able to induce a spirit of relative "relaxation" or compromise as
it has in neighboring Poland and in Kádár's Hungary. A similar
contradiction has existed in another area: despite the weakness
and perpetual shakiness of Ulbricht's government in the personnel and administrative fields, the DDR has in effect been
ruled by a centrally unified, relatively homogeneous and truly
omnipotent clique whose leader (the "Lenin of Saxony") has
never been exposed to de-Stalinization, and consequently has
never had to be personally re-Stalinized. Thus, while the phrase
"collective leadership" has been (somewhat loosely) applied to
the political leadership of the DDR, it must be remembered that
this leadership group has always been under the steady control
and strict surveillance of Ulbricht's Stalin-like figure. This phenomenon in itself has presented a contradiction in political terms.

"Negative" is an equally challenging aspect of the country's
evolution. It can be illustrated by the absence of a major wave
of de-Stalinization; of a "New Course" following Stalin's death;
of a "Thaw" which would have paralleled that of the neighboring
East European countries (again during the 1953–1956 period);
of the open, formal show trials so characteristic of the Stalinist
purges; of the formal and mass execution of political competitors;
of an unconcealed and naked tug-of-war, thinly camouflaged by
the phrase "struggle for succession," usually involving top party
—and top government—leaders. To summarize: there could have
been no antiparty faction on the Soviet political pattern, since
as yet there have been no serious contenders or challengers of
Ulbricht's extraordinary power position.

This host of negative features should not be interpreted in

absolutes or extremes on the political spectrum of internal developments. Life in the DDR has not oscillated between a set of black-and-white positions. There has been a modicum of de-Stalinization, a small thaw, a few purges (usually ending in suicide rather than execution), and some behind-the-scenes infighting among a few younger and ambitious party functionaries. The point of emphasis should be the difference in scope, timing, and basic tactics between the DDR and other East European satellites, particularly in the crucial period following Stalin's death.

In order to retrace the tortuous and complicated political path travelled by the masters of Germany's Soviet Zone of Occupation, we must focus the spotlight on East Germany's ruling satrap and military district governor, Walter Ulbricht. Born in 1893, Ulbricht joined the German Social Democratic party as early as 1912, but switched to the newly formed Communist party (KPD) shortly after World War I. He also participated at an early date in the activities of Lenin's Third Comintern in Moscow and has, at least since 1920, been closely identified with the Leninist-Stalinist line of international Communism. Between 1928 and 1933 Ulbricht served in the German *Reichstag* (Parliament), but was lucky enough to escape from Hitler, first to Czechoslovakia and subsequently to the Soviet Union. As Stalin's agent and a Comintern representative of high rank, Ulbricht then participated in the Spanish Civil War. Upon his return from that assignment, considered a major setback for world Communism, he was able to survive Stalin's ruthless purges of both the Comintern leadership and of the now-exiled hierarchy of the German KPD. With his characteristic political nimbleness and opportunism, Ulbricht thus managed not only to escape Stalin's wrath, but also to achieve a top position in the German National Committee for Liberation, a group of reliable exiled Communists groomed by Stalin to return to Germany after the war and preside over its long-term Sovietization.

In running his small (12 to 15 men) *Gruppe Ulbricht* and preparing the ultimate take-over of East Germany, the leader was materially helped by the fact that he was the only major German Communist (KPD) figure of prewar times who had survived Hitler, Stalin, and the war itself. A revealing comment on Ulbricht's personality is his famous remark to Stalin, who was interested in getting the prewar leader of German Communism, Ernst Thälmann, out of the notorious Dachau concentration camp during the brief (1939–1941) Nazi-Soviet honeymoon period. Ulbricht successfully opposed this plan, stating that "Communism needs martyrs in Germany!" Thälmann indeed was shot by the Nazis in Buchenwald concentration camp in 1944, and Ulbricht had removed his potentially most dangerous rival as far as postwar Communization was concerned.

Berlin was still burning in utter devastation when Ulbricht brought his *Gruppe* in on May 2, 1945; in the uniform of a full colonel of the Red Army, he marched right behind Marshal Zhukov. Since that ominous and triumphant victory march of the Soviet military forces, Ulbricht's career has followed a well-known and widely publicized path of tyrannical one-man rule in the so-called DDR. First sharing some of the formal powers and working closely with the President of East Germany, Wilhelm Pieck, Ulbricht has held on tenaciously to the following top positions: First Secretary of the Socialist Unity Party (SED), First Deputy Minister President (Prime Minister) in the government, and after Pieck's death, also as Chairman of the Council of State.

While Ulbricht's first two jobs are self-explanatory, the third requires some comment. It was the result of a constitutional amendment which replaced the presidency with a Council of State *(Staatsrat)* consisting of a collective executive of 24 members, led by a Chairman and six Deputy Chairmen. The Council of State was also authorized to interpret laws and enact resolutions having the force of law. Its Chairman was assigned the customary ceremonial responsibilities which had belonged to the President prior to September, 1960. As of that date, the functions of Chief of State, Chairman of the Council of State, and Communist party boss have been combined, to an extent unheard of even in the Soviet Union, in the person of a single individual.

Although a man of complex characteristics, two principal features emerge sharply in Ulbricht's personality. One is that throughout his lengthy tenure of power he has been more of a fanatical Stalinist than Stalin himself. His political and economic policies have been undeviatingly truculent and uncompromising, while his toughness and self-centered approach have never allowed room for friends and at best for only a few loyal supporters (mostly in the top echelons of his ruling SED). His tactical bluntness can probably best be described in the colloquial terms: "Never a kind word to anyone!" This operational principle, shared by the entire ruling elite of the DDR, is extremely easy to illustrate. One by one, the major socioeconomic groups among the population are reminded that while conditions have not been too good in recent years, the worst is yet to come. Ulbricht himself enjoys sounding such clarion calls of warning. When asked, for example, why the DDR kept on using a German phrase (abbreviated as LPG) to describe a collective farm, instead of calling it a *Kolkhoz* (Soviet style), Ulbricht promptly suggested that LPG sounded better to the East German farmer since it gave him a chance to "glance back into the past for a little while longer." It was made clear to the audience that while the semantics of the situation may be transitional, the basic institutions of Communism were certainly there to stay.

Ulbricht's notorious toughness has been accurately labelled by the press of the German Federal Republic as the "pressure cooker" complex operating in the DDR. Prior to the erection of the Wall on August 13, 1961, the escape avenue provided by the city of Berlin was properly seen as a safety valve which prevented the pressure cooker from blowing up by allowing a suitable opening to the regime's opponents. Conversely, population pressures in the DDR have often increased to the danger point after the abrupt closing of the major safety valve.

The second characteristic of importance is Ulbricht's hardheaded pragmatism. He has never been a theoretician and has not concerned himself with complex ideological problems, but has been cast rather in the role of an economically minded and oriented Stalinist. Until the agricultural and industrial crises of the mid-nineteen sixties overwhelmed Ulbricht, he used to boast that under his direction the DDR had become the sixth most important industrial power in the world, following the United States, the Soviet Union, the Federal German Republic, Great Britain, and France. This would place East Germany second in the entire Communist bloc while making it the leader in chemical industry, the supplier of half of all Soviet industrial imports and of about 30 percent of its uranium. The principal fact to stress is that Ulbricht continuously brags, pushes, threatens, cajoles, deplores, and implores—concerned in an almost monomaniacal manner with the economic production, industrial and agricultural achievements of his truncated and badly exploited land.

Ulbricht's threat-and-promise, carrot-and-stick policy has led to endless contradictions in the country's domestic affairs, particularly in the economic and social realms. The West German press has been right in raising the justifiable query: "Can Ulbricht truly coexist with Ulbricht?" Consequently the DDR elite has often been appraised as a veritable two-platoon system: one group would hand out one set of party-line instructions on the top, while another would sharply modify, or mollify, it on a considerably lower level where issues of practical application have to be considered with more attention to detail.

PURGES AND POLITICAL RESISTANCE

From the picture painted so far, it would appear that a *total* absence of political opposition has marked the first 20 years of the DDR's existence. This would be a misleading impression, however, because occasional removals of high party functionaries, arrests, long-term imprisonments, and even a few suicides punctuated the frequently rocky road of the country's political evolution. In order to achieve a precarious equilibrium between the usual foundations of a Communist society, the Ulbricht regime has been forced to balance the tenuous relationships between four supporting pillars: the party hierarchy, the state bureaucracy, the economic apparatus and, last but not least, the military organization. Whenever one of these forces seemed to lose its sense of proportion or get out of line, the ubiquitous instrument of DDR terror, its *Volkspolizei* (People's Police) was compelled to step in.

Viewed in this organizational framework, Ulbricht can well be characterized as being in charge of a permanent, repressive operation. According to an observer of the East German political scene, he has proved to be "a clever practitioner of the preventive purge." This kind of purge consists of removing the competitive leadership before it can become too dangerous or threatening to the leader himself. It can be viewed as a form of de-Stalinization in which potential future Stalins are being silenced and neutralized before they could even begin the long climb to the "cult of personality" pinnacle of power. In Ulbricht's DDR the years 1956–1957 and 1958–1960 represented the two major phases of political vulnerability. Although each was marked by a wave of purges aimed at the liquidation of various anti-Ulbricht groups, the two rounds of purges actually had different characteristics.

The 1956–1957 round was aimed at an opposition group of intellectuals, mostly university professors and journalists whose resistance to Ulbricht crystallized around Professor Wolfgang Harich. An able young sociologist, probably also suspect on account of his upper-middle-class origin, Harich had demanded a "specifically German road to socialism," extolled the Hungarian revolution, denounced the "reactionary role" of the U.S.S.R. not only in the Polish and Hungarian events of 1956, but in effect ever since 1945, and—last but not least—urged the SED leadership to carry out important internal reforms leading the party away from Stalinism. Harich then reached the dangerous conclusion that "all Stalinists must be excluded from the Party!" He was arrested in November 1956 and after a brief trial was given a 10-year prison sentence.

The 1958–1960 round of purges involved two different groups. One was a clique of high-level bureaucrats within the party who had directly challenged Ulbricht's political control and demanded more flexibility in party affairs. The group was led by Ernst Wollweber and Karl Schirdewan, both men occupying excellent positions from which to challenge Ulbricht's "cult of personality" within the SED. As Minister of State Security, Wollweber was actually in charge of the secret police, while Schirdewan had overall control of party personnel as "cadre" (or personnel) secretary of the Central Committee of the SED. This must have been a high-level intraparty battle of the top *apparatchiki* of East Germany; rather obviously, it ended with Ulbricht's victory as the two leaders were expelled from the party for *factionalism* and for trying to undermine the state hierarchy.

Along with the bureaucrats there also occurred a purge of the so-called economic group of expert planners centering around the Minister of Heavy Industry, Fritz Selbmann. For a few months in 1958 these people formed a "managers' front" and effectively challenged Ulbricht's economic policies as being unduly harsh and his administrative reforms as directing the country along wrong lines of development. The economists were broken up and severely punished. To avoid long-term prison sentences, at least one member of the group (Gerhart Ziller, economic secretary of the party Central Committee) committed suicide. Ulbricht was later forced to admit that these incidents marked the real danger point of his regime. At the Fifth SED Party Congress, held in East Berlin in July 1958, he clearly stated that: "The discussions of this period showed that the conflict between the development of a socialist base and the evolution of our ideology became steadily more profound. . . We must acknowledge that the softening up process had progressed quite a long distance."

The group purges described here inevitably led to a large-scale and more systematic chastisement of the party membership. The massive re-examination of the party rank-and-file, often described in the Communist literature as a "purification purge," lasted throughout 1958 and 1959 and resulted in the expulsion of 60,000 members, the wholesale removal of SED district leaders, and the "re-election" of about 300,000 party functionaries who were presumably considered reliable after the purification—and verification—campaigns. Thus the DDR's "permanent purge" process, so characteristic of all totalitarian forms of government, has asserted itself on two different levels:

1. It was aimed first of all at different types of groups with rather specialized professional interests, led by fairly strong-willed and decisive personalities who appeared ready to challenge Walter Ulbricht, but failed in their attempts, and
2. it involved a quiet mass purge of party members and functionaries whose "softening up" activities could have been catastrophic for the DDR. In the long run, these "purification" purges have succeeded in keeping in line the almost 1.5 million members of the SED.

CULT OF PERSONALITY IN THE DDR

As we have seen above, a continuous and skillfully conducted process of *preemptive* de-Stalinization has contributed materially to keeping the "Stalin of the DDR" on his shaky throne. Time alone will eventually de-Stalinize Walter Ulbricht who, while politically untouchable, is now in his seventies. For at least the past decade and a half this man has been surrounded by a carefully nurtured "cult of personality" which, while not as blatant and all-pervasive as Stalin's was during his 31-year rule, has certainly followed a steady party line of obedience and adulation. In effect, whenever the now-departed Khrushchev leadership tightened and accelerated its relentless de-Stalinization campaign, Ulbricht seemed to step up—in a contradictory direction—his own DDR-wide "cult of personality" drive. For example, immediately following the Twenty-Second Party Congress of October-November 1961 at which Khrushchev denounced Stalin with unusual ferocity, new governmental measures were published to strengthen Ulbricht's super-constitutional status.

Young Pioneers, the most youthful members of the FDJ (or Free German Youth Movement), were now given a new official anthem: "Forward with our Comrade Ulbricht who is our friend and model!" They were also encouraged to set up special "places of honor" for Walter Ulbricht in their homes. High school students in Leipzig founded their own "Ulbricht" regiment and FDJ membership meetings were ordered to devote all of their spring meetings (the year was 1963) to the general theme: "What is your contribution to the leadership and policies of Comrade Ulbricht?"

Simultaneously party leaders kept comparing Ulbricht in their speeches to Goethe, Schiller, and Heine as one of "the Heroes of German History," a true promoter of German national culture and a leading figure in the workers' international movement. Completely overshadowed by this excessive adulation of Ulbricht, a quiet de-Stalinization of Joseph Stalin himself was carried out in the DDR, obviously on Soviet orders. Its formal aspects were held to a minimum: in November 1961 East Berlin's notorious

Stalin Allee was renamed Karl Marx Allee and the country's first "socialist city," Stalinstadt, was changed to Eisenhüttenstadt.

After 1961, DDR politics have actually changed in the direction of re-Stalinization or of a peculiarly non-Soviet type of neo-Stalinism, far more abrupt and rigid in its ideological orientation than that of the European bloc's fellow Communist members, (except for Albania). In the meantime, as long as the Ulbricht regime can buttress its position by such an all-pervasive "cult of personality" campaign, it is unlikely that—at least in the ageing leader's lifetime—major personnel changes will occur on the highest levels of political leadership. As a student of modern totalitarianism remarked: "How can there be changes in the political 'superstructure' of a society if the institutional 'infrastructure' remains unchanged?" Answering this justifiable question, one can cautiously forecast more stability and viability for the DDR leadership in the next decade than the shaky foundations of this Zone of Occupation would normally warrant. The major exception to this generalized prediction would be the recurrence of a revolt against the regime on the pattern of the exciting events of June 17, 1953. Such a truly *popular* revolt could destroy the very bases of the Ulbricht regime's existence and eventually liberate the Zone's millions of captive Germans. Consequently, a brief review of the 1953 developments is of particular importance in assessing the long- or short-term trends of durability of the current SED regime in East Germany.

IMPACT OF THE POPULAR REVOLT OF JUNE 17, 1953

The factual background of the June 17 revolt is too well known today to merit a detailed account. Rather than an analysis of the stormy events surrounding it, its overall ideological and political impact is worthy of reassessment for the 1960s. The East Berlin revolt occurred a mere three months after Stalin's death as a result of the protest movement of construction workers on the Stalin Allee, this monument to the Soviet dictator and gift of the "German people" to Russia. The popular mass movement spread like wildfire and within 48 hours engulfed more than 200 urban communities throughout the Soviet Zone of

Occupation. It erupted in large-scale workers' strikes, popular demonstrations, riots approximating major uprisings and leading to the arrest of secret policemen, and to the wholesale release of innocent political prisoners.

The SED and the government handled the workers' initial protest demands with extraordinary clumsiness, and at first refused to change the unjust production quotas which had been the source of irritation and despair. Subsequently the authorities wavered, whereupon the riots intensified and spread through East Berlin. At the moment when it appeared that the Ulbricht regime was losing its grip, the East German Communists called for help from the Soviet occupation forces and the Red Army moved in with full force. Overnight the East Berlin revolt was brutally quelled and in less than 72 hours popular resistance to the occupation and the Communist regime collapsed throughout the Zone. The Red Army then withdrew to its barracks and the Ulbricht regime was allowed to crack down on the major figures of the countrywide rebellion. Soon the secret police was fully reinstated, the jails were again filled to overflowing with the previous inmates and a brand new crop of "political prisoners." An ominous silence prevailed among the frightened people of the DDR.

In retrospect, three major characteristics emerge from the chaotic events of June 1953. It is significant to note that while the revolt had suffered from a lack of centralized leadership and certainly from a lack of communications among the diverse and widespread places where the individual, local eruptions had taken place, it affected every major social and economic group within the DDR. With the exception of a few completely agricultural and remote areas, Soviet military authorities were forced to declare martial law and emergency conditions throughout *the entire Zone*.

As a second feature, we must point to an interesting contradiction in terms. The revolt was both spontaneous and largely leaderless, and yet it had a few definite, clear-cut objectives. It was not born in the midst of the deepest misery of a concentration camp atmosphere, but—on the contrary—seemed to have been closely linked to a post-Stalinist atmosphere of slow but steady psychological and physical improvement. It was the slowness of the *rate* of improvement that disappointed the East German population which had expected faster fulfillment of the many economic and political promises made by the regime in the weeks of "relaxation" following Joseph Stalin's death. These popular yearnings for immediate improvement had rapidly "overtaken and surpassed" (to use favorite Communist expressions) the actual socioeconomic and political performance of the regime.

To generalize, it has been true of other Eastern European popular revolts (notably of those in Poland and Hungary) that a sudden and widespread hope that the country's condition would improve drastically in the near future was an essential precondition. Thus in East Berlin the optical illusion that a silver lining was visible in the dark clouds of totalitarianism was a major reason for the spirit of spontaneity and recklessness without which such revolts cannot be generated.

The third factor of importance was the long-term impact of the revolt. Placed in its historic perspective, this particular revolution now appears as both the end and the beginning of a significant process of ideological evolution. It was immediately preceded by eight years in a Communist prison in which freedom of speech and of expression had been painfully curtailed; this era had in turn been preceded by five years of more or less total war and seven years of Nazi terror with an imprisonment of a different type for many Berliners. As a beginning of a new chapter, the date of June 17, 1953 looms almost equally large. It certainly marked the dawn of an era of "Thaw," of massive restlessness, of a "New Course" which subsequently produced not only de-Stalinization, but also led chronologically and logically to the Polish revolts of June and October 1956, and to the more meaningful and violent Hungarian revolution of October and November 1956. These two latter-day revolts reflected several key features of the first one: its spontaneity, its largely leaderless nature, its unplanned background and yet, despite all of these fundamental shortcomings, its clear-cut popular objectives. These objectives seemed to have been a composite of negative and positive forces—an element of strong social protest coupled with a nationwide dynamic vigor and ideological élan. The East Berlin—and

Soviet Zone—uprisings have set the precedent for these later eruptions and thus serve as useful prototypes for the study of future revolts against alien-imposed tyrannies.

Economic and Social Repression in the DDR

Seldom has theory been more divergent from practice than in the economic and social aspects of everyday life in East Germany. The relevant constitutional provisions are conceptually satisfactory and eminently democratic. Article 19 of the Constitution of 1949 provides, for example, that "Economic life must correspond to the fundamental principles of socialist legality," while Article 20 claims that "the State will support *the private initiative* of farmers, and of commerce and industry." Article 24 then adds: "The farmers will be guaranteed private property on their land," while in the realm of social and cultural life Articles 34 and 37 stress that: "The arts, science and all learning must be free," and "Youth must be educated to become independently thinking, in the spirit of humanism, and responsibly mature as men."

To contrast the last 20 years' practice with this classically resplendent doctrine, three phrases can best set the stage. Directed by Soviet manipulators and overlords, the economic and social development of the DDR has been heavily *centralized, socialized, and militarized* ever since 1945. All three characteristics have been the obvious outgrowth of a crudely managed military administration, bureaucratically centralized in the Soviet Zone of Berlin and entrusted with such extraneous, but from the colonial occupier's point of view essential, functions as economic planning and social regimentation for the entire Zone. Between 1945 and 1949 (prior to the artificially set October 7, 1949 "birthdate" of the DDR), the entire complicated military government setup was obviously directed from Moscow, with the Soviet *Kommandatura* in East Berlin acting as a superagency in the economic administration of the several hundred large industrial plants which had been promptly transferred to Soviet government ownership.

The industrial take-over clearly preceded agricultural collectivization. For a while it seemed that the farmers would be left alone and even be allowed to enjoy the fruits of a major land reform measure redistributing and subdividing the large baronial estates among thousands of small landholders. In order to encourage food production, the deceptive illusion was created that the constitutional provision concerning independent land ownership would be carefully observed. While agriculture was thus slowly put back on its feet, the major industrial plants were earmarked for "Soviet reparations" from the outset. Such reparations were then exacted either in the form of "current production"—that is, the entire output of a factory going directly to the Soviet Union —or by physical removal of the plant (with management and labor) to the Soviet Union where it was set up and operated directly under U.S.S.R. management. It is obvious therefore that the captive population of the Zone was plagued right from 1945 on by a frightening shortage of consumers' goods, since all of its industries which had not been destroyed in World War II were now directly expropriated by the U.S.S.R. Even while the food supplies improved, these local shortages coupled with the damaging absence of all interzonal trade, set a most depressing tone to economic life.

After 1949 the nature of political controls on economic development changed substantially and Soviet pressures assumed an indirect nature while the actual, day-by-day direction of DDR policies rested in the hands of the East Berlin government. From the inception of semisatellite status, East Germany's economic and social evolution can best be described as one of a *dialectic* progress during which fairly steady forward spurts of improvements alternated with deep and unsettling crisis situations. As an example, the 1954–1959 era brought industrial progress, with the DDR's production running 25 percent above the prewar rate and the agricultural output slowly improving. During this transitional period only 47 percent of the Zone's farmland was controlled by the state, leaving a relatively large area available for private farming. As long as incentives for profits and private production were thus within reach, the development trend pointed upward. The major danger signal at this point consisted of the steady refugee exodus which drained the DDR of its most valuable and vigorous manpower resource. The refugee outflow affected particularly the industries which relied on skilled workers and the agricultural sector of the economy which was weakened by the large-scale loss of farmers to the West. After 1959 the dialectic process swung the other way, with agricultural and industrial crises marking the early sixties.

Throughout these crucial years the SED regime practiced two diametrically opposite sets of policies and kept alternating them at regular intervals; judging from the results, neither socio-economic approach showed signs of improvement or of long-term solution.

One of these policies can be described as that of "relative leniency." It was based on the assumption that some of Walter Ulbricht's forced superindustrialization projects were not only irrational in character, but also dangerous to the economic development of the DDR. Several members of the elite group (economists Dahlem, Selbmann and others) who advocated at least a system of economic decentralization with a lessening of police terror, were periodically purged for their unorthodox views. Advocates of this policy maintained that the farmers must be encouraged to cultivate their "private sectors" assiduously and that the rate of agricultural collectivization should be slowed down, rather than stepped up, with the maintenance and possible enlargement of the peasants' private plots. They also insisted that the working conditions of industrial labor ought to be improved and that, in general, the "narrow-minded" attitude of terrorizing the working class with a Stalinist "wooden mallet" policy be abandoned. This policy, in short, would appeal to the *voluntary* efforts of the worker, spurring him on with such ubiquitous slogans as: "Produce more in the same amount of time for the same amount of money!"

Here a noncompulsory pattern of the social mobilization of the masses seems to be stressed, while terror and compulsion are—at least temporarily—replaced by voluntarily fixed production goals. The incentive offered the population is the all-out effort to improve the general standard of living and assure the average worker of more consumer goods at the expense of the previously immense heavy industrial investment. At this point the government kept running into serious trouble since the standard of living had been so low for so many years that consumer-good shortages continued to be appalling. This dilemma then produced the official explanation that the very existence of the many consumer-good shortages proved in reality that a steady improvement was taking place in the country's standard of living. "High living standard equals shortages!" seems to have been the SED's governing slogan for a while. It led to such ludicrous newspaper statements as the assertion (in a 1963 statement of the party's official *Neues Deutschland*) that consumer good shortages *on the whole* were not really serious because they showed up only in the "one thousand little things of one's daily needs." This is a semantically fascinating justification of a "steadily improving" living standard as seen by the manipulators of a totally controlled economy.

The second and more recent policy pattern has been that of a Stalinist economic toughness. The building of the Berlin Wall on August 13, 1961, marked the reinstitution of certain harsh and involuntary measures which augured the dawning of a truly neo-Stalinist era in East Germany. In order to understand the new "line," we must first consider the social and economic implications of the mass exodus of DDR citizens between 1948 and 1961.

Using reliable West German statistics concerning the background of this enormous mass migration, it is now clear that approximately four million East Germans fled their homeland during this period. More concretely, about 30,000 DDR refugees have crossed the Iron Curtain border *each month*, year in and year out, thus "voting with their feet" against the Soviet-imposed tyranny. This steady exodus has dealt such a damaging blow to East German prestige and manpower that, at least in retrospect, it seems to have made the building of a wall, the closing-off of a wide-open escape hatch, a foregone conclusion by 1960 or 1961. The economic damage to the country becomes even more apparent if we consider the three social groups which have played the most conspicuous part in this large-scale and dynamic process of political defection. The steady flight of leading intellectuals, college professors, editors, prominent lawyers, engineers, and doctors, has been emphatically noted by the West. The medical profession in particular has taken a firm stand in rejecting the Ulbricht regime. Annually between 1500 and 2000 doctors had escaped to the West, and even in the course of a "slower year," like 1959, about 400 left. The doctor shortage has become one of East

Germany's major headaches. In numerous semiempty hospitals and clinics, Bulgarian and Czech medical students, imported to help out a fellow Communist country, are posing as doctors and perform medical tasks. Frequently even North Korean and Albanian researchers have been called upon to fill appointments in high-level technical institutes and universities from which most of the permanent (and competent) staff had already fled to the West.

The second group has been the youth, particularly of college age. Here the principal reason must have been the all-pervasive dreariness and minute regimentation of everyday life, coupled with the unpromising, limited economic opportunities of East Germany as contrasted with West Germany. No Western observer who has witnessed the dreary marching and Nazi-type behavior of the Free German Youth Movement, or glanced at the depressing Humboldt University in East Berlin could have doubted the sincerity and determination of youth to improve its living conditions and search for a freer and more pleasant atmosphere elsewhere. Leaving their families behind, groups of young men and women escapees have lined up daily at the reception centers maintained for refugees in West Berlin.

While industrial workers have never appeared en masse among the refugees, the 1960 agricultural collectivization drive and the threatened collectivization of the independent artisan class led to a sudden spurt in the flight of artisans, farmers, farm laborers, and apprentices in state production cooperatives. Some 1150 farmers left their farms in March and April 1960 compared with 332 in January and February. In a period of one week in May, more than 16,500 East Germans fled to West Berlin, while for the comparable period the 1959 figure was merely 8100. On the whole, these disastrous attempts to communize the land as well as the people's major economic activities, were not likely to accelerate the pace of reconstruction. On the contrary, as a result of this mass exodus, the Communist party had been forced to stage a temporary and purely tactical retreat.

The retreat by the regime did not halt either the process of agricultural collectivization or the socialization of industry. The SED's "march toward triumphant and complete socialism" continued relentlessly. The end result was predetermined and inevitable indeed: by 1963 some 200,000 small businesses, employing about 600,000 people, were gradually compressed into the collectivized mould of what has become the most Communistic state in Europe outside the Soviet Union.

In the meantime the problem of redefectors, refugees from the Soviet zone deciding to leave the West and return to the East, had concerned both the West and East German governments. Statistics on this sensitive issue are particularly exaggerated and frequently misleading. The East Berlin regime claims that one out of every four defectors actually redefects to East Germany, while the Federal Republic figures refer to one out of ten "returnees." Of the two, the latter statistic seems to be far more acceptable. Difficulties in locating jobs, loneliness, and homesickness seem to have been the primary reasons motivating the redefectors. After all, most of the four million who have left East Germany through the years had personal and family ties to the East, and they were constantly renewing these connections through correspondence and occasional visits which were possible until the erection of the Berlin Wall in 1961.

West Berlin operators of mass-media communications, particularly officials of RIAS—Radio in the American Sector—have repeatedly stressed that a fair percentage of the redefectors had been directly involved in espionage for East Germany, and indirectly for Soviet authorities. The story of many redefectors merely camouflages a West German expulsion order after the originally *bona fide* refugee has been caught gathering intelligence materials in the West. West Berlin has served not only as a showcase of democracy, but also as a primary battleground in the current Cold War. Thus it has been saturated by agents and operators of all types from behind the Iron Curtain. It seemed rather logical that a number of them would pose as legitimate political refugees, would be flown out of Berlin to Frankfurt or Munich at West German expense, and having accomplished their espionage mission, would then request return transportation to the East, claiming this time to be genuine re-emigrants. Unhappily, not even the strictest and most thorough political checks or de-Communization proceedings in West Berlin were able to eradicate this pattern of infiltration behind the forward bastions of the Free World.

Since August 1961 neo-Stalinist (or in Communist parlance "left-wing extremist") measures have circumscribed the everyday life of the walled-in population ever more tightly. A newly appointed triumvirate of tough-minded bureaucrats announced the new policies of strictness, austerity, forced savings, and higher workers' productivity as early as July of that year. As of that date food rationing was reintroduced with butter, eggs, milk, and flour carefully rationed under a "local" system which considerably aggravated the plight of the consumers. As British author Terence Prittie observed:

Families had to register with certain shops, and if they bought rationed items elsewhere, the contravention of the local regulations was sure to be discovered by the army of state inspectors (estimated at 47,000 and tending to increase). The actual market supply of vegetables has been pitiful this year . . . no choice, a complete lack of quality, and an even more striking lack of interest on the part of the sellers. Butcher shops have often been sold out of meat by 11 o'clock in the morning, and in some towns the authorities imposed two "meatless" days per week.[3]

Despite severe governmental measures, the growth rate of industrial production has steadily declined while food and power shortages (ever since the winter of 1962–1963) have persisted in a nearly catastrophic manner. The recent state of the DDR's economy has been described as mixed, composed of uneven doses of exhortation and compulsion. The manpower problem has been illustrative of both methods. The country has been plagued with a growing manpower shortage which neither the drastic termination of the refugee exodus after 1961 nor the availability of about 60,000 workers who had previously been employed in West Berlin and lost their jobs, was able to offset. On the contrary, the introduction of military conscription in 1962 syphoned off a large number of younger workers who could have been of direct help to the faltering economy. "Today we face the task that with fewer workers we must produce more and simultaneously feed more people. This can be achieved only through considerably higher workers' productivity," observed an

[3] *Problems of Communism* (November–December, 1961). An even more up-to-date discussion of this problem is given by Martin Janicke in "The Persistence of Stalinism," *Problems of Communism* (July–August, 1963), pp. 1–8.

SED party leader in 1963. Subsequently working norms were raised and wages lowered in order to achieve the projected 5.8 percent rate of annual economic growth. Considering the basic technological strength of East Germany, originally well balanced between industry and agriculture, this must be viewed as a fairly low rate. When even this growth seemed impossible to achieve, and the overall industrial production did not rise by more than 3 percent, the grandiose Seven-Year Plan, adopted with so much publicity and fanfare in 1959, was quietly dropped and a new Seven-Year Plan with more modest and realistic goals adopted for the years 1964 to 1970.

On the whole, the ruling party's economic posturing has resulted in two distinct, and essentially contradictory, phenomena. One has been the mobilization of the three million member Free German Youth (FDJ) to combat the economic crisis of the country. For the past several years now the FDJ has been fanatically sponsoring "Youth Into Industry!" and "Youth Back to the Land!" movements. The latter campaign, involving each year several months of "voluntary" work in the villages, has been pushed with particular vigor as a possible antidote to the agricultural plight. The youth leaders are seemingly eager to reverse the strong urbanization trend that sends young people streaming to the cities in search of better opportunities, and hopefully talk of resettling them on the collectivized land. On several recent East Berlin TV programs FDJ chief Schumann strongly criticized young people who insisted on moving to the cities as being "exceptionally poor students of their country's history." The "voluntary brigade" work also extends to the collective farm members, and farmers are being forced to put in 400 to 500 hours of extra work on major agricultural projects without any compensation or credit toward their collective farm work. The widely publicized slogan exhorting both workers and farmers is "Self-obligation for Work," as an after-hours, voluntary, and special effort.

The other symptom of social unrest can best be characterized as ideological indifference and political apathy. This pattern of behavior is itself a composite of several personal attitudes: a reluctance to obey the dictates of an essentially alien regime; the painful memories of the June 1953 events; and an intense dislike of the pressure, push, exhortation, and compulsion accompanying, with the steady din of an all-pervasive propaganda apparatus, a slowly and almost reluctantly rising standard of living. Last but not least, there is the painful long-term separation of families divided by the Berlin Wall. The comment of a prominent West German newspaper, *Christ Und Welt*, interestingly sums up the prevailing popular attitude: "There is a great ideological stillness in the Zone since no one knows whether what he is doing today will not be wrong the next day." Indeed this stillness, the lack of a fresh breath of air, is probably the most distinctive political feature of the DDR in the 1960's.

Special Problem-Areas of the Ulbricht Regime: Intrabloc Relations and Contacts with the West

The spectrum of DDR problem areas ranges from the question of relations with the Soviet Union and other Communist countries to the issue of policies toward Western nations, including the German Federal Republic. Each of these areas is characterized by a major policy goal or expectation articulated by Walter Ulbricht himself in the past two decades. In intrabloc affairs the DDR has endeavored to maintain good relations with the U.S.S.R. and the Communist countries of Eastern Europe, attempting to camouflage its own status of satellite dependency on the U.S.S.R. In its policies toward the West the DDR has feverishly tried to achieve a minimum of respectability and acceptance while particularly emphasizing in recent years a friendly rapprochement toward various Asian and African countries. Along the line of West German policy, it has set its primary goal in the neutralization and take-over of West Berlin.

Soviet-DDR relations present a complicated picture since the Ulbricht regime basically cannot afford to disagree with the Soviet leadership. At the same time the East Germans have clearly voiced their policy differences on two or three major issues. On these, they disagreed both with Khrushchev and, after the events of October 1964 leading to the removal of Khrushchev, with the dual leadership of Brezhnev and Kosygin. Among the bones of contention the problem of de-Stalinization must take first place. Khrushchev's vigorous policy, particularly following the pronouncements of the Twenty-Second Party Congress of 1961, was a source of acute embarrassment to Ulbricht whose own regime had not only been singularly devoid of such a process, but had even witnessed a recent campaign of *re-Stalinization*. Thus the issue of a "cult of personality," so bitterly denounced in the Soviet Union, seems to be as irrelevant in the DDR as it has been in Communist China where Maoism is clearly based on the personality cult of Mao Tse-tung.

The SED leadership has also reacted in a panicky manner to the Soviet Union's Khrushchev-inspired pro-West German policy. The former Soviet leader's repeated attempts to seek a rapprochement and full understanding on important issues with the Bonn government have clearly frightened Ulbricht and his colleagues. Any reference to *direct* negotiations between Moscow and Bonn, any mention of the "Rapallo Complex" [4] irritates the DDR's opinion-makers and arouses their antagonism. One of the more revealing statements was SED party functionary Gerhard Kegel's East Berlin TV speech which stated that "there were differences in the policies of the Soviet Union and the DDR," and that the latter strongly disagreed with recent Soviet-West German negotiations. When the news that the then Soviet Premier Khrushchev had agreed to meet with West German Chancellor Ludwig Erhard was officially published in August 1964, it evoked a typically ungracious response in East Germany. The East Berlin Radio Service issued the following statement: "It is said that in the very near future, Soviet Premier Nikita Khrushchev may visit Bonn. Why not? Years ago, Adenauer was in Moscow. Nikita Khrushchev might very well pay a visit to Bonn. In the past, talks and exchanges have proved to be useful and correct."

Beyond the fear that these superficial negotiations between Moscow and Bonn might lead to some concrete results, there lies the Ulbricht regime's profound dissatisfaction with the Soviet leaders' stand on Germany. The DDR government has insisted on an all-German reunification plan on completely Communist terms. Under Khrushchev, the Soviet Communist party's approach to this issue was negative or at least one of cautious approval

---

[4] At Rapallo, Italy, in 1922 the German Weimar Republic was the first major European country to recognize the New Russian Bolshevik government.

with great delays involved. Khrushchev articulated this view most clearly in a speech delivered at the Leipzig Fair on March 7, 1959:

> We are for the unity of Germany which is a burning need for the German people. However, can the peoples of the world live without this reunification? Yes, they can and they can even live without it quite well. Can the Germans themselves live without reunification? Yes, indeed they can and they can even live well without it. Consequently, while this is an important issue, it is not a fundamental question.

While this statement is a denial of the Ulbricht view and a contradiction of one of the DDR's basic policy goals, in other areas the Soviet leaders' intention has been of a friendlier nature. They have obviously endeavored to bolster the often-faltering East Berlin regime and to lend a hand to the complex process of stabilizing it. They have repeatedly applied the "peaceful coexistence" doctrine to the DDR, denying the warlike views of China and Albania, and they have pressed (although slowly and with surprising moderation) for the signing of a peace treaty with East Germany. Support has also come on the Berlin issue in which the then party boss Nikita Khrushchev expressed approval of the Wall and of Ulbricht's "Let's keep the pressure on the West and on the West Berliners!" type of brinkmanship policy, with all the attendant dangers of a *permanent* crisis. To the extent that the NATO allies can be kept off balance in Central Europe, the Soviet and East German master strategists agree on this ominous and unsettling policy.

Turning to DDR-Peking relations, an interesting ambivalence in attitudes can be noted. On the one hand, along with Czechoslovakia and Bulgaria, the Ulbricht regime has been increasingly sympathetic to the so-called "Chinese line" with its belligerent Stalinist outlook, its domestic and foreign hardness, and its belief in a monolithically organized international Communist bloc. Such a tough line would theoretically suit Walter Ulbricht, and would probably be a useful justification for his politically unstable regime. On the other hand, the SED has been forced to watch the Soviet Union closely and has been too dependent on Soviet support to be able to afford the open label of being *pro-Chinese* or to develop its own road to socialism. Consequently, DDR leaders have gone out of their way to denounce officially the Peking regime and its role in the Sino-Soviet dispute, even while making subtle mental reservations concerning the validity of these ideological attacks.

The Sino-East German dialogue is of interest to the student of Communism. Speaking through their Albanian mouthpiece, the Chinese have insisted that the basically weak Communist system of the DDR must be strengthened by the immediate signing of a peace treaty between the Soviet Union and East Germany. Then party leader Khrushchev and First Secretary Ulbricht were bitterly criticized by Albanian party boss Enver Hoxha in a public address of November 7, 1961, and ridiculed for mistakenly applying the "peaceful coexistence" concept and a policy of conciliation in postponing the signing of a peace treaty. Not to be outdone by the Albanians, East German Communists have forcefully denounced Peking for a number of ideological "crimes." The year 1964 saw particularly vituperative attacks by the DDR regime which repeatedly claimed that the Chinese Communists were intent on undermining Walter Ulbricht. In a July 16, 1964, statement it stressed, for example, that the Chinese leadership "mixed boldly in the affairs of other fraternal parties, including our party. Indeed, it does not shrink from stirring up the membership of other parties in order to push out their Marxist-Leninist leaders."

East Germany's relations with other bloc countries must be viewed first within the context of Communist international organization, and then of the legal recognition of a country which is essentially a satellite and a Soviet Occupation Zone. East Germany is an important member of both European Communist organizations currently in operation. On January 28, 1956, it was admitted to the Warsaw Pact, the military network for Soviet and East European armed forces and the then Minister of Defense (present Prime Minister) Major General Willy Stoph became Deputy Commander of the Warsaw Pact forces for the DDR. The country has also performed a significant role in the economic integration network of Eastern Europe, CEMA, where it has been assigned key functions in the shipbuilding, chemical, and textile industries, supplying other bloc countries with its technologically more advanced industrial products.

In recent years the West German Federal Republic has solidified its earlier practice of promptly severing ties with any country which has extended recognition to the DDR. Indeed, this pattern of retaliatory action has been raised to the level of a diplomatic principle and is described as the Von Hallstein doctrine (bearing the name of a distinguished German foreign affairs specialist). As a result of rigid enforcement of this doctrine, so far only the Soviet Union, the Eastern European Communist states, Communist China, and Yugoslavia have extended recognition to East Germany. Of these countries, the DDR embassies in Warsaw, Prague, Budapest, Sofia, and Bucharest have played important roles, while the Soviet Embassy in East Berlin, residing in a tremendous building which had been unharmed in World War II, acts as a super-ministry of foreign affairs for this truly satellite "government." In turn, only the most experienced and top-level SED functionaries and party specialists are ever sent to Moscow to staff the large-scale operations of the DDR's embassy to the U.S.S.R.

The non-Communist world has so far presented a solid phalanx against East Germany, both in terms of legal recognition and political relationships. Although there have been rumors that President De Gaulle may recognize the DDR and raise its trade mission in Paris to an embassy by giving it diplomatic status, there has as yet been no concrete move in this direction. Not only have Western and Central European, Latin American, and Middle Eastern countries pointedly ignored Walter Ulbricht, but even the newly emergent African states have so far assumed diplomatic relations with the Federal Republic to the exclusion of the DDR. The *economic* prestige battle, on the other hand, proved to be less hazardous and more remunerative for East Germany. Sidestepping the touchy issue of legal recognition, *de facto* and commercially speaking, the DDR now trades with approximately 100 countries and has concluded particularly profitable trade agreements with such key nations as the United Arab Republic, Iraq, India, and Indonesia, as well as with strategically located new African and Asian states such as Ghana, Guinea, Mali, and Ceylon. East German trade experts and industrial equipment have made their way, as part of aid programs to underdeveloped areas, to Cuba, Colombia, Burma, and Tanzania, to mention just a random sample. Large DDR missions can be found in such cities as Helsinki, Cairo, New Delhi, Djakarta, Baghdad, and Rangoon. They are "trade delegations" in name, but actually operate as political missions in a murky twilight area so characteristic of our Cold War era. Such commercial relationships are carried on, in this case, in a legal vacuum and in a shaky framework of quasidiplomatic recognition. Members of the trade delegations are allowed to fly their nation's flag on the "consulate" buildings and frequently act upon political problems. Thus, the DDR has carved out a place for itself where it is allowed to carry on commercial and political relations with 100 nations, without ever assuming a state of mutual legal recognition. We can evaluate the foreign policy line described here as a two phase policy consciously developed and practiced by the Ulbricht regime: the first goal is to obtain some form of social recognition, while the second step is full diplomatic recognition for the DDR. The main instrument in accomplishing both goals has been East Germany's skillful foreign trade policy.

In DDR-West German relations the real stumbling block appears to be Berlin. One of the SED leaders observed years ago that: "In the class struggle there can be no neutrality." The phrase is worth remembering since this much-tortured term is now being applied to the divided city as the predominant goal of the East German regime. In the viewpoint of the Ulbricht clique Berlin must be "neutralized." Such a neutral or neutralized status implies a treaty terminating Western "occupation" in West Berlin, the removal of all Allied troops, the suspension of West Berlin's current municipal government and legislature, a joint customs zone for both Berlins and—last but not least— an extension of the East Berlin government into West Berlin on German Communist terms. West Berlin, the DDR leaders point out, is in the middle of the customs and sovereign territory of the "German Democratic Republic." It does not belong to the German Federal Republic nor can it continue under indefinite Allied military supervision and control. West Berlin, as Walter Ulbricht angrily stated on the eve of building his Wall in August 1961, was a gaping hole which for years had prevented him from carrying his system to completion.

Needless to say, neither the neutralization of West Berlin through the extension of Communist rule nor the withdrawal of

NATO troops from the beleaguered city, have been acceptable bases for negotiation between either Bonn and East Berlin or—against a broader setting—between Washington and Moscow. Both in the Khrushchev and post-Khrushchev periods Soviet reluctance to draft and sign a separate peace treaty with East Germany, has been a clear-cut indication that the Russian party elite views Walter Ulbricht's overly ambitious plans with regard to Berlin (and ultimately to German reunification) with dismay and caution, if not with outright alarm. In the meantime, American and NATO presence in the Federal Republic and in the Communist-surrounded city of West Berlin, is a solid guarantee that Ulbricht's belligerent aims will be frustrated and exuberant expectations properly deflated.

Conclusions

The following conclusions can be drawn from our survey of East German government and politics.

1. The DDR can be truly classified as a reluctant satellite. The immense gap separating the East German population from its Soviet-imposed leadership has not narrowed in recent years. Indeed this political, ideological, and cultural gap has assumed an additional physical dimension with the construction of the "Wall of Shame" in August 1961. For the past two decades one of the most salient features of the SED cadres and leadership has been "their complete severance from their own nation, and from its feelings and interests."

2. As a result of this antipopular and fanatically Communist attitude, the nature of the regime can rightly be characterized as Stalinist and totalitarian. Neither the anti-Stalinist policy changes of 1953–1956, nor the measures relaxing terror have penetrated beyond the surface; on the contrary, the personalized dictatorship exemplified by Walter Ulbricht has not been eliminated. It has actually undergone a subtle, but obvious, process of steady re-Stalinization.

3. The general climate of popular feeling has not improved perceptibly in East Germany in the past few years. "In strictly human terms," as one expert recently noted, "there has probably been as much frustration and unhappiness in the last decade as

under Stalin, even though it has been of a different order." Two
additional points must be stressed here. The Wall has been of
tragic significance in reminding both West and East Germans of
the prolongation of a divided Germany. This reminder has
acted both as a depressant and as a call for violent action. On
the other hand, it is also obvious that the prospects for any
recurrence of the popular revolt of June 1953 have dimmed in
the DDR. The crushing of that revolt by the Red Army and
the total inability or unwillingness of the West to intervene
have not been forgotten by the captive people of the DDR, and
these developments are not likely to spur them on to future
revolutionary heroics. Of the socioeconomic groups spearheading
a silent opposition to the Ulbricht regime, the intellectuals and
professional people must be mentioned first. Youth is also
antagonistic, and while the Wall has largely eliminated mass
flights to the West, even drastic coercive measures have failed
to end opposition or to kindle enthusiasm for the youth movement (FDJ) or SED.

4. To balance the stark picture painted under the first three
headings, it must also be noted that in the past five years East
Germany's industrial progress has been quite remarkable. Industrial output in 1964–1965 has almost equalled that of all of
Germany in 1936 and consequently living conditions have risen
substantially. Despite the oppressive political atmosphere, cultural and scientific progress has also been significant. This fact
was recognized even by the United States government which in
July 1964 admitted—for the first time—ten East German scholars
to an International Congress of Biochemistry in New York.

However unpleasant the political complexion of its government,
the economic and even cultural potency of East Germany can
no longer be denied. As reported by Paul Wohl in *The Christian
Science Monitor*, when Soviet Secretary Leonid I. Brezhnev visited
East Berlin in October 1964, on the occasion of the fifteenth
anniversary of the East German "state," he was forced to make
the extraordinary admission that the Soviet Union "extensively
applied East German experiences in chemistry, shipbuilding, and
agricultural production." [5]

[5] See his excellent series of articles published in November and December,
1964. The citation here is from "France Detours Toward Pankow," *The
Christian Science Monitor* (December 18, 1964).

Thus the image currently projected by the DDR is a mixed one: it reflects a gray zone, rather than the pronounced black (and little white) of an earlier period which, at least in open terror and oppression, seems to have been worse than the slowly improving years of the 1960's.

BIBLIOGRAPHICAL NOTE

Books

For good background reading five major works appear to be particularly useful since they illuminate several major aspects of the formation and early years of the DDR, this truncated and artificial sector of partitioned Germany. Arnold J. Heidenheimer's *The Governments of Germany* (New York: Crowell, 1961) discusses the broad political features, while John P. Nettl's *The Eastern Zone and Soviet Policy in Germany, 1945–1950* (New York: Oxford University Press, 1951) covers the economic aspects. Wolfgang Leonhard's *Child of the Revolution* (Chicago: Regnery, 1958) is a unique account of the organization of the Ulbricht group which first returned to Germany in 1945; his subsequent *The Kremlin Since Stalin* (New York: Praeger, 1962) analyzes in interesting detail the current Soviet-East German political and military relationships. A recent publication of Georgetown University's Center for Strategic Studies, *Détente, Cold War Strategies In Transition*, edited by E. L. Dulles and R. Crane (New York: Praeger, 1965) contains important essays on the DDR's general position in Eastern Europe (by Klaus Mehnert) and on the perennial Berlin problem (by Eleanor L. Dulles).

In an attempt to keep these notes selective, only recent and specific additions to East German political literature have been cited. Students should also consult such *general* works in the field as Z. K. Brzezinski's *The Soviet Bloc: Unity and Conflict* (Cambridge: Harvard University Press, 1960), and his *Alternative to Partition* (New York: McGraw-Hill, 1965, for the Council on Foreign Relations), as well as Stephen Fischer-Galati (ed.), *Eastern Europe in the Sixties* (New York: Praeger, 1963).

Constitutional aspects are examined in the German-language *Selbstzeugnisse des SED-Regimes* by A. Riklin and K. Westen (Cologne, 1963), and in English by Hans-Heinrich Jescheck, *Justice and the State: Penal Law and its Application in the Soviet-Occupied Zone of Germany* (Tübingen, 1965). The exciting moment of the June 17, 1953 popular uprising is well covered by Stephan

Brandt in his *The East German Uprising* (New York: Praeger, 1955), while Carola Stern sheds light on the ruling party and on its dictator-leader in *Ulbricht: A Political Biography* (New York: Praeger, 1965). This work is not only a revealing portrait of a Stalinist *apparatchik*, but is also invaluable for a further understanding of the Rákosis, Paukers, Gottwalds, and other Soviet satraps of the 1944–1956 period.

Articles

Of the welter of excellent articles dealing with the ideological and political evolution of East Germany, the following deserve special mention: Günter Bartsch, "Die Kommunisten und das Generationsproblem," *Osteuropa* (May, 1964), pp. 329–340; Melvin Croan, "East Germany," from *The Communist States at the Crossroads*, edited by A. Bromke (New York: Praeger, 1965), pp. 126–139, and also his "Soviet-German Relations," *Survey* (October, 1962), pp. 12–28. Dealing with cultural and political problems, Martin Janicke's article, "East Germany Today—the Persistence of Stalinism" presents a panoramic view of life under Ulbricht in *Problems of Communism* (July–August, 1963), pp. 1–8. Noteworthy is Hans Rogger's essay on "East Germany: Stable or Immobile?" in *Current History* (March, 1965), pp. 135–141. Last, but not least, we should stress the brilliant, incisive study by one of the foremost students of contemporary world Communism, Richard Lowenthal's "The Prospects for Pluralistic Communism," in *Dissent* (Winter, 1965), pp. 103–143.

For special issues of leading periodicals dealing with East Germany in the broader setting of Eastern European politics, consult the following: "East Europe in Flux," *Current History* (March, 1965), pp. 129–182, and *East Europe*, especially the issues for June–December, 1965. From *Problems of Communism* (a bimonthly publication by the United States Information Agency, Washington, D.C.), consult "Ten Years After Stalin," a Special Issue, Vol. XII, No. 2 (March–April, 1963), pp. 1–108; "New Winds in Eastern Europe," (May–June, 1964), pp. 1–88; and "The Iron Curtain Today," (November–December, 1964), pp. 1–67. All of these issues are useful; many of the articles have been contributed by experts with long residence and experience in a particular Iron Curtain country.

CHAPTER FIVE

Hungary

The General Setting

THE TERMS of the 1945 armistice, generally confirmed by the 1947 Peace Treaty of Paris, deprived Hungary of all the territories "returned" to it during World War II, reducing the country to its Treaty of Trianon size.[1] It is today the second smallest state of Eastern Europe, its territory comprising almost 36,000 square miles, which is somewhat smaller than the state of Indiana. As of January 1, 1961, Hungary had over 10 million inhabitants, almost entirely of Magyar nationality. The only prewar sizable minority, the German one, has been reduced by the postwar partial expulsion based on the 1945 Potsdam Agreement. Almost two-thirds of the population are Roman Catholic, the rest being divided among different Protestant churches, the Calvinists being by far the largest.

Perhaps the most significant postwar economic and social development has been the rapid industrialization of the still predominantly agricultural country. To this day around 35 percent of the population is dependent for its livelihood on agriculture, the country possessing rather favorable conditions of climate and soil for agricultural pursuits. Despite its relatively small power basis, and (with the exception of bauxite of which Hungary has the greatest deposits in Europe) a conspicuous lack of raw materials, the industrial production has risen enormously, reaching by 1960 over 60 percent of the total national product and providing for the livelihood of over 30 percent of the population. Accompanying the process of industrialization has been

[1] The Treaty of Trianon, signed June 14, 1920, deprived Hungary of two-thirds of its pre-World War I territory and three-fifths of its population.

a pronounced trend toward urbanization; by 1960 almost 40 percent of the total population lived in cities, with 18.1 percent being settled in Budapest.

Twilight of Democracy

Hungary started its postwar existence under most unfavorable circumstances. It was not only treated as a defeated German satellite but, in the last year of the conflict, was also devastated by the war which took place on its territory. The country suffered immensely under the Red Army occupation, the expenses of which it had to bear. The Soviet government proceeded to a merciless exactment of the provisionally fixed reparation bill, demanding immediate delivery of great quantities of manufactured goods. Last but not least, there was the Soviet demand that all German assets located on Hungarian territory be delivered to the Soviet Union as "war booty."

From the point of view of Communist theory and practice Hungary seemed to provide an excellent opportunity for the application of the classical Bolshevik social revolution. Military defeat and bankruptcy of the old regime appeared to favor action by a small but determined and highly disciplined group of professional revolutionaries. But the tragic experience under the Communist Béla Kun shortly after World War I had left a definite imprint in the minds of the Hungarian people. This, coupled with the traditional fear of Russia, prevented the still very weak Hungarian Communist party (hereinafter referred to as HCP) from any immediate violent action.

No doubt in the period of the Popular Front and later, the Communists were able to renew rather small-scale activities within the country, but it was only in the last year of the war that they began to show more determination and strength. Yet in the Hungarian Independence Front—a wartime resistance organization—the HCP, represented by Laszlo Rajk and his group, played the role of a junior partner, being overshadowed by the much larger and more experienced Smallholders' and Social Democratic parties. The CPH position was greatly strengthened after the Red Army conquest of Hungary east of the Tisza, which made it possible for the well-trained and highly indoctrinated Communist exiles, who since 1919 had lived in Moscow and performed relatively important services for the Comintern to move to Debrecen, the temporary capital of "liberated" Hungary. It was then that the CPH assumed a position of what seemed to be equality with the other political parties. Conscious of its many weaknesses, however, the party followed a policy of moderation, both in its tactics and final aims. Thus the provisional National Assembly and the provisional government of General Béla Miklos were declared to be a genuine coalition based on the wartime underground cooperation of the Smallholders, the Social Democrats, and the Communists, to whom representatives of the National Peasant and Citizen Democratic parties were added. The 12-member cabinet included five nonpolitical members, some of definitely conservative leanings. Moreover, as in the other Eastern European states, so in Hungary the Communist party followed a preconceived policy characterized by emphasis on close friendship with other "democratic" groups, intense patriotism, religious tolerance, and apparent devotion to the ideals and practices of democracy. Some CPH policies, such as the transformation of the antiquated social system which was to be achieved by a radical land reform, were identical with those of the other parties and corresponded to the wishes of the great majority of the nation. In a similar fashion there was a general understanding among the existing parties as to the nationalization of key industries.

Yet even the first steps aiming at the restoration of organized life in postwar Hungary bore the definite imprint of Soviet practices. This was true of the nature of the provisional National Assembly which was based on the "election" by acclamation of an equal number of representatives designated by the Smallholders, the Social Democrats, and the CPH. The seemingly representative composition of the provisional government belied its true nature. The share of the Communists, which was to be equal to that of the other coalition members, was in reality much larger. One nonpolitical member proved to be a Communist of long standing; also Francis Erdei who, as representative of the small National Peasant party, held the all-important Ministry of the Interior, proved to be a willing tool of the Communists. Thus from the very beginning the police apparatus was open to CPH infiltration. As in the other liberated states of the area, the Communists managed to seize control over the trade unions which in the past had been dominated by the Social Democrats. The National Federation of Trade Unions assumed important political functions in the public life of the country, being given representation in the National Committees and other organs of the revolution. Last but not least, the left-wing Social Democrats, led by Árpád Szakasits, gradually eliminated the moderate prewar leadership of the party which soon changed into a staunch supporter of Communist policies.

In retrospect it must be said that the elements of democratic constitutionalism—represented in the first place by the Small-holders' party—fought a desperate defensive struggle, a rearguard action in which they had little chance of success. It was the Soviets and their military might who enabled the CPH to play its role in the grand strategy of totalitarian infiltration. The presence of Russian troops alone enhanced the Communist chances by creating an atmosphere of despondency and weakening the will of the less determined adherents of democracy. Even those who were resolute opponents of Communism had nothing left but to accept the promises of the HCP at their face value and regard its relatively far-reaching departure from Soviet practices and theory as genuine. Being shielded by its powerful protector, the CPH could afford such concessions without risking the success of its future bid for power; at the same time it could profit from its liberal and tolerant stand. Later, when the Communist party tactics changed and the time came for a frontal attack against the greatly weakened forces of democracy, the availability of immediate aid from the Red Army guaranteed the victory of any policies the CPH decided to pursue.

Yet almost until the end of 1946 the prospects for internal order and stability under the coalition of the existing political parties—the so-called Hungarian National Front—seemed to be relatively good. The land reform, for which the Communist Minister of Agriculture, Imre Nagy, claimed credit, failed to sway the peasant masses to the extreme left. Nor did harassment by the Communist-infiltrated Ministry of the Interior divert the population from supporting the non-Communists who were represented by the Smallholders' party. Perhaps the only gain of the Communists was their seizure of a large degree of control over the leadership of the Social Democratic and National Peasant parties with whom the CPH formed the so-called leftist bloc. On the other hand, the ruthlessness of the Soviet occupation and the willingness of the Communists to disregard vital national interests tended to awaken the Hungarian people to the danger of the Soviet type of totalitarianism.

When the test of strength came, in the November 1945 election, the leftist parties suffered a crushing defeat. Against the 57 percent majority of the Smallholders, the CPH and the Social Democrats received only 17 percent each, and the National Peasant party a mere 5 percent. The declaration that Hungary was a republic, which followed, was a foregone conclusion unopposed by any of the political parties. Yet this highly democratic election was not expressed by a democratic division of power. While the majority received the offices of the President (Zoltán Tildy) and the Premier (Ferenc Nagy), the leftist bloc was allotted the same number of ministers as the Smallholders, the CPH keeping at the same time the Ministry of the Interior.

As subsequent developments proved, the feeling of optimism and belief in the possibility of establishing a constitutional democracy after departure of the Soviets proved utterly unwarranted. Failure to gain a majority by democratic means caused the Communists to replace their "mild" methods by outright terror, forceful repression, and intimidation.

The Communist Seizure of Power

The story of the Hungarian Communist seizure of power is not different from that of the other Eastern European countries. What gave it a peculiar flavor was not the decisiveness of Soviet intervention (without which no country of the area would have succumbed to Communism), but the fact that the CPH—while supported by its two partners in the leftist bloc—alone represented only 17 percent of the electorate. It has been pointed out that the Communists made use of two methods: "The discovery of anti-democratic conspiracies and the forced merger."[2] While by no means original, the first method proved to be particularly suited to the nature of the only opposition party. No doubt the number of adherents of the old regime in the Smallholders' party was no larger—and probably much smaller—than in the CPH which welcomed anyone to its still rather thin ranks. The main advantage of the majority party, namely its ability to combine in one organization almost 60 percent of the electorate, proved to be its main shortcoming. In their postwar form the Small-holders, one of the traditional Hungarian political parties, suf-fered from a lack of internal cohesion and ideological firmness. This relative ambiguity, while understandable in a party which had greatly increased its size and suddenly assumed a leading position, offered a unique opportunity for Communist attacks against its integrity and later its very existence.

The repressive action, which started at the end of 1946, was undertaken with utmost brutality by the Communist-controlled political squad of the army, the security police and, when neces-sary, by the Soviet authorities. The arrest of a number of alleged conspirators against the Republic was followed by the imprison-ment of their "accomplices" among the Smallholders deputies, and reached its summit in the arrest by the Soviet secret police of Béla Kovacs, the party's Secretary General and one of the staunch-est defenders of Hungarian democracy. While greatly disturbed, the remaining leaders of the Smallholders' party refused to abandon the coalition in the vain hope that they might still be able to stem the tide of Communism. While often criticized for having accepted the Communist-imposed process of "self-liquidation," the leaders of the Smallholders' party, apart from armed resist-ance, had no other choice. In June 1947 the resignation of Ferenc Nagy brought about a sudden collapse of whatever organ-ized political resistance to the CPH practices might have remained. There followed further arrests and many opposition leaders were forced into exile.

Having eliminated its main competitor, the CPH made its second bid for more popular support. Interestingly enough, in the August 1947 election six opposition parties were allowed to

[2] Paul Kecskemeti, *The Unexpected Revolution* (Stanford, Calif.: Stanford University Press, 1961), p. 201.

participate, ostensibly in order to prevent the emergence of a large non-Communist party. Despite electoral manipulation the CPH received only 22 percent of all votes, but the Communist-dominated National Front of which the Communist Party was the principal component, secured 60 percent. The odd forty percent of the electorate, who voted for the non-Communist opposition parties, were soon deprived of their parliamentary representation. By the beginning of 1948 only the parties of the National Front remained.

As elsewhere, so in Hungary the development toward total Communist supremacy was concluded by the merger of the Social Democrats with the Communists. This last act of consolidation was greatly aided by the efforts of the opportunist leader of the Socialists, Árpád Szakasits, who clearly dominated his less astute colleagues in Social Democratic Party. In June 1948 the "Hungarian Workers party" (hereinafter to be referred to as the HWP) emerged. A postscript to this development was the February 1949 creation of the Hungarian Independent People's Front. It was the single list of this Front which, in the May 1949 "election" won an overwhelming victory over the forces of Hungarian "reaction."

The Period of Stalinism

From the point of view of the history of Hungarian Communism, the "transitional" year 1948 prepared the ground for systematic Stalinization. This cataclysmic development can be identified with the personality of one man—the Secretary General of the HWP, Mátyás Rákosi. A member of the Béla Kun government and an official of the Comintern, he was a veteran of Hungarian prisons; since 1940 he had lived in Moscow, becoming the leader of the Hungarian Communist exiles in the Soviet Union. While eager to devote his not inconsiderable intelligence and knowledge to the task of the Sovietization of Hungary, Rákosi's main asset was his understanding of the power machinations within the CPSU and his ability to read the mind of Stalin better than any of the Hungarian Communist leaders. This fact alone qualified him to become Stalin's lieutenant in Hungary. Compared to the leaders of other Communist parties of the Eastern European countries, Rákosi's control over his party and country was infinitely greater, being in certain respects similar to that of the Russian dictator. Indeed, there was a certain similarity between the two men. While capable of putting on an appearance of friendliness and even good nature, in reality their minds were warped by vindictiveness, deceitfulness, and ruthlessness bordering on the sadistic. Heading the so-called "Muscovite" group in the HWP, Rákosi regarded Communism as an unswerving and almost mechanical transplantation of Stalinist concepts and practices to Hungarian soil. His dictatorship, far from being that of the proletariat, was not even that of the party. As in the Soviet Union, it assumed a peculiarly personal character. Even the more influential members of the Political Bureau were pressed into the background by the dynamic personality of the otherwise unattractive and dwarfish Rákosi.

It was this narrowing of the basis of power that soon made crude and barbarian terror inevitable. As a result, the years of Stalinism in Hungary saw a tremendous growth of the instruments of coercion. In December 1949 the dreaded State Security Section (AVO) in the Ministry of the Interior was replaced by the State Security Authority (AVH). This new organ, with which also the Frontier Guard units were amalgamated, was subordinated directly to the Council of Ministers and headed by one of the most ruthless members of the "Muscovite" group, Gábor Péter. In reality, however, the new police acted under the direct orders of Rákosi himself, establishing at the same time close contacts with the Soviet security organs, the MVD and the MGB. The functions of the AVH soon were extended to cover the entire Hungarian nation in all aspects of its societal life. Starting in 1947, severe punishments, including deportations, forced labor, and even executions, which originally were meted out only against war criminals and Hungarian pro-Nazis, were directed against all anti-Communist elements in the democratic parties. By 1949 the persecution changed into a ruthless campaign of terror carried on—in a truly totalitarian manner—against both real and potential enemies of the regime. While forced collectivization made relatively little progress (by the end of the Stalinist period collective farms covered only 26 percent of all arable land), the struggle against the *kulaks* was conducted with great brutality, exposing independent farmers to different types of persecution and resulting in the stagnation and even relative decrease of agricultural production. This policy, which caused a considerable lowering of the standard of living, was further aggravated by a senseless increase of the heavy industrial production without regard for the actual needs of the people or the economic potentialities of the country.

Equally distressing was the persecution of the churches initiated in the middle of 1948 by the nationalization of all Catholic schools. In 1949 the regime started an all-out campaign against the Roman Catholic Church, sentencing Cardinal Mindszenty, the Hungarian Primate, to life imprisonment. In keeping with the time-honored practice of Communist governments, a special State Office for Church Affairs was created and the organization of a pro-regime Committee of Catholic Priests was enforced. Amid continuous persecutions of the clergy and of members of religious orders, including the ranking head of the Catholic Church, Archbishop Grösz, a decree was published empowering the government to appoint church dignitaries. Only then, in July 1951, did the bishops take an oath of allegiance to the constitution of the People's Republic. The Protestant churches, having first accepted a compromise with the Communist government, eventually found themselves in conflict with the regime, their bishops being forced to vacate their positions in favor of men more "adaptable" to Communism.

The disruption of the churches was accompanied by a fundamental reorganization of the entire educational system which was to become one of the main weapons of class warfare. Also, all means of communication were subordinated to the ultimate aims of Stalinism. Above all, literary creation was put under the control of the HWP, Hungarian authors being forced either to subscribe to the tenets of "socialist realism" or to be silent.

Becoming an aim in itself, terror which was aptly administered by Gábor Péter soon turned against the members of the HWP itself, exacting the terrible toll of around 200,000 victims. Of course, the action of the organs of state security did not take place in isolation, but was closely coordinated with the policies of the Kremlin. Most characteristic of Rákosi's terror was the fate of Árpád Szakasits, the Social Democratic leader who did his utmost to destroy his own party and merge it with the Communists. While his Czechoslovak counterpart, Zdenék Fierlinger, managed to maintain his position, Szakasits was not only deprived of his functions but also subjected to the indignities of the Communist police. Another characteristic of the Hungarian purge was the speed with which it changed into what might be described as a domestic *Yezhovshchina*, engulfing the fanatical leader of the interwar Communist underground, former Minister of the Interior László Rajk.

It is not easy to explain the mystery of Rajk's execution. His relationship to Rákosi was that of a potential competitor—not dissimilar to that of the Czechoslovak Secretary General Slánský to the party leader, Klement Gottwald. It may well be that, like Gottwald, Rákosi did not expect his purge to go that far. Granted his vindictiveness and violent nature, Rákosi would have been hardly opposed even to the death of his rival. On the other hand, like Gottwald he must have been fully aware of the ominous precedent-making quality of Rajk's trial and execution. The visit of János Kádár in Rajk's prison, where on behalf of Rákosi he promised Rajk his life if he made a full confession, might be regarded as a confirmation of this theory. The fact that Rajk did not escape execution may be explained by Rákosi's inability to stop the Soviet-Hungarian police machine.

It is impossible to underestimate the overall impact of the period of purges on the Hungarian people. It may have imposed the deadly silence of a cemetery, but at the same time it entirely destroyed what little moral justification the HWP might have had.

The "New Course" and Its Effects

There were basically two reasons why the "New Course" policy, inaugurated after the death of Stalin, was much more effective in Hungary than in the other satellites of the Soviet Union. In the first place, Rákosi's policy of terror and economic adventurism, which brought the entire Communist system into disrepute, endangered the very foundations of the regime. Secondly, and more importantly, Hungary had a Communist leader who presented an alternative to Rákosi. This man was Imre Nagy, the scholarly professor who spent the war years in Russia and was known to be especially critical of the economic policies of the regime. The CPSU leadership took the matter into its own hands, inviting both men to Moscow in June 1953. The Soviet rulers were unprepared to repudiate Rákosi, preferring a compromise solution by allowing him to retain the position of First Secretary of the party and entrusting the office of Prime Minister to Imre Nagy.

The duumvirate imposed on Hungary, however, resulted in a seesaw struggle between the two leaders. While rebuked by Moscow, Rákosi refused to accept defeat and with the support of party functionaries started a systematic sabotage of Nagy's reforms. The New Course program of the Prime Minister was announced in July 1953. It consisted of abandoning the overemphasis on heavy industrialization and forcible collectivization; also, it promised support to individual farmers and artisans and, above all, the undoing of the many violations of legality and the excesses against elementary concepts of justice.

In the political power contest between Rákosi and Nagy the leadership of the CPSU played the role of an umpire. As usual in Communist societies, the contest assumed the form of an ideological dispute which ran parallel to that between Malenkov and Khrushchev. Against Nagy's learned arguments, based on the teachings of Lenin, Rákosi rather demagogically accused his antagonist of trespassing against the main principle of Leninism —that of the leading role of the Communist party. Using the disintegration of the collective farm system which followed Nagy's speech as a pretext, Rákosi maintained that the reform program, if put into effect in its entirety, would endanger the very foundations of Communism in Hungary. Yet his intrigues and even complaints to the Kremlin masters proved to be of little avail. Nagy managed to prevail over his rival even on such politically delicate issues as the dissolution of concentration camps and the release of hundreds of their Communist and former Social Democratic inmates. It may well be that the sudden emergence of these writers, journalists, intellectual workers, and party functionaries was to be one of the ingredients of the 1956 revolution.

What these innocent victims of Hungarian Stalinism had to say about their experiences in the horror chambers of the AVH demonstrated the sadistic nature of Communist terror and exploded as base lies all the accusations levelled against them. Among the party functionaries who were released was János Kádár who, in the turbulent days of the revolution and after, was destined to play a role of great political significance.

Despite the attractiveness of the reforms promised and partly introduced by Nagy, he remained isolated in the party leadership and received little support from the masses. Thus he continued to be dependent on the goodwill of the Kremlin. This humiliating subordination was demonstrated by his April 1955 dismissal from all state and party functions. His demotion, which was dutifully performed by the same Central Committee that had brought him to power, resulted from the change in the political power equilibrium in the Soviet Union, as expressed by Khrushchev's victory over Malenkov. Nagy's fall and the subsequent discontinuation of his New Course were explained as results of his erroneous policies emphasizing the production of consumer goods at the expense of heavy industry. His industrial reconversion policies, it was stated, were too expensive and incompatible with the economic potentialities of Hungary. In addition, he was accused of "rightist opportunist" tendencies and "anti-Party factional methods" that were contrary to the principles of Marxism-Leninism. The treatment of Nagy, however, was much harsher than that of Rákosi after his 1953 demotion. One month after his removal from all positions of power, the former Prime Minister was expelled from the party. However unsuccessful it might have been, Nagy's tenure marked the beginning of a split in the Communist leadership. What was more important, however, was that he was the first to provide an alternative to the Soviet type of Communism.

The Hungarian Uprising of 1956

The Hungarian revolution occupies a special position among the major Eastern European attempts to shake off Soviet domination. While Yugoslavia declared its political independence of the Soviet Union, it developed its own brand of Communism which continued the principle of the power monopoly of the Communist party. Poland secured for itself a relatively high degree of political and economic autonomy, but in the realm of ideology limited its reforms to less important deviations from Soviet orthodoxy. Hungary alone challenged not only the power of the Kremlin but also the ideology of Communism. Only in Hungary was there an attempt to do away with the first of the basic laws of orthodox Communism, namely that relating to the dictatorship of the proletariat. In the last days of its existence, the revolutionary regime replaced the Communist party monopoly by a genuine multiparty system. Concepts of economic collectivism were to be combined with the all-important procedural principles of Western democracy. It was this attempt, no less than the foreign policies of the revolutionary government, that brought about the disastrous Soviet intervention.

PRELUDE TO REVOLUTION

After Nagy's elimination, the separation of party and chief state offices was continued, but the fact that the new Premier was a political nonentity created the impression that Rákosi might be able to return to the concept of one-man rule. In reality, however, his power was only a shadow of what it had been in Stalin's lifetime. No doubt heavy industry was returned to its position of priority, but there was no resumption of forced collectivization. Outright enemies of the regime were persecuted, but the secret police acted with relative restraint. While tending toward dogmatism, Rákosi's regime was no longer in a position to restore the terroristic methods of Stalinism. On the contrary, the Hungarian leader was forced to follow painstakingly Moscow's policy of gradual decompression.

What was most painful for Rákosi was his inability to reduce to impotence those functionaries of the party who had managed to survive the sufferings of the AVH prisons and concentration camps and were rehabilitated during Nagy's premiership. Indeed, as time passed, some of these men assumed relatively important positions in the party. Nor was it possible for the regime to take any action against Nagy and his supporters. No wonder that the latent split within the HWP continued to grow. The main shortcoming of Rákosi's opponents was lack of internal unity and coordination of action. Thus the Party Secretary was able to paralyze the first significant action of protest, the November 1955 Memorandum of writers, which severely criticized the cultural policies of the party and government.

It seems that the Hungarian ruler remained unaware of the enmity of the masses and of the gradual undermining of his position even within the HWP leadership. While definitely "orthodox" in its political views, the group of former prisoners, headed by János Kádár, never forgave Rákosi and was determined to do its utmost to limit his power. The second group, composed of the intellectual elite of the party, were not only anti-Stalinists but also men who had serious doubts about the Soviet application of Marxism-Leninism. It was this group that began to look to Imre Nagy as a potential savior of Hungary.

Curiously enough, the man who in his previous struggle for power seemed to have put up practically no fight, suddenly became a symbol of defiance against the Rákosi regime. The fact that he refused to follow Malenkov's example and recant his "mistaken views" gained him the admiration both of the Communist intellectuals and of the broader masses of the people. Rightly or wrongly, he was regarded as "the providential statesman of Hungary"[3]—a man destined to lead his nation toward a happier future.

In political retirement, Nagy was engaged in writing a defense of his policies which he believed he would be able to submit to the Central Committee of the HWP. This defense, which in 1957 was published in the West,[4] was characterized by a firm belief in the possibility of combining Hungarian patriotism with Communism. Nagy's Communism, however, was nearer to Titoism, or even Western socialism, than to Khrushchev's version of Marxism-Leninism. Great emphasis was laid on respect for national tradition, equality among socialist states, and patriotism which he regarded as a necessary ingredient of proletarian internationalism. He wrote with scorn about those who willingly

[3] Ferenc A. Vali, *Rift and Revolt in Hungary* (Cambridge: Harvard University Press, 1961), p. 201.
[4] Imre Nagy, *On Communism: In Defense of the New Course* (New York: Praeger, 1957).

accepted "slavery" in order "to insure their own specially privileged status." Nagy's writings were circulated among his friends, especially those representing the opposition within the party, and greatly contributed to the intellectual ferment of the time.

The struggle against Rákosi and his clique assumed an entirely different character after the Twentieth CPSU Congress. The rejection of the cult of the individual made it possible to attack not only Rákosi, but also some of the basic assumptions of the then orthodox version of Marxism-Leninism. What before was regarded as "rightist and bourgeois democratic deviationism" suddenly changed into an honest endeavor to achieve intraparty democracy, socialist legality, and to return to the time-honored principles of Marx and Lenin. After his return from the Moscow Congress, Rákosi shamelessly associated himself with the new policies of Khrushchev, announcing that the Rajk case has been reviewed by the party and that this "victim of Gábor Péter's gang" has been already rehabilitated by the Supreme Court. He promised similar treatment to all other innocent victims of the violation of the principle of socialist legality.

The opposition forces found a powerful instrument for the presentation of their views in the Petöfi Circle, a discussion society founded under the auspices of the Communist Youth League. In it students, scientists, and influential party writers subjected the entire governmental system to scathing criticism and openly called for Imre Nagy's return to office. No doubt the final ouster of the "Hungarian Stalin," on July 18, 1956, was again decided in Moscow, but its main cause was the nationwide series of demonstrations by his Hungarian opponents. Yet Rákosi's demise was only a partial victory, Khrushchev selecting as his successor Ernö Gerö, well known as a former Stalinist and Rákosi's close associate.

But the liberalization trend continued, being marked, above all, by the monumental demonstration on the occasion of the reburial of Rajk. This macabre spectacle enabled hundreds of thousands of people to demonstrate openly against the regime for the first time since the Communist seizure of power. By then the outcry for immediate reforms became irresistible and the opposition, influenced by the victory of Polish nationalism over Soviet domination, began to formulate a more definite program. The

16-point resolution of the Budapest students, which listed the main aims of the reformers, included such demands as the evacuation of Soviet troops from Hungary, return of Imre Nagy, multiparty elections, and many other liberal democratic claims. While the situation slowly approached a climax, the oppositional forces very carefully avoided the use of violence.

THE SPONTANEOUS REVOLUTION

One of the main weaknesses of the HWP opposition had been its inability to gain full support of the workers. This aim was achieved on October 23, when a student demonstration in Budapest ended in an outburst of mass violence. To use the words of Paul Kecskemeti, "the clash between the police and street crowds attracted by a student demonstration" represented the "juncture between the 'elite pattern' and the 'mass pattern' " which helped to precipitate the Hungarian revolution.

The scope of this study precludes even a cursory examination of this first major armed uprising in a Soviet satellite which—after short-lived initial success—was crushed by the might of the Russian army. It is possible, however, to indicate at least some of the characteristic features of the revolution.

As has been pointed out, it was not planned, but a spontaneous, action determined by a number of circumstances of which the refusal of the army to fight against the rebels, the behavior of the AVH, and Soviet intervention were the most important. After the first shots were fired on October 23, the violent clash snowballed into a revolution, acquiring a life and existence of its own. In a sense, there were two revolutions. The first consisted of continuous changes in the composition and thinking of the Hungarian leadership; this revolutionary development, however, proceeded at a very slow pace, constantly lagging behind the mood of the people. The second revolution—the real one—took possession of the broad masses of the Hungarian nation and was marked by both firmness of belief and clarity of aim. It was only in the first days of November that the two revolutions fused into one, adopting under the leadership of the new Premier, Imre Nagy, a program aiming at domestic democratization and eliminating the humiliating subordination to a foreign power.

Whatever the reasons of the initial withdrawal of the Soviet Army—it might have been the losses sustained in combat or the indecisiveness of the Kremlin—the fact remains that in the desperate encounters with the Russian tanks the juvenile freedom fighters managed to more than hold their own, putting up a magnificent struggle against a stronger and better-armed adversary.

The third characteristic of the revolution concerned developments within the Communist party. Once deprived of its organs of coercion, the AVH being crushed in the course of the fighting, the Communist party melted away, its administrative network disintegrating and its members leaving what they regarded as a sinking ship. It was this sudden collapse that forced the new leadership to make far-reaching concessions which were basically incompatible with the Communist point of view. Only thus can it be explained why even János Kádár, who succeeded Gerö as First Secretary of the party, expressed agreement with the restoration of the multiparty system, thus abandoning the idea of the dictatorship of the proletariat. This he did in the knowledge that a free election would reduce the Communists to an insignificant role. It was perhaps awareness of this weakness that prompted Kádár to proclaim, on November 1, the formation of a new party—the Hungarian Socialist Workers' party (hereinafter referred to as the HSWP)—which both in the composition of its leadership and program still reflected the mood of the revolution.

Despite the tremendous and highly diversified intellectual activity in revolutionary Hungary, it is possible to identify two basic characteristics of its ideology—those of national independence and internal freedom. With regard to these two aims the nation, speaking through the different National (or revolutionary) Councils, displayed an astonishing degree of unanimity. The insurgents resolutely refused to use the term "counterrevolution," insisting on being the "national movement of the Hungarian people." In other words, the great majority opposed the abolition of such basic economic and social changes of the past decade as land reform and the nationalization of key industries. Indeed, the emergence of workers' councils, who soon assumed a decisive role in the entire movement, indicated a trend toward the improvement of the management of nationalized enterprises. Forced collectivization, however, was firmly repudiated. Generally speaking, the revolutionary ideology was marked by emphasis on social and political reforms to which demands of a purely material-istic nature were strictly subordinated. Thus there was absolute unanimity in favor of a return to formal democracy, and partic-ularly to the multiparty system and free elections. In the last five days of the revolutionary government the demand for a complete withdrawal of the Soviet army, for Hungary's neutral-ization, and for the dissociation from the Warsaw Pact—as voiced by Imre Nagy himself—expressed the Hungarian desire to achieve complete national independence. All in all, some of the demands and their formulations were highly reminiscent of the ideology of Hungarian populism. This was best expressed by the plan of the populist István Bibó, written shortly after the Red Army suppressed Hungary's heroic revolutionary effort.

Last but not least, it is necessary to mention the behavior of the Soviet Union which from the very beginning followed a policy of devious deception. It may well be that Khrushchev would have accepted the Hungarian changes, had they been limited to the reforms introduced by Gomulka in Poland. It was toward this end that Mikoyan and Suslov, as well as the Russian ambas-sador, carried on elaborate negotiations with Imre Nagy. The deceptiveness of the Soviet leaders, however, is shown by the fact that they used the delay caused by the negotiations to prepare for a large-scale invasion which was ruthlessly put into effect when the Hungarians refused to meet the Soviet demands.

The Victory of Tyranny and Its Aftermath

The tragic irony of the "victory" of the Hungarian revolution was manifested by the fact that less than three days after the release of the last political prisoners, including Cardinal Minds-zenty, Imre Nagy found his government and country imperilled by a second Soviet intervention. It was then that he appealed to the United Nations, particularly asking the four Great Powers to help Hungary defend its neutrality.

All pleas, including the moving appeal of the Hungarian

Writers' Association, remained unanswered, Hungary being left alone to bear the brunt of the Soviet attack which started on November fourth. While there was no organized army to resist the Soviet onslaught, groups of workers, students, and elements of the military continued to fight for a number of days. Nagy and some of his associates escaped to the Yugoslav Embassy, while Mindszenty was granted diplomatic refuge by the Americans. At the same time János Kádár broadcast from eastern Hungary an appeal to the Hungarian people, asking it to give full support to a new "revolutionary worker-peasant government" which was constituted when it became clear that "the government of Imre Nagy had come under the sway of reaction." As it turned out, the "new government" was composed entirely of Communists and their fellow travelers.

Being totally dependent on the power of the Soviet army, which for many weeks controlled the administrative services of Hungary, Kádár was regarded with utmost contempt. In order to gain at least some degree of sympathy, he took great pains not to dissociate himself entirely from the revolution and some of its original aims. He continued to proscribe the Rákosi clique and to promise a regime of moderation to be based on full cooperation with the workers' councils and even with other parties loyal to the People's Democratic system. As it appeared later, Kádár's moderation was dictated by the fact that the elaborate edifice of prerevolutionary "socialism" had been entirely shattered, that the Communist party lay in ruins, and that the country was in sore need of economic aid. To promote political stabilization and economic restoration required not only loans, which were rather generously granted by the members of the Soviet bloc, but also the cooperation and goodwill of the Hungarian people.

But soon it became clear that the Communists, strengthened by Soviet support, were unwilling to exercise moderation in dealing with the adherents of the former Imre Nagy government. When, on November 22, Nagy and his close collaborators left the Yugoslav Embassy, provided with safe-conduct assurances from the Hungarian and Yugoslav governments, they were arrested by the Soviet authorities and deported to Rumania. It was in this period that a mass exodus from Hungary started; the number of refugees, mostly consisting of young people, reached almost 200,000 by April 1957. In the following two years Kádár, faced with resistance and the sullen opposition of the overwhelming majority of the nation, returned to the Stalinist methods which he himself had exorcised. The one-party rule was re-established, the Writers' Association disbanded, and the worker's councils, "the last institutional citadel of the insurgent nation," dissolved. Thus the consolidation of the party and state was accompanied by an energetic repression against the revolutionary associations and their individual members, particularly the intellectuals, who were subjected to outright persecution. While the reorganized Security Police did not return to the excesses of Stalinism, deportation, long-term imprisonment, and even death sentences were not lacking. The persecution reached its climax in the June 1958 secret trial and execution of Imre Nagy and two of his associates, the others receiving heavy sentences. As pointed out by one observer, this action "constituted a breach of faith almost unprecedented in the history of civilized nations."[5]

This "streamlined" terror eventually resulted in a certain degree of political and economic stabilization. Thus, by the time of the December 1959 (Seventh) HSWP Congress, Kádár was able to inaugurate a policy of concessions. The Writers' Association was reconstituted, mild criticism of party methods (but not aims) was allowed, and the People's Patriotic Front, a mass organization created in the Nagy period, was revived. Despite this apparent liberalization, the regime "kept its powder dry," meting out harsh punishments whenever necessary, and following a policy which retained the substance of orthodox Communism. In its attitude toward the writers, the party only grudgingly and never entirely gave up the requirements of "socialist realism." As a result, only in the last four years did the "wall of silence" between the most prominent *literati* and the regime begin to break down. On the other hand, in the economic field the government relentlessly pursued the aim of complete socialization, the collectivization of agriculture being accomplished by 1962 and bringing about the usual disastrous effects, which for a time changed Hungary into a wheat-importing country. Of special significance was the resumption of the struggle against the churches whose representatives were exposed to

[5] Stephen D. Kertesz, "Hungary," in Stephen D. Kertesz (ed.), *East Central Europe and the World* (Notre Dame, Ind.: Notre Dame University Press, 1962), p. 137.

systematic harassment and persecution. In addition to promoting antireligious propaganda, the regime gave renewed support to the Peace Movement of Hungarian Catholic Priests and comparable government-sponsored organizations. This wave of anti-Catholic measures was brought to a halt by the September 1964 agreement with the Vatican, heralded as the first re-establishment of relations between the Holy See and a Communist country. While solving a number of problems, such as the appointment of bishops, the question of the oaths of priests, and the position of the Hungarian College in Rome, the agreement did not entirely stop the persecution of individual priests.

Budapest today is considered the most lively, outspoken, and liberalizing capital of Eastern Europe. However tempting the atmosphere of "new Hungary" may be, the mementoes of 1956 —"the pathetic appeals of Free Radio Kossuth, the Judas act of Kádár, the 'safe conduct of Imre Nagy' and his judicial murder later on"[6]—cannot be forgotten, either by the Hungarian people or the free world.

The Hungarian Political and Governmental System

As in other Communist societies, in Hungary the foundation of the political system is the Communist party. However, it can hardly be regarded as the personification of "the unity of proletarian principles, will, and revolutionary action." For its development has been marked by internal convulsions and lack of political and ideological continuity. This was true of all three phases of Hungarian Communism—of the ill-fated movement of Béla Kun in 1919; of its post-1944 successor, the party of Mátyás Rákosi, who vilified Béla Kun's memory and declared Stalin to be the model for the Hungarian Communists; and of the party of János Kádár, organized after Rákosi's downfall and the 1956 disintegration of Communism. Even his Hungarian Socialist Workers' party went through profound internal changes, abandoning the heritage of the Hungarian revolution in whose name it was created.

Another feature of Hungarian Communism has been its inability to be accepted as a domestic movement. The parties of Kun

---

[6] Editors of Survey, *Hungary Today* (New York: Praeger, 1962), p. 3.

and Rákosi were regarded as agents of a foreign power; even the regime of Kádár, because of its role in the 1956 events, failed to gain the support of the Hungarian people. Hence the small size of the HSWP is not due to the application of the elitist principle, but to the reluctance of Hungarians to become associated with a party which invited foreign intervention against their nation.

THE COMMUNIST ELITE—ITS ORGANIZATION AND LEADERSHIP

Outside of Russia, Hungary is the only state to have had a Communist regime prior to World War II. The short-lived dictatorship of Béla Kun, however, ended in total collapse which dealt a heavy blow to Hungarian Communism, limiting it almost entirely to the group of exiles living in the Soviet Union and Western Europe. Like their Polish comrades, the Hungarians incurred the wrath of Stalin, Béla Kun succumbing to the paranoia of the Soviet dictator in 1938.

On the other hand, there remained at least some continuity between the 1919 experiment and postwar Communism which soon after 1941 gave rise to the emergence of two factions within the Hungarian Communist party. The more influential were the so-called "Moscovites" led by the former People's Commissar in the 1919 government, Mátyás Rákosi, who spent the war years in the Soviet Union. Rákosi's dynamic and autocratic personality tended to overshadow all the other members of the Muscovite group, including the scholarly Imre Nagy and the world-renowned Marxist philosopher, György Lukács. The second group, whose main representative was László Rajk, consisted of those Communists who spent the interwar and wartime periods in Hungary, being engaged in perilous and hopeless underground activities. The two groups merged only after the liberation of Hungary, on February 25, 1945.

At first the Communists followed a policy of rapid expansion, which they regarded as important in their surge to power. While very small at the beginning, the party soon began to pick up strength, partly through the voluntary cooperation of the poorest elements of the agricultural population who profited from the 1945 land reform, and partly by attracting those who chose to support Communism because of fear or opportunism. It would be inaccurate, however, to deny the party's initial power of attraction which, in the period preceding the seizure of power, was greatly enhanced by its ability to parade as the main representative of the deepest wishes of the Hungarian people. Its universalist and humanitarian appeal, its patriotism, as well as its generosity in judging the sins of Nazi collaborators, greatly contributed to the growth of the party.

Thus the original membership of 30,000 in February 1945 rose by the middle of 1947 to 700,000. The tendency to sacrifice quality for quantity continued until the June 1948 absorption of the Social Democrats by the Communists resulted in the new Hungarian Workers' party with almost 1,500,000 members. Marking the completion of the seizure of power, the merger signalled the advent of the period of socialist construction. It was then that the HWP and its leader, Rákosi, threw off the mask of moderation and proceeded to a series of measures bringing about a fundamental change in the existing institutional, social, and economic patterns of life. Of course, this enormous task could not be accomplished by a party composed of people who had only recently become members (in many cases for politically and ideologically irrelevant reasons), or of those who failed to acknowledge the ideological monopoly of the party leadership. To remedy this basic shortcoming and to become an elitist party, the HWP was subjected to a drastic purge so that by 1951 its membership sank to about 860,000. The expulsions were accompanied by a regime of terror against all who were real or potential menaces to the rule of the "Muscovite foursome," Rákosi, Ernö Gerö, József Révai, and Mihály Farkas. Indeed, Rákosi soon assumed the position of the "Hungarian Stalin," displaying an inclination toward violence and brutality similar to his Moscow master's. His totalitarian despotism reached its zenith in the execution of László Rajk and the subsequent repressive action against other leading members of the party. For a long time it seemed as if terror, accompanied by the "immense victories of socialism," would be sufficient to keep the Communist party membership under control and in line with Rákosi's policies. But when after Stalin's death, Imre Nagy's New Course reforms demonstrated the possibility of an alternative to the horrors of Stalinism, the Hungarian party was suddenly recognized for what it really was, namely, an agent of a foreign power. It was then that its members, many of whom, in the period of terror, "effectively divested themselves of independent judgment and entrusted their moral conscience to the Party for safekeeping,"[7] indignantly turned against it and its main representative. The fact that Rákosi managed to retain his office for so long was due not only to his shrewdness but also to the blindness of his Moscow protectors. The final crash of the Stalinist leadership at the end of October 1956 pulled down the entire edifice of the party which proved to be nothing but an empty shell.

Announcing, on November 1, 1956, the dissolution of the "old" Communist party, Kádár spoke not only for himself, but also for six other Communists, including Imre Nagy, who stood in the forefront of the revolutionary movement. While warning against counterrevolution, he declared that the new Hungarian Socialist Workers' party (HSWP) fully accepted the ideas of the "glorious uprising" which was prepared by Communist "ideological and organizational leaders." Yet of the new HSWP leadership only Kádár, who switched loyalties from the revolution to the Soviet interventionists, remained less than three days later; the other six leaders were dispersed and finally ended in prisons. Instead, a new revolutionary center, headed by Kádár emerged, asserting that the "glorious" revolution was nothing but a counterrevolutionary plot endangering the very foundations of socialism in Hungary.

Whatever its true motivation, the initial policy of moderation adopted by the Kádár regime was perfectly suited to the reorganization of the Communist party, which for many weeks consisted of little more than those party leaders who offered their services to the Soviet occupation authorities. Of course it was fairly easy to reconstitute, under the protection of Soviet bayonets, the central party organs—the Central Committee, an eleven-member Politbureau, and the Secretariat—composed mainly of close associates of Kádár, many of whom had been imprisoned or purged in the Rákosi period. Also the re-establishment of the medium and lower party organs presented no insuperable obstacles. The functionaries of the "old" party, who in most cases were tainted by Stalinism, were only too eager to return to their old jobs.

[7] Paul Zinner, *Revolution in Hungary* (New York: Columbia University Press, 1962), p. 134.

Much more difficult was the membership problem, the majority of former Communists refusing for a long time to apply for admittance to the new party. While in the subsequent years the total membership increased to around 400,000, this success was only relative, as approximately one-half of all members were either in the pay of the HSWP or otherwise closely associated with the Kádár regime. Kádár's boast that "smaller membership preserves the vanguard character of the Party" was, at least in part, a tacit recognition of defeat; the traditional backbone of Communism—genuine industrial workers and representatives of the intelligentsia—were conspicuously missing. The fact that the HSWP became a "party of functionaries" can be regarded as a source of both strength and weakness. It secured the loyalty of its members by a common interest in the preservation of their privileged position. On the other hand, the party remains more distant from the Hungarian people than its prerevolutionary forerunner.

In order to create an impression of basic continuity, the HSWP Congress which met in November 1959 declared itself to be the seventh in the troubled history of Hungarian Communism, disregarding the many cataclysmic disruptions of its development. As pointed out by Tibor Meray, the main aim of this maneuver was to gain both respectability and tradition for the badly damaged reputation of the party:

It accepted Bela Kun's dictatorship of the proletariat of 1919, no less than Bela Kun's subsequent assassination in the Soviet Union; it accepted the recruitment of volunteers for Spain in the thirties, no less than the execution of these volunteers in 1949–50; it accepted even the ten years' dictatorship of Matyas Rakosi, previously denounced by Kadar as the blind and reckless policy of guilty men, but now vindicated in the theses of the congress with the usual qualification that "though some mistakes had been made, it nevertheless had been an era of great democratic and socialist achievements under the guidance of the Party."[8]

This obvious attempt to achieve unity of the Communist movement, going so far as to seek excuses for the 1956 events and to minimize their traumatic significance, resulted from the intra-

[8] Tibor Meray, "Genealogical Troubles," in Editors of Survey, *Hungary Today* (New York: Frederick A. Praeger, 1962), p. 32.

party struggle conducted by Kádár on two fronts for the purity of Marxist-Leninist ideology—against revisionism and against dogmatism. The 1959 policy of the HSWP, while assuming a middle-of-the-road position between these two extremes, was balanced in favor of the former pro-Rákosi dogmatics who, having escaped from Hungary, were (with the exception of Rákosi) allowed to return home. On the other hand, the fight against the very numerous former pro-Nagy revisionists was much more intensive, many members of this group still languishing in prisons. Thus the "centrist" line of Kádár, while serving the needs of the Hungarian party, seemed to coincide with the still strongly antirevisionist policies of Khrushchev.

It was perhaps the unequivocal friendship of Khrushchev, who attended and addressed the congress, that enabled the Hungarian leader to make the bold statement that the Soviet troops would remain in his country "as long as the international situation requires it." In all fairness, however, it is necessary to admit that Kádár made this gesture in order to gain Soviet permission to rid the HSWP of the many glaring defects that made the "old" party detested by the overwhelming majority of the people. He even went so far as to speak of the necessity of the Communists "becoming humane in the right sense of the word."

The Eighth HSWP Congress, which met in November 1962, took place in an atmosphere which in many respects was different from that of 1959. The tenor of this congress, which was preceded by a purge of "sectarian dogmatics" on all levels of the party, was emphasis on the finality of the breach with the old concept of Stalinism in whatever form it might appear. The reiteration of the watchword "whoever is not against us is with us" clearly indicated the party's eagerness to base its policy on the concept of national unity. The 1956 revolution was hardly mentioned, the HSWP considering itself strong enough to continue to build on the foundations of the Kádár brand of socialism. While extremes of revisionism and dogmatism were again condemned, the express rejection of the theory of the sharpening class struggle and a degree of liberalization in cultural affairs demonstrated the measure of self-confidence of the party whose membership had risen to over 500,000.

In the following year the party continued its de-Stalinization policy which was referred to as Kadar's program of "Socialist national unity." Hungarian society, it was stated, had reached a new stage in which the main task was the actual construction of socialism. "The class struggle, naturally, continues at the present stage, but its forms and methods are changed." It is not to be applied "against former kulaks, or in general against members of the former ruling classes." The party carefully avoided the use of the term "liberalization," but at the same time it tolerated and even promoted changes which did away with the most burdensome aspects of Communist totalitarianism. Most significant was the broadening of the base of Hungarian society by admitting to leading positions, especially in the economic organization of the country, nonparty members. The discussion that arose over the issue of *meritocracy*—in which the old-line Stalinists protested against the promotion of such persons to top administrative jobs—ended in the recognition of expert knowledge as the main criterion in the personnel policies of the government. To impose this requirement on all levels of state organization became an extremely difficult problem.

The organizational structure of the HSWP differs little from that of the other Communist parties of the area. While the core of power is vested in the Politbureau, ever since the 1956 revolt the Central Committee has been rising in stature. The party is divided into territorial units on the county, district, and village levels. The basic organizations in the armed forces, frontier guards, internal police, and in the railroad system, are directly subordinated to the national Central Committee. The central party organs have been moulded into effective and highly disciplined tools of Communism. On the other hand, the lower strata of the HSWP organization still suffer from a number of serious shortcomings, ranging from lack of interest to ideological vagueness and heresy.

The discussion of the HSWP would be incomplete without mention of its present leadership. Enough has been said of János Kádár, who is perhaps the most complex and pathetic figure among the Eastern European leaders. He is definitely respected by the party members over whom he exercises full control; even for the masses of the Hungarian people the last years of Kádár's rule compare very favorably with the horrors of the Rákosi period. Yet Kádár's name is indelibly connected with the 1956 destruction of the short-lived Hungarian independence and the draconic repressions that followed. The second in command in the HSWP is the intellectual Gyula Kállai, Politbureau member, the party's chief theoretician, and since July 1965 Prime Minister in the government. The other members of the party leadership are Kádár's close collaborators, the only exceptions being the "Muscovite" Ferenc Münnich and Antal Apró, who occupied an important position under Rákosi.

One of the main characteristics of prerevolutionary Hungarian Communism was its inability to gain genuine support among the youth. The young people, especially university and secondary school students, stood in the vanguard of the reform movement and in the 1956 revolution became the most dedicated fighters for freedom. At the same time, the official youth organization disintegrated to an even greater extent than the HWP itself.

Thus, after the defeat of the revolution, the new HSWP was faced with the difficult problem of turning the youth away from the ideals for which they had fought and suffered. The newly created Communist Youth League, in order to avoid the mistakes of its predecessor, was to combine two concepts. It was to be more closely associated with the party. Secondly, its policies were to be such that they would attract even children of bourgeois origin. Speaking at the League's 1960 congress, János Kádár referred to the youth organization as a "loyal auxiliary of the HSWP, . . . to which the Party will grant all possible aid in the future so that a large number of talented youths can fill leading posts in socialist construction."

On the surface the Communist Youth League was very successful, being able to concentrate in its ranks a relatively large proportion of young people and relegating the formerly independent student organizations to the background. By the beginning of 1965 the League had around 800,000 members. Yet, as was repeatedly admitted by the Communist leaders, the attitude of the young people toward politics and the HSWP remained essentially negative. While many have lost their 1956 enthusiasm, the "cold realism and cynicism" for which they are often criticized are nothing but protests against a system which has brought them bitter disillusionment and a spiritual void.

NONPARTY SOCIAL ORGANIZATIONS

By the beginning of 1949 Hungary started an energetic campaign against what remained of the non-Communist parties. The Independent People's Front which emerged in April 1949 acted as an electoral agent for the HWP, giving only nominal recognition to the non-Communist parties. In 1954 the new Premier, Imre Nagy, being isolated both in the party and government, replaced the Independent People's Front by the so-called Patriotic People's Front. However, his hope that the new organization, which entirely abolished the old political parties, might bring him mass support, remained unfulfilled. The Front played no role during the revolution and practically ceased to exist. It was revived by Kádár only in March 1957 to serve as one of the tools of political consolidation. Embracing, in addition to the HSWP, all mass, social, cultural, and even scientific organizations, the Front was meant to demonstrate the unity of the Hungarian people behind the Kádár government. At the same time it assumed the same electoral functions as its predecessor. Thus in the 1957 and 1963 elections it presented a single list of candidates, acting at least theoretically as an agent of the entire Hungarian people. While even individual membership in the Front has been made possible, it is clear that both its organization and policies are determined by the HSWP.

Of the mass organizations the most important one is the Council of Trade Unions with around 3,000,000 members. In the last ten years it has gone through a development not dissimilar to that of the HSWP. During the revolution it changed temporarily into a genuine workers' association. Beginning with the end of November 1956 it gradually came under the control of its old functionaries and helped the government in the repressive action against the workers' councils. Last but not least, Hungary possesses mass organizations similar to those in other Communist societies. Of these the National Council of Hungarian Women, the National Peace Council, and the Society for the Dissemination of Scientific Knowledge deserve to be mentioned.

CONSTITUTION AND GOVERNMENT

In the period preceding the Communist seizure of power Hungary adopted a provisional constitutional law (Law No. I—1946) which associated the new political organization with past attempts to establish a democratic system of government. Despite its brevity, the new law provided for the introduction of fundamental concepts of Western liberal constitutionalism, paying special attention to the "natural and inalienable rights of man." However, within less than a year and a half the provisional constitution became a dead letter, the country gradually changing into a full-fledged dictatorship of the Communist party. Thus for over a year Hungary had disregarded the rules of its basic law, the political and institutional changes taking place on the basis of Communist party decisions. The adoption of the August 1949 constitution, which was to be one of the external marks of the final victory of Communism, made little change in the current theory and practice of government. Its importance lies in its position in the historical development of People's Democratic constitutionalism. Having been written after the split between Tito and the Cominform, the Hungarian basic law is much nearer to the Soviet model than are the preceding constitutions of Yugoslavia, Bulgaria, Rumania, and particularly Czechoslovakia. On the other hand, it lags behind the more recent Polish, Rumanian, and the 1960 Czechoslovak constitutional documents.

Unlike its democratic predecessor, the Hungarian constitutional charter makes no reference to previous domestic efforts at establishing a politically and socially more adequate system, but derives the "new democracy" entirely from the Red Army liberation and the example and assistance of the Soviet Union. It has all the markings of a document serving a society which has taken more than mere preliminary steps in the building of socialism. Thus it is permeated by the idea of class struggle which by inference can be regarded as the main aim of its substantive provisions. For instance, Hungary is not a state in which the power belongs to the "people" but to the "workers of town and country." The actual purpose of all economic activity "is to dislodge capitalist elements and consistently build up a socialist system of economy." This sweeping statement is a much more accurate description of the actual developments than the confusing provisions of the older People's Democratic constitutions which, rather euphemistically, referred to the state's right of expropriation and nationalization.

Even more outspoken are the provisions dealing with the organization of the judiciary and public prosecution which have closely conformed to the Soviet 1936 constitution. All judges have been made elective and may be recalled by their electors. The provisions relating to the Chief Public Prosecutor were so drafted as to enable him to assume the leading role in the actual administration of justice. Perhaps most far-reaching—as an expression of unmitigated class struggle—is the provision of Article 41 which determines the goals of the Hungarian judicial system. While it speaks of the punishment of "the enemies of the working people," the protection of the state and its economic and social order, and the education of "the working people in the observance of the rules governing the life of a socialist commonwealth," no mention is made of protecting the rights of the individual. No express reference is made to the Communist party, but the statement about the special role of "the working class led by its advance guard" clearly refers to the privileged and monopolitic position of the HSWP.

Even before the adoption of the constitution, measures were taken to remake the legal system so that it would conform to the new social and political conditions. The process of legal change, while somewhat delayed on account of the revolutionary events of 1956, proved in the final analysis to be as thorough as in the other states of Eastern Europe. A large part of the new legislation (even on very important matters) took the form of decrees of the Presidential Council of the National Assembly; their subsequent confirmation by the National Assembly became a matter of form. The law, both substantive and procedural, continued to change in keeping with the shifting needs of the state, as determined by the party. Thus it became the most effective instrument of class struggle.

The initial purpose of the law was to provide the external

framework for the merciless destruction of the antagonistic classes and all opposition to Communist rule. In the course of further development of socialist society, law was used to break peasant resistance to the collectivization drive. Simultaneously, it was turned into a watchdog over the labor discipline necessary to carry out the industrialization drive. While more intensive in the pre-1956 period, the enforcement of labor discipline still looms large in the activities of the courts. Another special category of laws, ordinances, and numerous regulations concerns the protection of "socialist property." To this day the Hungarian public has been unable to think of socialist ownership as it thinks of personal property or the now obsolete private property. Despite the continued progress in the construction of socialism, crimes against state property, such as thefts, irregular practices, etc., are on the increase. This fact has been reflected in the May 1960 Criminal Code. Compared to its predecessor, it has been greatly reduced in size, but it continues the trend toward granting special attention to the defense of the state and the socialist social order, and it also introduces a number of new crimes. The relative decrease in the activities of the courts is due to the introduction, outside the formal legal system, of "social courts" and "trade union tribunals" to deal with a whole variety of offenses. Some, like "violations of rules of social coexistence," are so vague that they may cover almost any action. The use of these extrajudicial bodies, whose competence was greatly extended in October 1963, is a mixed blessing. They are limited to matters of lesser significance and their decisions are subject to judicial review. Yet the fact that the members of the new quasijudicial institutions do not have any legal training opens the way to misuse and political persecution. Of similar significance are the activities of the People's Inspection Committees, created in every county and entrusted with ferreting out not only common crimes, but also such offenses as "liberalism, irresponsibility, indiscipline, and the seeds of demagogy."

The "liberalizing" tendencies of the last years of Kádár's rule had little effect on the position of the National Assembly which is to act as "the highest organ of state authority" and is endowed with supreme legislative power. As in the past, however, the National Assembly possesses at best the shadow of power, its importance and prestige being overshadowed by its Presidential Council, Council of Ministers, and ultimately by the all-powerful HSWP. This fact alone is the most important reason for the inferior status of the parliament. While much work is supposed to be done in its committees, the short duration of the plenary sessions—at times only two days—strengthens the suspicion that the parliamentary function is more decorative than real. Nor does the manner of election contribute to the reputation of the National Assembly, the balloting being limited to a single slate of candidates running under the auspices of the People's Patriotic Front which is entrusted with the entire electoral procedure and campaign. The nomination of candidates is reserved to a number of mass organizations and institutions, but only the HSWP and the nonparty candidates can be recommended. Even if more than one candidate might be nominated for each seat, this change would hardly improve on the basically unopposed single slate ticket.

In the election of February 1963, 340 members were sent into the National Assembly. The majority were neither workers nor peasants, but officials of the party and persons belonging to the managerial, professional, and general intellectual strata of the population. While representing a cross section of the Hungarian public, the National Assembly has a comfortable HSWP majority which is supported by many fellow travelers who often are more eager to comply with the wishes of the regime than are genuine party members.

One of the most important functions of the National Assembly is the election of the Presidential Council which acts as a collective president, its many powers being almost identical with those of the Soviet-type presidium. In keeping with the Communist constitutional concept of the unity of power, its competence covers the legislative, executive, and judicial spheres of action. In practice, however, the Council is only little more important than the National Assembly. It enjoys the external paraphernalia of power rather than its real substance and has practically no say in the actual policy-making process.

While constitutionally subordinated to the National Assembly and the Presidential Council, the Council of Ministers is the most important organ of government. As in other Communist states, in Hungary the government has gone through significant organizational and political changes. Soon after the Communist seizure of power, in the period of Stalinism, there was a tendency to concentrate the chief governmental offices in the hands of the party leaders. Thus the dictator Rákosi combined membership in the government as Deputy Premier and Prime Minister, with the office of the Secretary General and later First Secretary of the party. Other leading members of the political hierarchy occupied the most influential positions in the cabinet.

When the period of the New Course ushered in the concept of collective leadership, Rákosi was forced to give up his position in the government, and for some time it seemed as if Imre Nagy might present a real challenge. Nagy's demotion, precipitated by the fall of Malenkov, demonstrated that in reality the political power was firmly in the hands of Rákosi, the party boss. As has been pointed out by Andrew Gyorgy, under the principle of collective leadership, power which was supposedly divided between party and government "was essentially monolithic in shielding a strong Party leader behind the relatively thin facade of the new collective." This interpretation is perfectly suited to the present situation in Hungary. János Kádár, who after the revolution controlled the two leading positions of power, twice—first in the period between 1958 and 1961 and again in 1965—relinquished his premiership. His political authority, however, remained unimpaired. The fact that on the second occasion Kádár considered it unnecessary to remain as a Minister of State in the cabinet shows the subordination of that body to the party and its leader.

The same is true of the other important personalities in the party. They no longer regard it as imperative to seek influential positions in the cabinet which to a large extent is composed of those party members whose main qualification is administrative ability. Only the most decisive posts are held by members of the highest party hierarchy.

The local government, which is organized territorially on three levels, does not differ significantly from that of the other states of Eastern Europe. It is composed of representative organs, the local councils (which are under the supervision of the Presidential Council), and their executive committees actually entrusted with the different tasks of administration. The ultimate responsibility of these committees to the central government by far overshadows their relationship to the councils which they are supposed to serve. In the last local elections, in which over 100,000 councilmen were elected (almost one half for the first time), the campaign was reported to have been somewhat livelier, perhaps due to the fact that 62 percent of the candidates were not party members. However, the report that in only 179 cases were there actually two candidates approved by the party clearly shows the totalitarian character of the electoral system.

Conclusions

It is next to impossible to venture a judgment on the future development of the Hungarian state. However, one may consider those factors which, it is fair to assume, may determine the future behavior both of the government and the people.

1. It would be ludicrous to deny a definite and far-reaching liberalization of the present regime, as compared to the Rákosi period and the four years of Kádár's postrevolutionary government. The relaxation of pressures can be explained by the greater strength of the HSWP which—although numerically smaller—is a more cohesive and disciplined body than its prerevolutionary forerunner. Without risking its position of control, it can eliminate or alleviate the most oppressive features of traditional Communism.

2. The party, however, has by no means given up its absolute monopoly of power. There are still political prisoners in Hungary, and all the liberties granted are subject to important limitations. Nonparty members may be appointed to important positions in the state administration, provided that their expert knowledge is combined with unconditional fidelity to the cause of socialism. Class origin no longer determines eligibility for university studies, but political conviction, as ascertained by a variety of methods, has become the decisive criterion. However important the relaxation in the sphere of literature may appear, the fact remains that the party has not given up its right "to sit in judgment on literary products" and to suppress them if they "question the

hallowed ideological tenets or basic practices of Communism."[9] In fact, the party has been able to use the "new literary freedoms" for its own benefit by insisting that only such writings as are permeated by firm faith in the future of Communism may be published.

3. To say that the Hungarians have won a "victory in defeat" —as some Western observers have stated—is a gross exaggeration. As pointed out by Imre Kovács, the three main points of the revolutionary program—"national independence, the withdrawal of Soviet troops, and free elections"—are exactly those which the Kádár regime "has left undone."

4. However "realistic" the Hungarians may have become, one can hardly assume that a people which ten years ago went through the agony of a hopeless struggle for emancipation has entirely forsaken its national aspirations. Despite disillusionment, which has a special hold on the young people, at least one visible ingredient of defiance has remained. That is nationalism, to which Kádár's regime has been forced to make at times relatively significant concessions.

BIBLIOGRAPHICAL NOTE

Books

The literature on the political development of postwar Hungary, and particularly on the 1956 revolution, is voluminous. While Andrew Gyorgy's essay on Hungary in his *Governments of Danubian Europe* (New York: Holt, Rinehart and Winston, 1949) covers mainly the constitutional and political evolution of the immediately post-1944 period, Stephen Kertesz's *Diplomacy in a Whirlpool* (South Bend: Notre Dame University Press, 1953) deals with the international position of Hungary, particularly its subordination to Soviet political and economic interests. The third important source, especially on the Communist seizure of power, is Ferenc Nagy's *The Struggle Behind the Iron Curtain* (New York: Macmillan, 1948). Ernest C. Helmreich's *Hungary* (New York: Praeger, 1957) contains a survey of prerevolutionary legal and political conditions. Of special significance for the study of

[9] Laszlo M. Tikos, "Hungary: Literary Renascence," in *Problems of Communism*, Vol. 13, No. 3, p. 33.

the "New Course" policies and the Hungarian brand of "National Communism" is Imre Nagy's documentary book *Imre Nagy on Communism: In Defense of the New Course* (New York: Praeger, 1957).

Of the large number of volumes analyzing the political significance of the Hungarian revolution only a few can be mentioned here. First is Ferenc A. Vali's monumental *Rift and Revolt in Hungary* (Cambridge: Harvard University Press, 1961), a brilliant discussion not only of the revolution, but also of its prelude and aftermath. Paul Kecskemeti's *The Unexpected Revolution* (Stanford: Stanford University Press, 1961) considers the influence of totalitarianism on the different social strata of the Hungarian population and their behavior during the revolt. Paul Zinner's *Revolution in Hungary* (New York: Columbia University Press, 1962), based to a large extent on interviews and other materials assembled by the Columbia University Project on Hungary, tends to throw a new light on the 1956 events. Useful is the same author's *National Communism and Popular Revolt in Eastern Europe* (New York: Columbia University Press, 1956), providing a selection of the most important documents relating to the Hungarian revolution. Another important documentary source is the *Report of the Special Committee on the Problem of Hungary*, issued by the United Nations General Assembly in 1957.

Monographs and Articles

A large number of shorter studies and articles have been published dealing with different aspects of the Hungarian political development. Among these Hannah Arendt's excellent essay "Epilogue: Reflections on the Hungarian Revolution," in her book *The Origins of Totalitarianism* (Cleveland: Meridian Books, 1958) deserves to be mentioned. Of the more recent studies, F. A. Vali's "Hungary," from *The Communist States at the Crossroads*, edited by A. Bromke (New York: Praeger, 1965), pp. 71–86, considers the influence of the revival of nationalism in Eastern Europe on the regime of János Kádár. G. R. Urban's "Hungary," in Walter Laqueur and Leopold Labedz's *Polycentrism* (New York: Praeger, 1962), pp. 72–80 deals with the influence of the Sino-Soviet dispute on Hungarian internal policies.

CHAPTER SIX

Yugoslavia

The General Setting

OF ALL THE countries considered in this book, Tito's Socialist Federal Republic consists of elements by far the most heterogeneous. Its history has been greatly influenced by the conflicting goals of its different ethnic, cultural, and social groups. Its principal continuing problems may be classed as demographic, ethnic-cultural, and socioeconomic in nature.

DEMOGRAPHIC IMBALANCES

With its population of 18.5 million and a territory of 98,766 square miles, Yugoslavia is the second largest Eastern European country (after Poland), approaching in density the European average but exceeding only that of Albania and Bulgaria among its neighbors. The annual birth rate, down from 28 in the thirties (and 35 in the twenties) to 22 in 1962, is still one of the highest in Europe, resulting in an annual growth rate of 12.5 per thousand despite an infant mortality rate of 83.9 which is unexceeded on the continent.

Several imbalances, however, make the demographic situation less than desirable. In the first place, the population pyramid shows severe indentations in the 20–30 and 40–50 age groups as a result of birth deficits of the World War I and II periods and an officially estimated loss of life during World War II of 1.7 million—one out of nine of the prewar population. This means that the population of working age as a whole, already burdened with the regime's experiments in rapid industrialization and on-and-off collectivization, must carry along a heavier load of inactive population than would normally be the case.

Moreover, this situation will continue to worsen at least until the children of those now in their thirties enter the labor market.

The war losses account also for a higher than normal disproportion between the male and the female populations, but the pattern varies regionally, ranging from a surplus of 310–360 females for every 1000 males of the 35–40 age group in the northern and central parts of the country to an actual surplus of males in all age groups in the extreme south. Since both the regional differences in the population growth rate (from 6.1 per thousand in the north to 28.9 in the south) and the distribution of surviving males happen to be in reverse relationship to the regional levels of the economic and cultural development, the regime is faced with a severe dilemma. A would-be model socialist society requires both rapid economic progress as a whole and the elimination of "contradictions" between its various parts. Yet massive investment in the south, to compensate for the fast population growth rate and to utilize the surplus manpower, is bound to be both politically unpopular in the more advanced areas (from which the capital must be extracted) and economically wasteful. To concentrate on expanding the existing industrial base in the north and west would mean a further increase in interregional stratification. This would not only violate ideological postulates, but in the long run it would be politically explosive, because the economic differences would further reinforce the existing ethnic prejudices. A third solution, resettlement of excess southern population in the confiscated farmland of the fertile northern plains, already attempted in an agrarian reform under the royal government in the twenties and resumed with more vigor in the early post-World War II period, proved to be only a drop in a bucket as far as the south was concerned. In the north, however, in addition to the resentment of the indigenous people, who saw the newcomers as usurpers of property and as a threat to the existing ethnic character of the region, the result was a decrease in productivity of the redistributed farmland. For the future, in any case, this alternative is not available, since the size of farms is already reduced to the bare subsistence requirements of the present farm population. Thus the regime is faced with the formidable task of administering socialism to a population decimated in its most productive age groups in the most advanced regions, and of providing employment and education to the rapidly growing population of the most backward areas at the price of slowing down the economic growth of the country as a whole. Yet, even more difficult are the problems arising from the ethnic and cultural structure of the population.

THE NATIONAL QUESTION

The most striking feature of the Yugoslav population is the lack of Yugoslavs. To be exact, there are some of them: of the 18.5 million people enumerated in the census of 1961, a total of 317,125 or 1.7 percent (down from 998,698 in 1953) claimed to be Yugoslavs. The others were Serbs, Croats, Slovenes, Macedonians, Montenegrins, or members of a Slavic-speaking Moslem group afraid to declare their nationality and classed as "ethnic Moslems." Finally, there were non-South-Slavic minorities, of which, after the expulsion of ethnic Germans, the Albanians and Hungarians are the largest; indeed, each of these two minority groups is more numerous than the entire population of the constituent republic of Montenegro, and the combined minorities exceed each of the five recognized South Slav nationalities except the Serbs and Croats.

The regime's nationality policy follows the Soviet pattern of recognition of cultural identity and a nominally federal state structure—an apparent advance compared to the prewar regime, which, in Tito's words, "ignored [the national question] completely, persistently preaching that the Serbs, Croats and Slovenes are one nation, paying no attention whatsoever to the Montenegrins and Macedonians." Since World War II Yugoslavia is, accordingly, divided into six republics—one for each of the five South Slav peoples plus Bosnia-Hercegovina, which represents no particular nationality but is a historically well-defined area of mixed population in the mountainous central zone between Serbia and Croatia. There are also two autonomous provinces with purely geographic designations, Kosovo-Metohija in the south of the Serbian republic, corresponding to the area inhabited by the Albanian minority, and Vojvodina, comprising the major part of the Danubian plain in the northeast, again an area of mixed population including most of the Hungarian minority in Yugoslavia.

TABLE 1. Nationality Structure of Yugoslavia
(In Thousands of Population)

	Slovenia	Croatia	Bosnia-Hercegovina	Serbia[a]	Montenegro	Macedonia	Total SFRY
Slovenes	1522	39	6	20	1	1	1589
Croats	31	3340	712	196	11	4	4294
Serbs	14	625	1406	5705	14	43	7806
Montenegrins	1	8	13	105	384	3	514
Macedonians	1	4	2	36	6	1001	1046
Moslems[b]	1	3	842	94	31	1	973
Yugoslavs[c]	3	16	276	20	2	3	317
Others[d]	19	125	21	1467	29	350	2011
Total	1592	4160	3278	7642	472	1406	18549

[a] Includes autonomous provinces Vojvodina (pop. 1855 thousand) and Kosovo-Metohija (964 thousand).
[b] "Ethnic category," applying to Bosnian Moslems, not to all persons of Moslem religion (of which there are about two million).
[c] "Undecided Yugoslavs," largely same as "ethnic Moslems."
[d] Includes 915 thousand Albanians, 504 thousand Hungarians, 182 thousand Turks, and other national minority groups.
SOURCE: *Statistical Yearbook of the SFRY,* 1963, pp. 335–336. Totals do not add up exactly because of rounding.

There are several reasons why the federal state structure, such as it is, does not resolve but aggravates the national antagonisms among the South Slavs. In the first place, as long as the decision-making power is a monopoly of the Communist party, within which democratic centralism (with emphasis on the latter word) is the unchallengeable rule, the federal form of the state organization can serve no other purpose than to provide a more efficient administration of central policies. Secondly, whatever discretionary powers may remain at the local level—and central policy-making can never exclude all bias in local execution—the system is clearly rigged so that behind the slogan of "brotherhood and unity" and the legal equality of all nationalities some are more equal than others. This can be seen both in the pariah status of certain groups, in the structure of public committees and assemblies, and in the drawing of boundaries between the units of the federation. It also shows in the nationality composition of the central instruments of power, such as the army, the police, and the chain of public prosecutors and party secretaries (where the government does not make any comparative statistical data available and therefore need not even try to make their composition appear balanced).

Two cases may serve to illustrate the point. In the Socialist Republic of Bosnia-Hercegovina, where "ethnic Moslems"—called "Turks" by the Serbs—constitute about one-third of the population, their representation in the public assemblies decreases with the level of government from a maximum of 10 percent of all seats in the local assemblies to 7.5 percent at the district level and only one-half of one percent in the Republic's assembly in Sarajevo, whereas not a single person is listed as an ethnic Moslem among the 670 members of the Federal Assembly in Belgrade. The data on "undecided Yugoslavs" reveal that Moslems who declare themselves as Yugoslavs are favored over those who remain plain Moslems, but the group as a whole remains heavily underrepresented. Moreover, it is not necessary for the Serbs to put up a Yugoslav façade to do quite well in the government of Bosnia and Hercegovina. With only 43 percent of the population, they hold 55 percent of the seats at the local level, 56 percent in the districts, and 59 percent in the assembly of the Republic. The case of Bosnia-Hercegovina is particularly interesting, because the province was given the status of a republic ostensibly as a neutral zone—since both Serbs and Croats claim it as part of their historical and ethnic territories—yet by *de facto* exclusion of Moslems, it has become a Serbian administrative preserve. A similar result was obtained by gerrymandering and other methods in the autonomous province of Vojvodina, the rich agrarian plain in the northeast. Here, after the expulsion of the German minority, the colonization of substantial numbers of peasants from the mountainous areas in the south, and the exchange of the Baranya district with its few Serbs for the formerly Croatian district of Srijem and its substantial part of the Serb minority in Croatia, the number of Serbs was increased from 35 percent of the population in the prewar province to 50.7 percent at the time of the first postwar census.

The point is, of course, not that the Communists themselves are suddenly more involved in national prejudices than in supranational class warfare, but that even an internationalist regime in Yugoslavia cannot avoid catering to those national groups that support the existence of the state—if not always its current rulers. It is necessary to understand that the citizens of Yugoslavia are members of their particular nationality groups in a different sense than an American citizen from Indiana is a "Hoosier," or possibly also "Scotch-Irish," while he is also an American. The national allegiance, in the case of the five South Slav nationalities, lies with the parts rather than the whole. A Serbian speaks the Serbian language (not "Serbo-Croatian," unless he is a diplomat or a tourist guide), attends the Serbian Orthodox Church, may read the publications of the Serbian Academy of Arts and Sciences in Belgrade (not the Yugoslav Academy, which is the name of the equivalent Croatian institution in Zagreb), and derives his national myths from the history of the Serbian states of the Byzantine era. He looks upon the Serbian occupation of the formerly Austro-Hungarian areas inhabited by other South Slavs—whom he considers denationalized Serbs—as the rightful prize for Serbia's sacrifices in shaking off Ottoman rule after 500 years of oppression and in liberating the South Slavs from Austro-Hungarian and more recently German and Italian occupations. Being the largest in number among the South Slavs (except for the Bulgarians, who, being outside Yugoslavia, do not matter) and *ipso facto* controlling the main instruments of power of the central government, the Serbs can keep a Yugoslav front vis-à-vis the outside world and demand a Yugoslav allegiance from the other nationalities without becoming any less Serbian themselves. Other groups, finding their past and present sacrifices hardly less glorious, but the rewards of South Slav unity hardly commensurate, tend to assume a defensive position, which makes them guilty of "separatism." To the degree that it is nationally motivated, the opposition cannot be a loyal one. Without any peaceful process by which the "outs" may become the "ins," the nationality question has kept the country in a state of permanent crisis ever since 1918.

The interwar regime's solution to the problem was a system which granted *de facto* autonomy to the third largest nationality, the Slovenes, bribed by extensive patronage the vocal but smallest (hence relatively inexpensive) group, the Montenegrins, into supporting the centralist concept, and crudely suppressed any sign of Macedonian self-identification. This left all the state's energy free to keep the Croatian aspiration to self-determination under control. The solution of the Communist regime is more of the same, with the variation of attempting to bribe the Macedonians too. The result, however, is that opposition sentiment, once manifested chiefly by the Croatians, is now equally if not more widely spread in the most economically and culturally advanced republic of Slovenia. Though public discussion of the nationalist question can take place only within the limits imposed by the Communist system—it flared up at first with reference to relatively innocuous matters, such as sports, culture, and language, but has recently spilled over into the fields of party strategy, economic policy, and the conduct of foreign affairs—there is little doubt that the issue is as alive as ever. The divisive influence cannot be excluded from the party monolith, for if there is a Yugoslav, hence Serbian, way to Communism, what else but a "Stalinism" of Belgrade vintage rules out a Croatian or Slovenian way? Indeed, if there was a single dominant theme at the party congress held in Zagreb in December 1964, it was the national issue. All major speakers took a poke at both the "bureaucratic-centralistic" and the "bureaucratic-particularistic" nationalistic deviations, declaring them to be as dangerous and counterrevolutionary as the "classical" bourgeois nationalism. Tito in person deplored the fact that certain individuals (presumably within the party) not only "take an irresponsible, nay, benevolent attitude towards various nationalistic phenomena," but even "employ the well known arguments of the bourgeois chauvinistic ideology." The conclusions of the congress, however, placed the greatest emphasis on the struggle against the particularistic variety of nationalistic deviations, recommending the remedy of "further strengthening of brotherhood and unity" by way of a "Yugoslav Socialist patriotism."

SOCIOECONOMIC QUESTIONS

If the demographic imbalances and nationality structure of Yugoslavia give rise to problems with which any type of government would have hard going, the difficulties caused by the socioeconomic background of the population are magnified by the subjective criteria which are necessarily applied by a Communist regime. The reference is not to the bourgeois class, which was dispossessed and made politically impotent in the Communist rise to power, but to the still predominantly agricultural character of the people in spite of the ideological requirement of a proletarian and industrial base for the "higher stages of socialism." The requirement was waived during the Partisan warfare and the take-over period by referring to the "alliance" of the "working people" with the "working class" or, for Communist forums, the skillful exploitation of the revolutionary potential of the peasants—not unlike the strategy used by Lenin and Mao. Indeed, in the first phase of postwar agricultural policy, we are told, the regime correctly applied a policy of redistribution of land instead of immediate collectivization, based on "political rather than economic criteria" and the "fulfilling of the party's obligations toward the peasantry, which had massively participated in the people's liberation struggle."

Phase two was precipitated by the Moscow-Belgrade dispute of the late forties, when a forced collectivization drive was attempted but, under the pressure of heavy crop failures, had to be abandoned for a modus vivendi reducing the maximum size of private farms to 10 hectares and postponing collectivization until the government's investment, taxing, and pricing policies induced the farmers to join the collectives voluntarily. A decade later, as the new constitution of 1963 was about to attest that the country has progressed well into the socialist stage, the government felt it necessary to reconcile social reality with the socialist image by attempting to prove that the socioeconomic structure is rapidly shifting in favor of the nonfarm population, and that in the villages, despite continued private land ownership, the socialist forces have taken a firm and increasingly controlling foothold. This was accomplished by several means, from redefining statistical categories and watering down the concept of the socialist sectors to redrawing district boundaries to produce proletarian majorities in a maximum number of districts. The constitution itself reinforced the system of representation introduced in the fifties, which is based on the value of the marketable output of different social strata instead of on the number of people in each community. For all practical purposes this system disenfranchises the independent farmers. Introducing the draft of the socialist constitution, Edward Kardelj, President of the Federal Assembly and until recently heir apparent and second in command to Tito, announced that, as of 1961, the number of people who were dependent on private farming had decreased to less than 50 percent of the total population, and further, that the total output of the private sector (essentially agriculture) was reduced to 24.9 percent of the gross national product. Yet, while there can be no meaningful argument with the manipulated output value, as far as the population ratio is concerned, a special census of agriculture of 1960 found 12,590,000 people living on farms; though nearly one and one-third million of them held jobs outside the farm, those working on the farms alone outnumbered the combined industrial, mining, and handicraft workers by nearly three to one. Since at the same time 88 percent of the tillable land and 96 percent of the total work force engaged in farming remained in the private sector (despite government policies that permit no private acquisition of farm machinery and peg the output of 5120 collective and state farms at 203 billion dinars, as compared with 302 billion for 2,623,223 private farms) there was a defeat on two fronts: not only are the farmers still by far the largest social class, but they are of the stubborn kind who refuse to be educated in the benefits of collective farming.

The party takes solace in the existence of "general cooperatives" (serving as government purchasing and distributing agents) and various forms of cooperative arrangements between the socialized and the private farms, which are widespread; these are considered semisocialist phenomena and a learning mechanism, as distinguished from the preferred "working cooperatives" (equivalent to *kolkhozes*), in which membership is nearly nil. Over the years the number of independent farmers has, indeed, decreased by a small fraction, as some of the least efficient who left the collectives in the mass exodus of the early fifties had to rejoin them or seek employment in the cities. But this creeping socialization of individual substandard farms cannot be seriously considered as a step towards the socialist transformation of agriculture which the party has in mind.

There is at present little that the government can do to speed up the process. Surplus land population is already crowding the cities, where it can be given employment only at the price of inflated payrolls or the creation of inefficient, "politically motivated" industries. After three agricultural redistributions, resulting in a current average farm size of 4.3 hectares (10.6 acres), of which less than 50 percent is tillable, the government is well aware of the economic and political risks of any new redistribution or collectivization drives. Meanwhile, the continued existence of private farms is reconciled with Communist goals as an "extension of the period of contemplation" granted to the farmers until the capital needed to resume socialization of the argicultural sector becomes available. But the demands on capital accumulation are many, and the agricultural area, traditionally a low priority item under Communist regimes, will have to wait. Characteristically, agriculture has a 10-year improvement plan rather than a plan of five years or less. Government spokesmen have pointed out that the farmers receive more for their products now than they did in the thirties, and agricultural production is growing, though slower than that of industry. Yet the fact remains that from 1924 to 1939 the agricultural surpluses of Yugoslavia, under the bourgeois regime, corrupt as it was, produced a positive balance of trade in every year except three, the depression and draught periods included, whereas the growing agricultural production of the Socialist Federal Republic must constantly be bailed out with American grain.

Needless to say, the passive resistance of the peasants has led to a political underrepresentation which, regardless of whether they constitute 70 or just below 50 percent of the population, is even worse than that of the "ethnic Moslems." Though the program of the LCY promises the peasantry an "equal status with other working people in the political and economic system," the agricultural representatives (collectivized and private farmers combined) occupy only 21 percent of the seats in the local assemblies and 7 percent in the districts. In the party, where they constitute 7.9 percent of the membership (which was down from

17.3 percent in 1957), their representation among the delegates to the Eighth Party Congress, in 1964, amounted to 2.3 percent.

The Dictatorship of the Proletariat

Although the period of Communist rule in Yugoslavia, like that in other Eastern European countries, formally falls into two phases, marked with the substitution in the state's title of the adjective "socialist" for "people's" in 1963, there were important differences from the very beginning. Except in the most ephemeral sense, Yugoslavia experienced neither a Soviet occupation nor a period of coalition government with step-by-step elimination of democratic forces and gradual intensification of political repression and social class struggle. Holding the monopoly of power practically since the day of German surrender in World War II, the Yugoslav Communist leaders could start the process of "building of socialism" without delay. Having remade the party and the accessory instruments of control in the Soviet image, they could withstand—in the absence of Soviet troops—Stalin's attempt of 1948 to replace them after he had expelled Yugoslavia from the Cominform, the Communist international organ. After a period of tightening the reins and intensifying the class struggle, the leaders of the CPY proceeded to an attack against centralism and bureaucratism—their own as well as Stalin's. As various changes in the economic and political management were introduced, the Marxist prediction of the withering away of the state, instead of being the final step which would crown the arrival of the Communist millenium, was declared a continuing process of the transitional, socialist stage. Not less dramatic, on the international scene the CPY moved out of and back into the fold of "fraternal parties" twice. Attempting to form an antiblocs bloc in one of the "out" periods, it earned the "revisionist" title just as its leaders had reason to believe that their theory of "separate roads to Communism" had become the universally accepted Communist doctrine.

Now, one could easily jump to the conclusion that such radical and frequent policy changes must sooner or later destroy the Communist regime. For have not even much smaller turns in the party line elsewhere called for a replacement of the leadership and a reshuffling of the entire membership of the party? And are not such measures as the workers' management of enterprises, the broadening of communal autonomy, the opening of party meetings to the public, and the transfer of various party functions to the front organizations offering the people the opportunity to sweep the party onto that scrap heap of history to which the Communists promise to discard the state once the antagonistic classes disappear and world conditions ripen for "real" communism? The elementary answer, of course, is that nobody knows for sure, not even the leaders of the CPY themselves. But in order to assess the likely consequences, one first has to understand how the changes came about and what really has, and what has not been changed. For the purpose of this discussion, more meaningful than an arbitrary division into people's democratic and socialist stages is to consider three major periods: the takeover of power and the Stalinist class struggle up to the excommunication edict of 1948; the soul-searching and experimentation with novel methods in the fifties; and finally, reconciliation with the Soviet camp and the attempted consolidation of internal reforms.

THE TAKEOVER PERIOD

As World War II was approaching its final phase, and the German army, under pressure of the Soviet advance towards the Hungarian plain and Allied progress in Italy, began to withdraw from the southern Balkans, Tito's guerilla army, its headquarters on the island of Vis protected by the British fleet, found itself in an ambiguous situation. On the mainland it held most of the central mountain massif, with the exception of major cities and communication lines, from southern Slovenia through southwestern Croatia and Bosnia to Montenegro. It also held scattered similarly inaccessible areas elsewhere. It had recently been strengthened with the acquisition of the equipment of the Italian occupation forces in the coastal zone, yet it had failed in its attempts to break through into the German occupied Serbia or to take a foothold in the northern plains. There, although they were still allied with the German army, the Serbian forces of General Nedić and the Croatin regular army were likely to switch to the allied side any day. Moreover, since the Chetniks of General Mihajlović were still somewhere in the Serbian mountains, all these forces could at least offer enough resistance to a Communist takeover to invite Western intervention. Worse yet, under an interallied operational agreement of May 1944 Yugoslavia, together with Greece, fell into the British Balkan operational zone, and the Russians, reluctant as they were to recognize Tito's Anti-Fascist Committee of National Liberation (AVNOJ), could well stay within their own zone of Bulgaria and Rumania. Even if the Russians had to take Belgrade in the course of their military operations in the northern plains, their very presence in Yugoslavia could precipitate Allied landings in the western parts of the country and thus preclude a Communist take-over of its entire territory. Then, two windfalls came into the hands of Tito's Partisans. First, at the end of August 1944, German operations against the Partisan forces attempting to infiltrate Serbia from the west had to be called off as the Russians approached from the northeast through Rumania; in September, once the German troops from Greece had moved north through Serbia, they relinquished all of it except the capital city to the Partisans without a major battle. Second, the Moscow Conference of October 9–12 between Stalin and Churchill changed the operational agreement of May into a zones-of-influence agreement, placing Yugoslavia in the fifty-fifty category. A preceding meeting on September 21, when Tito secretly left his headquarters on the island of Vis for Moscow, had settled the issue of participation of Soviet troops in the Communist conquest of Yugoslavia. Thus, when the Soviet army took Belgrade on October 20, it had the right to be there, at least temporarily. This was long enough to facilitate the city's take-over by the "people's authorities" and the "People's Liberation Army," which reached the capital from the south almost simultaneously with the Russians. Still the situation remained uncertain. Stalin, mistrusting the Allied intentions ("Churchill is the kind who, if you don't watch him, will slip a kopeck out of your pocket," he had warned Milovan Djilas on an earlier visit to Moscow), continued urging the Yugoslav Communists not to rush matters and to keep their part of the interallied wartime bargains for the time being. In November an agreement between the Yugoslav government in exile and Tito was reached, which, endorsed by the Yalta conference in February, 1945, resulted in the addition of a scattering of prewar deputies to the AVNOJ and of three representatives of the exile government to Tito's cabinet on March 8.

Thus began the short-lived "unified government" period, which, as Tito explained to the Fifth Party Congress in July 1948, "had been set up on outside advice." He continued that the party "knew exactly how the whole affair would end," and added that because "having created, while the war was still on, the principal conditions and distinct prospects for setting up a State of a new type in place of the old one, we were unable to make any concessions . . . ; we had to move quickly along our clearly marked path, while they had been sent to hold us up. And we were not deceived. . . ." Needless to say, it was not necessary to prolong the pretense of cooperation once the war had ended with no Western Allied troops on Yugoslav territory. In March the Soviets moved on to Hungary, leaving to the Partisan army the task of accepting the surrender of the remaining German forces in western Yugoslavia on V-E day. The bulk of the Croatian army withdrew to the Austrian province of Carynthia, surrendering to the British, only to be disarmed and turned over to the Partisans. The war was over, but the class war was in full swing. The new regime could proceed, in preparation for the forthcoming election, to use the political monopoly of the People's Front, to suppress freedom of speech, press, and assembly, including the freedoms of the parties represented by the "Western" members of the cabinet, who thereupon resigned. "This was the last vigorous attempt to instigate so-called intervention by Western powers," Tito reported, "but this was not successful either." He added that the remaining Western ministers had "simply left . . . [whereas] the people's government remained and went full steam ahead."

The elections were held on November 11, 1945 without an opposition list but with a separate box into which anyone wanting to risk registering a protest vote could drop his ballot. They produced the familiar 96 percent aye vote. On November 29 the newly elected Constituent Assembly abolished the monarchy and, upon installing a Presidium on the Soviet model in December, wasted no time in preparing a people's democratic constitution, proclaimed on January 31, 1946. However, if there was a people's democratic phase equivalent to the early postwar years in other Eastern European countries, it had already ended with the resignation of the three "Western" members of the cabinet in the early fall of 1945. Surveying the situation three years later, Tito boasted:

The Constitution has only confirmed, or rather codified, what was won during the war. . . . Now we are in the possession of the basic elements for building socialism in our country. Let us once again see what these elements are:
(1) The state authority which replaced the old bourgeois authority is a real people's government. . . .
(2) The Army is a completely new, people's army. . . .
(3) The state security, the Militia, the OZNA [secret police], etc., are organs of the people's authority; their task is to keep a strict watch and vigil. . . .
Consequently, we have a completely new state machinery, which is a vital condition for further development in the direction of socialism, that is to say, the political conditions for that development have been created.
(4) Radical nationalisation . . . thus basic material conditions, that is economic conditions, have been created for building socialism in our country.
(5) A united standpoint has prevailed among the vast majority of people, rallied in the People's Front. . . .[1]

How different was the ranking of the building blocks of socialism—the state, the army, and the police first—in 1948, compared with what it would become shortly thereafter, once the hope of immediate reconciliation with Moscow was abandoned! However, these three main elements were indeed firmly in Communist hands after 1945. The fourth, nationalization, was initiated by AVNOJ already during the war. It took the form of confiscation of property of ethnic Germans (Yugoslav citizens of Austrian or German origin), collaborators (owners of enterprises which continued to operate under German occupation), absentee owners (refugees and displaced persons), and

[1] Josip Broz Tito, *Selected Speeches and Articles, 1941–1961* (Zagreb: Naprijed, 1963), pp. 83–84.

foreign owners, and was completed in several stages. By 1948, for all practical purposes the entire economy except small farms, was in state hands.

Actually, whatever the sentiment of the populace, internal threats to the consolidation of Communist power were surprisingly few. Among its many prewar politicians Yugoslavia had few political heroes ready to risk their lives by raising their voice against Communist terror. The fact is, that like the three "Western" members of the "unified" government, most of the prominent political leaders "simply left" their posts. That is, most of them preferred leaving the country or keeping quiet if they did not leave on time, to becoming Yugoslav Petkovs or Masaryks—though there was no guarantee that keeping quiet would keep them out of jail. There were no political plots except those invented by the party to conduct lynching atmosphere trials as a deterrent measure or for other political purposes. Mihajlović was caught in his mountain hideout abandoned by all but a handful of his men, confessed to collaboration with the Germans and was executed—again without protest by his own people. The Church had deliberate martyrs, attempting, like Stepinac, to turn their trial into a trial of their accusers, but with religion being one of the main divisive factors among the peoples of Yugoslavia, the churches were in no position to serve as action organizations of the opposition sentiment. Only attempts of misled youths infiltrating the country on hopeless missions continue to be discovered even to this day. The Communist party must love this; for, having spent 20 years in the underground, it knows all the tricks of the trade and can keep in shape by staging the capture and the trial (if indeed not planning the mission too) in the politically most useful way. But when the chips were down, in the last days of World War II and immediately thereafter, there was no significant opposition, military or political, domestic or foreign; and only weeks later, at a rate incomparably faster than the developments in Russia after 1917, the party had total control.

THE EXCOMMUNICATION

The first serious threat, therefore, far from being caused by the remnants of the fascists and reactionaries, or by democratic political forces, came from the least expected quarter. It is difficult to imagine the kind of shock that must have been caused in Belgrade by the letter of the Central Committee of the Communist party of the Soviet Union of March 27, 1948, addressed to Tito *et al.* Opening with an icy "We regard your answer as incorrect and therefore completely unsatisfactory," it went on with a barrage of accusations spiked with references to the errors of Trotsky, Bernstein, Vollmar, Bukharin, and the Mensheviks, and to what happened to some of them ("We think that the political career of Trotsky is quite instructive"). Finally, it linked the discovery of the absence of democracy and the spirit of class struggle in the CPY with the presence of English spies, known to the CPY, in the Yugoslav government. Until then, the Yugoslav Communists had been both subjectively and objectively the most loyal to the CPSU and Stalin and, in their domestic policies, the most advanced in creating a true copy of the Soviet system. "What could be more exciting for a Communist, one who was coming from war and revolution?" writes Milovan Djilas in retrospect about his first visit to Stalin. He goes on:

To be received by Stalin—this was the greatest possible recognition for the heroism and suffering of our Partisan warriors and our people. In dungeons and in the holocaust of war, and in the no less violent spiritual crises and clashes with the internal and external foes of Communism, Stalin was something more than a leader in battle. He was the incarnation of an idea, transfigured in Communist minds into pure idea, and thereby into something infallible and timeless. Stalin was the victorious battle of today and the brotherhood of man tomorrow. . . .[2]

Djilas must know what he is talking about, for he was not only one of the four top leaders of the CPY (with Tito, Kardelj, and Ranković) against whom the brunt of the Soviet attacks of 1948 was addressed, but also, as erstwhile party propaganda chief, the wartime creator of the Stalin myth among the partisans. Was not the CPSU letter just a nightmare which would vanish as soon as Stalin learned the truth? A year or so later the CPY leaders discovered areas of friction with Moscow going back to their wartime operations. But at first, to be rewarded for their struggle on the side of the Soviet Union and for their

[2] *Conversations with Stalin* (New York: Harcourt, Brace & World, 1962), p. 73.

theretofore unique idolatry of Stalin with an accusation of Trotskyism and Menshevism (and soon of being protectors of *kulaks* and capitalist elements while introducing a "Turkish regime" in the party) could only be the result of misinformation supplied by a traitor among the informants of the Soviet party. In any event, the meetings of the CPY and the speeches of its leaders continued to end with "Long live Stalin!" for the rest of the year, until the truth sank in.

The fact is that Stalin did have good reasons to attempt to get rid of Tito, though they were not the ones emphasized in the early published exchanges. There were several subordinate issues, including the abortive attempt at a Balkan federation, agreed on between Tito and Dimitrov, then retracted by the latter when denounced in *Pravda*. But the main reason was based on fundamental party principles, not on any disagreement in the interpretation of those principles from the start. That is, it was based on an identical Marxist-Leninist understanding, in Moscow and Belgrade, of the revolutionary developments in the Balkans during and after World War II.

It is necessary to keep in mind that Marxism, as Communists never tire of pointing out, is not a static system of thought, but dialectics, meaning that it can always digest new contradictions. Only because it includes continual modifications, it is able to solve continually novel problems of action, for which it has been created and in which it has to perfect itself. No effective action, however, could result if any adherent to the general theory were allowed to invent action rules of his own. Different historical situations require different dialectical prescriptions of strategy and tactics, supplementary to the general instruction for class struggle given by Marx and Engels. But in order to preserve the unity of the movement, to assure that it goes in the direction demanded by the laws of history and at a rate warranted by the circumstances of a given time, these more detailed prescriptions must be given by a central authority.

How can such an authority be chosen to assure that its interpretations and amendments—that is, its rules of action—will not slow down instead of speed up the historical course to the millenium? The issue is simple. It is chosen by history itself, by virtue of accomplishments in revolutionary practice. Thus the

Marxism that was based on Lenin's accomplishment in the Russian revolution became "Marxism-Leninism." This in turn, by virtue of Stalin's success in preserving the conquered base in Russia and developing it further in the direction of socialism (and not to be entirely overlooked, by his success in eliminating internal dissenters and competitors) evolved further into "Marxism-Leninism-Stalinism," or "Leninism-Stalinism," the basic theory being continually enriched by the thought and practice of the movement's historical heroes.

With this in mind, the underlying problem can be easily discovered in several topics debated at length in successive exchanges between the Soviet and the Yugoslav party. Leaving the allegations of deviationist domestic policies, hostility toward the Soviet Union, Menshevism and Trotskyism, etc., aside—they were more in the nature of insults than disagreement on substance—one of the most revealing issues was that of the role of the Soviet army in the liberation of Yugoslavia. Here again, there was a subsidiary matter that created a tempest in a teapot, caused by Yugoslav complaints about the behavior of Soviet soldiers in Belgrade. Rejected by the Soviet military commandant as untrue, Stalin took them as proof of an unfriendly attitude, especially by Djilas, who had pressed the point to the Soviet commandant. "Can't he understand it," Stalin once asked another Yugoslav representative, "if a soldier who has crossed thousands of kilometers through blood and fire and death has fun with a woman or takes some trifle?" But the main matter in dispute was whether or not the Soviet army "installed" the Yugoslav leaders in power, as the Soviet and Cominform letters had argued or, as it was interpreted by the CPY, had by its very existence (and incidental presence in Belgrade) merely "aided" the CPY, which had already accomplished the revolution before the Soviet army appeared on Yugoslav territory. Though to an outsider this may seem a hairsplitting issue or a matter of idle vanity it is in fact crucial from the Communist point of view. For if the Yugoslav party, as it took great pains to explain, had already developed its own People's Liberation "Army" (i.e., not mere partisan detachments) while still in the mountains of Bosnia, and if this army was supported by an "already existing state life, from a permanent center, from a permanent free territory," which was merely aided in its further development by the Soviet Union—if in other words, the CPY had carried out a *revolution* and established a dictatorship of the proletariat on its own, then the time for something called Leninism-Stalinism-Titoism had come. Since the Soviet army is a product of Lenin's revolution and Stalin's dictatorship of the proletariat in the Soviet Union, the liberation or the establishment of a people's democracy in another country by the Soviet army is nothing but a reaffirmation of the supreme dialectical authority of the Soviet leadership. But a new revolution, carried out independently and in circumstances radically different from those of 1917, places the Russian revolutionary experience back into its historical epoch. For future action the revolutionary experience of the latest successful forefighter for the speeding up of the "inevitable" law of history becomes decisive.

Needless to say, Stalin would buy none of this. If "anybody" fails to see the truth of the Yugoslav independent accomplishment, the CPY leaders argued in one of their postmortem tracts, "he really asserts that nothing essentially different has happened in Yugoslavia during the war than in other countries, e.g., Bulgaria. It is ridiculous that we have to argue about the revolution in Yugoslavia with the Communists, as if a four-year uprising were a needle which cannot be found in a sack of wool." But what Stalin wanted to prove was precisely that nothing different had happened. "We must . . . say," he had the Central Committee of the CPSU write to Belgrade on May 4, 1948, "that the services of the Communist Parties of Poland, Czechoslovakia, Hungary, Rumania, Bulgaria and Albania are *not less than those of the CPY.*" Worse yet, the letter went on to explain that the services of the Yugoslav party to the cause did not even compare to those of the French and Italian parties, though these were not yet successful in capturing power; for, after all, the Yugoslav success was "not due to any special qualities of the CPY," but was achieved "mainly because after the destruction of the Yugoslav partisan headquarters by German paratroopers, at a moment when the people's liberation movement in Yugoslavia was passing through a serious crisis, the Soviet army came to the aid of the Yugoslav people, crushed the German invader, liberated Belgrade, and in this way created the conditions which were necessary for the CPY to achieve power." In short, Stalin did not have to wait for the theses of the Fifth Congress of the CPY of July 1948 to see the light. It was not Tito's lagging behind, but the fact that he was trying to catch up with the Soviet Union too quickly that annoyed Stalin. For together with the charismatic authority inherent in Tito's revolutionary successes, here was a potential challenge to the legitimacy of Stalin's monopolistic authority in the international Communist movement. This was no less real in the winter of 1947–1948, when Stalin must have made up his mind, than in the following spring and summer, when assaults from Moscow and Bucharest forced the CPY leaders to play their trumps while formulating a platform for their survival.

That they did survive shows how right Stalin was, except that he acted too late, for the CPY leaders were even nearer to catching up with the Soviet system than he thought they were. A Stalin-type purge of pro-Stalin Communists occurred in Yugoslavia, complete with publication of letters of some spared middle-echelon "Cominformists," thanking the secret police for "helping" them understand their mistake, and with several higher-echelon leaders killed in attempts to flee the country or committing suicide during the investigation. After that, the simmering crisis forced a tight regime until the end of 1950; finally, the Sixth Congress held in Zagreb in 1952, where the party name was changed to that of a League of Communists (LCY), signalled the end of the crisis period and an attempt of the party to seek broader support by loosening the reins.

The inner circle of the CPY leadership, handpicked by Tito in carrying out Stalin's mandate to rid the underground party of the late thirties of "factionalists," and dependent on a common front against the assault of 1948, survived the purge of Stalinists almost intact. Among the rank and file members, well over 10,000 were expelled, according to figures made public at the Sixth Congress—which does not seem excessive in view of the fact that the party purged 97,000 members between 1958 and 1963. By then, however, it was the "anarchist-pseudo-liberal" deviation, inspired by Djilas and later exploiting the official anti-bureaucratic campaign, that produced most of the expulsions. Short of armed intervention, Stalin's attempt—"I'll move my little finger and there will be no more Tito," he is reputed to have said—never had a chance. And barely eight months after Stalin's death, the Presidium of the Supreme Soviet in a message to Tito saluted the tenth anniversary of the Second Congress of AVNOJ, thereby in effect acknowledging the existence of a "state life" under CPY control when the Soviet army, far from being in a position to install the Yugoslav Communists to power, was still fighting on Russian territory.

Socialist Democracy

THE FUNDAMENTALS

The Yugoslav theory of the political system of the "transitional period," spelled out in reply to the Cominform accusations, was an adaptation of Stalin's description of the dictatorship of the proletariat in his *Problems of Leninism*, written in 1926. The leaders of the CPY were proud to point out, however, that it was the Yugoslav party rather than the Soviets or the Cominform, who first made it clear that people's democracy is a form of the dictatorship of the proletariat. "Before the conclusions of our Fifth Congress were formulated," declared Moša Pijade, then the principal Yugoslav expert on Marxist-Leninist theory, "Soviet economic, philosophic and other writers did not even divine that the people's democratic state had any relation to socialism, not to mention a relation to the dictatorship of the proletariat. At that time our theory was taken over by Dimitrov, who impaired it somewhat, then by Bierut and Rakoszy with more impairment, eventually by Soviet writers. Now they know what people's democracy is."[3] Comparing the Yugoslav with the Soviet system, Pijade found the following four differences:

1. The number of mass organizations ("levers and belts") has been raised to six, with the People's Front and the Union of Anti-Fascist Women added to Stalin's labor unions, soviets (people's committees in Yugoslavia), cooperatives, and the Youth Organization.

2. The existence of the People's Front as the political organization of the working people, with its double system of

---

[3] "On the Thirteenth Anniversary of tre CPY," *Izabrani Govori i Članci* (Belgrade: Kultura, 1950), p. 261.

membership: individual members, directly, and all other mass organizations collectively.

3. Membership of the CPY in the People's Front in order to be the dominant force of the Front. Pijade was careful to point out that in Yugoslavia the Front has never been a coalition of different political parties. It has always been entirely dominated by the Communist party, which from the beginning of the new regime has been the only party with an independent organization reaching down to the lowest level.

4. Placing the people's committees on the top of the list of levers and belts, in order to recognize their revolutionary character since their very creation.

According to Pijade, the role of the Communist party in a people's democracy is twofold. First, it directs the people organized in the People's Front—the working class, the working peasantry, and the working intelligentsia—and leads it in the struggle for the building of the socialist society, the destruction of the remnants of capitalism, and the victory of Communism. Second, it directs the state, through organs of the people's authority (people's committees), using the support of mass organizations.

The CPY was, therefore, the vanguard of the Yugoslav people's democracy in the sense used by Stalin when he was defining the role of the Communist party in the Soviet dictatorship of the proletariat. For despite the differences mentioned, Pijade found "a profound similarity in principle" between the Soviet and Yugoslav systems:

> The basic levers and belts are the same, although some of them may be different in single characteristics or form. Their essential characteristics and tasks are the same. The leading force, assuring the hegemony of the proletariat is the same. In addition we should not overlook the fact that comrade Stalin's study has been written at a time when the peasantry of the system described by him had not yet become the present kolkhoz peasantry of the Soviet Union.[4]

The "profound similarity in principles" was accompanied by an equivalent similarity in practice. M. S. Handler, then a *New York Times* correspondent in Belgrade, had the following to say on the subject:

[4] "Mechanism of the People's Democracy in Yugoslavia," *ibid.*, pp. 12 ff.

Brief visitors to Yugoslavia often make the mistake of trying to establish a relationship between internal changes and the degree to which the Yugoslav Communists are supposedly moving toward Western theories and practices. . . . The problem should be put in the following words: To what degree are the Yugoslav Communist leaders deviating from the Soviet model? It is erroneous to suppose that the question concerns the degree to which the Yugoslav leaders are leaning toward the West; there is not a scrap of evidence that they have done so or ever intend to. In their present state of development the Yugoslav Communist leaders reject with equal vigor the two possible Western concepts of a political and economic state— the social democratic and the capitalistic.[5]

The changes in the form and style of the party's work introduced since 1952 have had little effect on the essential characteristics described by Pijade. Nor has the label "socialist democracy," appropriated by the CPY in the sixties—with the originator of the idea, Milovan Djilas, safely in jail—anything more to do with a Western social-democratic type of government than the term "people's democracy" used in 1940 and 1950 had to do with the concept of a government by the people. Stalin's "vanguard of the vanguard" concept, party-working class-working people, sometimes expanded with the interposition of the People's Front (now Socialist Alliance of the Working People of Yugoslavia), appears to this day with monotonous regularity in party programs and other fundamental policy statements of the Yugoslav Communist leaders. The adoption of the adjective "socialist" in the Constitution of 1963 was intended to indicate progress along the Marxist timetable beyond the capture of political power by the Communist party to the point where socioeconomic relations have become *predominantly* socialistic. Evidence of progress is based on such tests as the ratio of the private to the socialist sector of the economy in the GNP, the absence of privately hired labor, and the maintenance of such general conditions that the remaining "antisocialist forces" and other manifestations of "retarded social consciousness" are deprived of the means to obstruct socialist development or to restore the capitalist economy. The term "democracy" refers to the application of the concept of "democratic centralism," which, as re-emphasized at the Eighth Party Congress in 1964, (a) excludes such "pseudo-

[5] "Communist Dogma and Yugoslav Practice," *Foreign Affairs* Vol. XXX, No. 2 (April 1952), pp. 438–439.

liberal" concepts as self-government and minority rights, and
(b) requires that the "minority," beyond mere compliance,
actively participate in putting into effect the decisions of the
"majority." When Djilas argued in 1954 that "the Leninist form
of the party has become obsolete (the dictatorship based on the
party), and must always and everywhere become obsolete as
soon as revolutionary conditions no longer exist . . . ," he was
accused of "directing an attack against the monolithic columns
of the LCY" and "undermining the achievements of the Revolution by demanding 'more' democracy (i.e., democracy for all)."
In 1958 the new party program, which served as the basis of the
1963 constitution and is still in effect, while emphasizing indirect
methods such as "fostering the development of the social consciousness" as opposed to use of bureaucratic practices by the
party, did not fail to warn that "antagonistic forces are not
yet sufficiently weakened "to cease to be a danger to the existence
of socialism. Therefore," the working class cannot give up the
weapon of its class struggle—the dictatorship of the proletariat
and the leading role of the League of the Communists of Yugoslavia. . . ." Accordingly, the principle of the party's political
monopoly, under its authority as the spokesman of the working
class and the initiator and organizer of the socialist revolution,
was incorporated into both the new Yugoslav Constitution of
1963 and the new Party Statutes of 1964.

THE CONSTITUTIONAL FRAMEWORK

The political monopoly of the party leadership allows for a
variety of means by which its policy can be implemented. Complete monolithism at any rate is always as much a myth as is
government by the people literally conceived. Within a Communist party, "constructive" criticism and varying degrees of discussion can be permitted or required, as long as the fundamental
rule of unquestioned obedience is not challenged, once an
authoritative decision has been handed down. In the relationship
of the party to the people, the implementation of party policies
can switch back and forth between revolutionary terror and
"socialist legality"; between the use of state organs and mass
organizations; between bureaucratic methods and exhortation,

propaganda, and bribery; between central decrees and local manipulation; and between political and economic means. Djilas finds three overlapping phases in the development of Communist regimes: "Revolution, or the usurpation of power—Lenin; 'Socialism,' or the building of the system—Stalin; 'Legality,' or stabilization of the system—'collective leadership'"; and he adds that Yugoslavia passed through all three in a relatively short time. Power, however, remains the "quintessence of Communism" in all three phases, more or less the end as well as the means, though "Communist leaders, thinking that through power as a means, they would attain their goal, did not believe it to be an end in itself."

The advantages of legality, once power had been seized, are obvious. In the first place, since the party leadership owns the state and can make and unmake the laws at will, there is no sensible reason to renounce the use of this most efficient bourgeois invention for obtaining general obedience. Secondly, since after the destruction of independent political and economic organizations any effective threat to the regime could only come from inside its own machinery, strict adherence of the bureaucracy to the laws adds another "transmission belt" in the total power structure, thereby contributing to the perpetuation of party leadership in power. Indeed, that portion of the total power structure which falls in the category state can be organized in such a way that it would contain several separated chains of command—the political and economic administrative chains, the courts and the prosecutors, the independent (of each other) bureaucracies of the republics, etc. Since in addition, the party and its auxiliaries —not to speak of the secret police—remain separate organizations outside the state, a defection in any one of the chains of command could not muster enough organized power to constitute a threat to the regime and is therefore unlikely to happen.

Communist constitutional theory is made to fit these fundamental power criteria. Yugoslavia now has its third Communist constitution, not counting the temporary status at the end of the war. In each case, the actual changes in the state structure had been tried out and placed into effect, and had been operating for some time before being formalized in a constitution. Moreover, in the case of the second constitutional document, the

Fundamental Law of 1953, the regime did not even bother to use the existing amending procedure. The matter can only be explained in terms of the limited relevance of formal constitutional law in a system run by the Communist party, which, indeed, is what Communist theorists do—in the appropriate dialectical manner.

The Yugoslav constitutional reform of 1953 is an excellent example of Communist constitutional theory in practice. The Constitution of 1946 was a near-facsimile of Stalin's Soviet Constitution of 1936. It included a bill of economic and political rights, although its use "for the purpose of changing or disturbing the constitutional system in an anti-democratic sense" was proclaimed "illegal and punishable." It asserted conspicuously the principle of federalism, "including the right of secession," only to make it ineffective by a broad definition of the powers of the central government, including broad federal powers over the republican ministries. Finally, through fusion of the judicial and legislative powers and centralization of public prosecution, it guaranteed that there will be no delay on the road to "socialism." Thus the Constitution of 1946 served a dual purpose: it was a document of Yugoslav progress towards the Soviet model, way ahead of all other people's democracies, and it facilitated the take-over of remaining private property and the use of various radical methods to speed up industrialization and transform the social structure of the country. By 1953, however, the main tasks of the revolutionary period had long been completed. More important, the excommunication of 1948 had intervened and, after some vaccillation between a policy of more radicalism to prove orthodoxy and one of relaxation of internal pressure for reasons of expediency, the Yugoslav leaders had set out to prove that their system is different from and superior to, rather than a close copy of, that of the Soviet Union. This took the form of a series of changes in the governmental structure and the administration of the economy, widely publicized as measures of decentralization and liberalization, the essence of which is discussed below. Characteristically, however, these measures had been introduced largely between 1950 and 1952, so that the Fundamental Law of 1953 assumed the nature of a *description* of past accomplishments, rather than that of a *set of rules* binding for all in the future.[6] Likewise characteristic, the Fundamental Law repealed eight out of sixteen chapters of the old constitution but stopped short of changing the chapters on the chain of the people's courts and prosecutors or the restrictions upon the use of fundamental rights included in the 1946 document.

The same basic method was applied in the case of the constitutional reform of 1963, although the 1946 and 1953 documents were thereby repealed in toto. Because further reorganization had taken place since the last constitutional enactment, Kardelj could introduce the new document as an attempt "to express everything new and significant that has arisen and affirmed itself during the last ten years in our socialist society." As for the future, the constitution's lengthy introductory part, called "General Principles," acknowledges explicitly for the first time the directing role of the party and the auxiliary role of the Socialist Alliance (former People's Front). The Principles also call for international cooperation in the development of a "free community of all peoples of the world," in agreement with the "progressive strivings of humanity," the achievement of which is placed on a list of socialist desiderata designed to promote "the development of such social relations in which the principle of communism: 'from each according to his abilities, to each according to his needs' will be realized." The Principles conclude with the brave statement that they constitute not only the basis for the "interpretation of the Constitution and the laws" but also for the "activity of all and everyone." They are broad enough, however, to need an authoritative reinterpretation themselves from time to time; the party, as the "organized directing force," continues to be in charge of that.

The main body of the constitution falls into two parts, one defining the social and political system in general, the other the organization of the federal authorities. The general part separates the socioeconomic area from the sociopolitical, reaffirming the

[6] The descriptive nature of proletarian constitutions (with periodic bringing up to date) is considered a virtue by Communist theorists, who assert that a bourgeois constitution, by contrast, refers to a set of relationships which in reality never exists. The problem with this argument (and practice) is that, if the party leadership is allowed to introduce measures which are "ahead of" (hence, when expedient, in violation of) the existing constitution, the citizen can expect little dependable protection from the prospective working of the constitutional system—regardless of how accurately the latest constitutional instruments "describe" his current rights.

principle of the worker's self-management in the former and declaring the working people as the sole holder of public power in the latter. This part also includes chapters on civil liberties and duties, the functions of "sociopolitical communities" (communes, districts, republics, and the federation) and of the courts and prosecutors, and a chapter on "constitutionality and legality." Concerning civil liberties, the constitution retains in substance the general qualification of 1946 in addition to making most of them, in separate provisions, subject to legislative implementation. Moreover, the courts remain dependent on the people's assemblies which elect the judges and can fire them before the expiration of their term of office, and the public prosecutors of all levels of government are still a separate power pyramid under the sole authority of the federal prosecutor. The main changes, therefore, in relation to the early, Soviet type of constitution, are in the areas with which the regime has been experimenting since the early fifties—management of enterprises and organization of the administrative machinery, particularly in the economic field. The changes in the first area have generally become known as worker's management; those in the second began under the slogan of decentralization of the state, which, by the time of the adoption of the current constitution, was beginning to receive less attention than the need of "debureaucratization" of the party itself. Connected with these reforms are subsidiary changes, some designed to support them, others to serve as safeguards against any tendency of decentralization and self-management to get out of hand.

WORKERS' MANAGEMENT AND DECENTRALIZATION

Both administrative decentralization and workers' management are in some mysterious way supposed to be connected with the Marxist concept of the withering away of the state. The particulars are vague and the facts indicate experimentation at various subordinate levels in a search for the most expedient performance of the inflated public functions, rather than the abolition of any of them. Workers' management ("socioeconomic self-government," as distinguished from the "functions of state power" in the "Sociopolitical" field is, moreover, said to eliminate the phenomenon of state capitalism, which, incidentally, the Yugoslav Communists find in both the Stalinist economic system and the advanced stages of the "decaying" bourgeois "monopoly-capitalist state." The General Principles of the 1963 constitution provide, accordingly, that no one owns the means of production or other means of social work. They are declared "social property"—a self-contradicting concept, for the society does not exist as a legal person and therefore cannot be the subject of property rights. The operative principle, therefore, is not property, but "free collective work," which takes the place of the shareholders' rights as a foundation of the "self-government of the working people in the working organization."

The scope of such self-government, however, far from being equivalent to the shareholders' right to dispose of his property, is limited to the specific functions assigned to the workers' committees in the management of enterprises, which remain in reality state property and subject to control by the state and society. Stripped to its essentials, the self-management plan amounts to the participation of workers in the distribution of the net profit, that is, the surplus remaining once the enterprise has paid its costs, both real and those imposed by the government. The latter include predetermined depreciation and labor cost, interest, rent for the use of land, and federal and local taxes (of turnover as well as progressive income varieties). From what remains, however, a part still has to be separated for new investments and the enterprises' social, housing, sports and recreation funds, etc. At any rate, if the real labor cost falls below the theoretical wage level, and the enterprise sells its output at prices which (within the framework imposed by government planning and controls) the workers' representatives can set themselves, there may be a surplus that can be used to increase the wages or the firm's social and investment funds.

The advantage of the system is the possibility of using the market to perform a function of the capitalist economy in a Communist system, i.e., to increase productivity. However, the idea works only to a point, because of its built-in economic contradictions, and because extraneous political criteria (firing dissenters instead of surplus workers, diversion of investment funds into ideologically motivated government projects, duplication of industrial capacities, and payroll padding to change the economic and the class structure of agricultural districts, etc.) continue to override economic requirements. There is also the unavoidable temptation for the worker-managers to raise the prices of their products and to distribute all funds they can get control of, and the government is continually devising new ways to contain this tendency without abolishing the system. That such devices have limited success has been demonstrated by the recent devaluation of the dinar. Finally, workers' management has made a larger number of people aware of the government's favoritism toward the underdeveloped republics, thereby increasing the political difficulties discussed earlier in this chapter.

Decentralization of the administrative machinery is a complement of workers' management, since the committees in the enterprises are themselves organs of decentralized administration of the nationalized firms. Any functions assigned to them had to be taken out of the sum of functions theretofore exercised by the central bureaucracy and its previously existing subdivisions. Actually, the introduction of workers' management in 1950 was accompanied by a series of reorganizations of the central government. The cumulative effect was the disappearance of federal ministries with jurisdiction over various branches of the economy. Only a part of their functions, however, was transferred to the lower levels of government, because the central machinery created a variety of councils that could perform similar functions although they were not called ministries. The industrial firms, moreover, were organized by production branches into higher economic "associations," which, in turn, were by 1958 grouped into "chambers"; since these bodies, like Communist labor unions, represent primarily the "general social interest" rather than their particular membership, they serve as subsidiary channels for carrying out central policies and as tools to counteract undesirable trends in the firms.

Meanwhile, the remaining ministries were renamed secretariats, the number growing to two "state" and seventeen "federal" secretariats by the time of the adoption of the 1963 constitution. The constitution leaves the matter of creating any number of federal secretariats, councils, specialized "functionaries," and "other organs" of the federal bureaucracy to regular legislation, which, in fact, is a continual process of limited significance. It should be noted, however, that the federal and state secretaries are not the full equivalent of the traditional concept of ministers, as they do not collectively form an executive political body, equivalent to a council of ministers. Rather, they are considered mere "administrators." Instead of a council of ministers, the Yugoslav constitution provides for a Federal Executive Council, of which the state and federal secretaries are members ex officio, but additional members are elected to it from among the deputies of the Federal Assembly. This system had already been introduced in 1953, ostensibly to prevent bureaucratization; in fact, however, it makes the executive body a crossbreed between a council of ministers and a Soviet type of presidium. Since the presidents of the executive councils of the constituent republics are also included in its membership, the Council is, by a combination of formal authority and the informal principle of reverse representation, characterized by a *de facto* concentration of powers—legislative, executive, and administrative; federal and republican—second only to that of the Executive Committee of the LCY, to which it is directly linked in the person of its president. The President of the State, however, and the Vice-President ceased to be members of the Federal Executive Council with the 1963 reform. This fact indicates a drop in the status of this body which, in any case, is now too large to serve as the highest political and executive authority. The Executive Committee of the party now includes among its 19 members, beside the Secretary General of the LCY (Tito) and the three secretaries of the Central Committee (Kardelj, Ranković, and Vlahović), the heads of the three branches of government, the presidents of the front and labor organizations, the secretaries of the party's central committees in the larger republics, and the Secretary of Defense. This is clearly the place where the various power pyramids within and without the formal state structure interlock, and thus the logical body to serve as the *de facto* cabinet. In any event the central power structure does not at present reflect any particular tendency of the state to wither away.

The showpiece of decentralization, however, is to be found at the local government level, in the institution of the commune. Introduced with a reform of the local people's committees in 1952, the commune was declared the basic unit of self-government with the adoption of the Law on the Organization of Com-

munes and Districts in 1955 and was hailed as a great accomplishment in "direct democracy." Under the 1963 constitution, the
commune, in addition to various specified tasks, "performs also
other functions of the social community except those specified
by the constitution as the rights and duties of the federation
or the republic." This gives the communes in principle the
same relationship to the republics as the latter have to the
federation. The commune is also allowed to delegate "matters
of common interest to communes" to the district, and the organs
of the commune "directly execute the federal and republican
laws and other directives unless their execution is by constitution
or law placed under the jurisdiction of the organs of the districts,
the republics or the federation." Within such limits, the communes can exercise legislative and taxing powers, prepare their
own annual plans, and distribute their funds and those they may
receive as federal or republican subsidies. The assemblies of the
communes, moreover, are now the only representative organs,
except for one of the five chambers of the Federal Assembly,
elected by a direct vote of the citizens (for the communal chamber) and producers (for the chamber of working associations).

The primary losers in the decentralization process are the
republics, since, according to Kardelj, the aim has been "that
our society be an organic 'national community' of communes,
which is to say not a federation of, but an integrated organism,
within which the individual cells will live a full life and draw
their strength from society as a whole."

Since 1955 the districts have been decreasing in importance
and in two territories (Montenegro and Kosovo-Metohija) they
have been abolished altogether, but only as the size of the communes grew by continuing consolidation. By now the development has gone the full circle, with the present number of communes approaching that of the original districts and already
below the number of city-communes and districts combined
before the reform of 1955. The growing size of the communes,
aside from the fringe benefit of noncomparability of consecutive
statistical data because of constantly changing boundaries, has
thus removed any meaningful relationship of the communes to
the community and direct democracy for which they were introduced. In addition, the larger communes and districts, combining

TABLE 2. Administrative Decentralization: Number of Local
Government Units

Year	Districts	Cities	City communes	Communes
1947	340	85	—	7866[a]
1951	360	94[b]	142[c]	7104[a]
1954	329	24	244	3912
1955	107	—	—	1479
1958	95	—	—	1193
1960	75	—	—	839
1963	40	—	—	581

[a] Number of local people's committees
[b] "Cities outside districts"
[c] "Cities within districts"
SOURCE: Statistical Yearbook of the SFRY, 1963, p. 60, and 1959, p. 23.

city and farm population and, in areas of mixed ethnic composition, villages inhabited by different nationalities, serve the purpose of producing the desired class or ethnic group majorities, or of maximizing the number of administrative subdivisions in which the value of industrial output surpasses that of agriculture. Since the jurisdiction of the subunits is, not less than their boundaries, subject to continual changes, the simplest way to estimate the relative importance of the local, republican, and federal levels in governmental functions at any given time is to compare the funds these units have at their disposal. By this criterion again, the republics are in an unenviable position, ranking not only behind both the federal and the local level, but also behind the federally directed economic combines taken by themselves. Nor is there at present any indication that the squeeze on the republics will be relaxed. For after all, isn't the social product of Yugoslavia in Kardelj's "a creation of a united working class and a united peasantry, rather than individual nationalities"?

TABLE 3. Administrative Decentralization: Government Budgets, 1964
(In Billions of Dinars)

Level	Revenue	Expenditure
Federal budget	758.6	623.8
Budgets of the republics	145.9	157.2
Budgets of the districts and communes	396.9	393.1
Total	1301.4	1174.1

SOURCE: OECD, Economic Surveys: Yugoslavia (Paris: May, 1965), p. 18.

However, the situation will remain fluid, for under the general principle that makes Communist constitutions mere descriptions of conditions which in turn may be changed without following any written framework, the possibility of continual rearranging for reasons of expediency or ideology remains always open.

Trends and Prospects

Yugoslavia, as a recent observer put it, "harbours a family of nations united by the fear that their hatred of each other may be exploited by the outsiders."[7] It might be added that the outsiders have on occasion not been the initiators but have been drawn into the process of exploitation of mutual hatreds by one or the other of the native groups. For native concepts of a "mission" have tended to become stronger than the foreign creeds that may have inspired them in this area where, in their time, Rome and Byzantium, Christianity and Islam, imperialism and nationalism, Catholicism and Orthodoxy, or "East" and "West" have clashed and sought adherents through the centuries, and where survival has nearly always meant fighting thy neighbor. Characteristically, the idea of a bridge between creeds, civilizations, and empires is virtually unknown as a working political concept among the South Slavs. After centuries of rearguard and forefighter roles, always in direct confrontation of major forces, the habit of being holier than the pope—whether the pope of Rome or those of Vienna, Istanbul, or Moscow—has become so firmly ingrained that it had to show its marks even on the Communist monolith.

Communism in Yugoslavia rode to power on a platform against mutual slaughters (though not forgetting first to foster them to create the proper conditions for the take-over), but only to substitute class war for religious war and the pursuit of revolutionary ideology for national bulwark role playing. Moreover, unlike the old-fashioned gendarme, the secret policeman and the party activist have raised claim to the souls as well as the bodies and the pocketbooks of its subjects. But the soul is singularly difficult to get. Under the uniform Communist structure, superimposed over peoples of virtually different civilizations, the old

[7] George Bailey, "Where Titoism Was Tried," *The Reporter* (July 1, 1965).

conflicts remain, though the actual struggles are carried on in novel forms and supported with arguments in the approved vocabulary. Thus, integral Yugloslavism takes the form of support for the principle of "progressive unification of humanity" and "socialist Yugoslav integration," or of struggle against the "territorialization" of the means of production. Conversely, national aspirations for self-determination and opposition to the economic exploitation of nationalities take the form of programs to rationalize and "de-politicize" the economy. Liberalism, finally, must often masquerade as an attempt to seek broader support for the regime by more expedient implementation of decisions on the new style of party work and emphasis on the use of non-bureaucratic methods.

There is also an increasing uneasiness about the issue of succession. Tito has recently abandoned some of his multiple interlocking positions and the former head of the police apparatus and the organizational secretary of the party, the Serbian Alexandar Ranković has apparently edged out the chief party theorist and President of the Federal Assembly, the Slovene Kardelj, by becoming the single Vice-President of the state. However, since police chiefs such as Beria have been ineffective in obtaining decisive party support in past Communist succession scrambles, the situation remains uncertain. Kardelj shares with Ranković a position in the Secretariat of the Executive Committee. Having been in charge of successive state reorganizations, he has attempted to strengthen the Federal Assembly by introducing some of the party's organizational features into the representation system and the pyramid of local and republican assemblies, of which the Federal Assembly is the apex.

Much of the criticism recently voiced in Yugoslavia (such as that in the Zagreb Marxist journal *Praxis*) indicates that besides the economic and nationality conflicts between different parts of the country, there is a conflict of generations within party ranks. For the critics, far from being old reactionaries that have by some miracle survived the take-over period, are often young Marxists who grew up and were educated under the Communist regime but find the continued concentration of power and privileges in the hands of World War II Partisan fighters the main obstacle to any progress of socialism. The main strength of these critics is in the fact that, having mastered Communist theory better than the majority of the veterans of the Partisan war ever could, they consider themselves better Communists than their comrades in the party and state apparatus and their fight against "primitivism" and "dogmatism" in party work a fight for the advancement of Communist goals. The main danger in the situation is that the *apparatchiks*, unable to cope with the attack of the young Turks by better arguments, may increasingly rely on strong-arm methods and ultimately on support of the Soviet big brother for the perpetuation of their power monopoly. It appears thus that the Yugoslav party, while seeking a non-Stalinist platform in the fifties, released forces which it finds increasingly difficult to control in the sixties and which may well make an open clash inevitable when the charismatic leader disappears from the scene.

Summing Up

Yugoslav Communists were singularly effective in rapidly monopolizing power at the end of World War II and in surviving Stalin's onslaught of 1948–1949. In the sequel they sought novel methods of party work, resulting in some liberalization, particularly in the fields of economic management and intraparty discussion, without changing the fundamental reality of one-party rule. Since with a lag of several years an analogous relaxation of methods took place in the Soviet Union and in other European Communist states, gradual reaccommodation between Belgrade and the Soviet bloc, more or less on Yugoslav "polycentric" terms, became possible. On the domestic front, however, Yugoslavia is currently drifting into a triple crisis:

1. The political system, unchallengeable from outside party ranks in the absence of a democratic political process and of non-Communist political organizations, is subject to increasing criticism from within which the party leadership cannot entirely suppress without a wholesale abandonment of its non-Stalinist Official platform. There is increased evidence of disagreement on methods of party work, in particular a growing demand of full freedom of discussion, and there is a widening intraparty chasm

between the "liberals" and the "dogmatists," although the over-riding authority of Tito still keeps the party from breaking up into organized antagonistic factions.

2. The economy is riddled with contradictions between economic and political considerations, and the officially adopted program of a qualified market economy, with pay according to work and workers' self-management, is being sabotaged by *apparatchiks* and Partisan veterans. Consequently, far from being able to compensate for the dwindling subsidies from abroad, the economic system currently threatens the working force with unemployment and continual lowering of real wages and the state with international bankruptcy. A side effect, a mass exodus of workers and technicians to greener pastures abroad, adds a class of economic exiles to the political ones. This in turn, decreases the already low efficiency and international competitiveness of industrial enterprises. All of this is sharpening the intraparty dispute between those who advocate full implementation of self-management and those who see the only remedy in a return to rigid central controls.

3. The inherited problems, in particular the existence of pariah social and national groups, remain. While the largest social class, the peasants, remains for all practical purposes excluded from the "socialist" society and deprived of spokesmen, the nationality problem underlies most other controversies. This is because exploitation and mismanagement in the economy and dogmatism in culture and party work are inevitably identified with central, hence Serbian, rule. The choice of Ranković as Tito's deputy was in this context particularly clumsy, threatening in any forthcoming succession struggle to transform the intraparty crisis into a crisis of the state.

On balance, however, none of these problems need spell the doom of the Communist regime. For one thing, no organized effort to provide a feasible democratic alternative is in sight. As for the economic crisis, unless the dogmatists succeed in pulling the LCY overboard, it is likely to be eased again by some form of foreign aid. Based on past performance, it appears doubtful that the West will find a way to use this opportunity to strengthen continually the liberal tendencies, particularly in the political area rather than only in the economic. But the Yugoslav Communists have shown enough flexibility in the past to appear capable, in the event of an imminent threat to their regime, to seek a formula which would satisfy both intraparty critics and potential foreign donors. Such a formula may not solve any of the fundamental social, economic, and national conflicts in the country at large but it may postpone a conflagration, which, indeed, is the method that has kept the LCY in power ever since World War II.

BIBLIOGRAPHICAL NOTE

Among the Communist publications in English, *Yugoslav Survey*, a monthly "Record of Facts and Information" is the most useful. There is also an annual *Statistical Pocket Book of Yugoslavia* (Belgrade: Federal Statistical Institute) whereas the larger *Statistical Yearbook of the SFRY* (Belgrade: Federal Statistical Institute) has its headings translated in a supplementary volume. The government further publishes a bimonthly *Review of International Affairs*, a series of studies under the title *The New Yugoslav Law*, and a quarterly political and ideological journal, *Socialist Thought and Practice*. The Zagreb bimonthly *Praxis* appears also in an abbreviated quarterly edition in French, English, and German combined (Department of Philosophy, University of Zagreb). Though the official party organs, *Komunist* and *Socijalizam* are designed for domestic consumption, articles and speeches of party leaders, such as Tito and Kardelj, and monographs of semiofficial academic analysts, such as Jovan Djordjević and Leon Geršković, appear in Western languages and the full text of the Program of the LCY has been published in book form in a translation by Stoyan Pribichevich under the title *Yugoslavia's Way* (New York: All Nations Press, 1958). An official biography of Tito was published by Vladimir Dedijer (New York: Simon and Schuster, 1953), who has also written his own memoirs as an insider of World War II Partisan struggle, *The Beloved Land* (New York: Simon and Schuster, 1961), but has since fallen in disgrace along with Milovan Djilas. Three of Djilas' own books are of relevance here: *Conversations With Stalin* (New York: Harcourt, Brace, and World, 1962), *Anatomy of a Moral* (New York: Praeger, 1959), and *The New Class* (New York: Praeger, 1957). At the other extreme are the stories of pre-Communist politicians, of which two examples will suffice to give the Serbian and Croatian viewpoints. They are A. C. Fotich, *The War We Lost* (New York: Viking, 1948), by the former royal ambassador in Washington, and Vladko

Maček, *In the Struggle for Freedom* (New York: Speller, 1957), by the late leader of the Croatian Peasant party.

American sources include two general symposia, R. J. Kerner (ed.), *Yugoslavia* (Berkeley: University of California Press, 1949), and Mid-European Studies Center of the Free Europe Committee, *Yugoslavia* (New York: Praeger, 1957), both now dated but still useful on some historical aspects. F. H. Eterovich and C. Spalatin (eds.), *Croatia: Land, People, Culture* (Toronto: University of Toronto Press, 1964), though narrower in scope, represents a similar across-the-disciplines approach and an attempt to balance the works written from a centralist Yugoslav point of view. An older voluminous travelogue, Rebecca West, *Black Lamb and Grey Falcon* (New York: Macmillan, 1955), is a revealing guide to the style of life and history of the South Slavs. Other useful books for background reading include J. B. Hopter, *Yugoslavia in Crisis, 1934–1941* (New York: Columbia University Press, 1962); I. J. Lederer, *Yugoslavia at the Paris Peace Conference* (New Haven: Yale University Press, 1963); Jozo Tomasevich, *Peasants, Politics, and Economic Change in Yugoslavia* (Stanford: Stanford University Press, 1955), and two sociological studies, D. A. Tomasic, *Personality and Culture in East European Politics* (South Norwalk, Conn.: Stewart, 1948), and J. M. Halpern, *Serbian Village* (New York: Columbia University Press, 1958). All but the last are concerned with various pre-World War II developments. The most interesting eyewitness accounts of World War II Partisan struggle are found in F. H. Maclean's *Escape to Adventure* (Boston: Little, Brown, 1950), and S. Clissold's *Whirlwind: An Account of Marshall Tito's Rise to Power* (London: Cresset, 1949). Ivan Avakumovic, *History of the Communist Party of Yugoslavia*, Vol. I (Aberdeen: University of Aberdeen Press, 1964) so far also covers only the period until World War II and the still earlier background of what would eventually become the Communist movement is examined in W. D. McClellan's *Svetozar Marković and the Origin of Balkan Socialism* (Princeton: Princeton University Press, 1964).

On postwar government and politics, G. W. Hoffman and F. W. Neal, *Yugoslavia and the New Communism* (New York: Twentieth Century Fund, 1962) is the most complete text, and rather favorable to the regime; so is F. W. Neal's own *Titoism in Action* (Berkeley: University of California Press, 1958). From a more critical perspective, C. P. McVicker, *Titoism: Pattern for International Communism* (New York: St. Martin's Press, 1957); A. N. Dragnich, *Tito's Promised Land: Yugoslavia* (New Brunswick: Rutgers University Press, 1954); and D. A. Tomasic, *National Communism and Soviet Strategy* (Washington, D.C.: Public Affairs Press, 1959) also deal with domestic politics. An excellent account of the new Yugoslav system of local government is J. C. Fisher's "The Yugoslav Commune," *World Politics* (April, 1964).

The new Yugoslav system of economic management is described in I. L. O.'s *Workers' Management in Yugoslavia* (Geneva, 1962); B. Ward's "Workers' Management in Yugoslavia," *Journal of Political Economy* (October, 1957); and G. Macesich's *Yugoslavia: Theory and Practice of Development Planning* (Charlottesville: University Press of Virginia, 1964). See, further, A. Waterston, *Planning in Yugoslavia: Organization and Implementation* (Baltimore: Johns Hopkins Press, 1962), and B. Ward, "The Firm in Illyria: Market Syndicalism," *The American Economic Review* (September, 1958).

Soviet-Yugoslav relations have received much attention in the literature. The essential documentation is contained in the Royal Institute of International Affairs, *The Soviet-Yugoslav Dispute* (New York: Oxford University Press, 1948), and in V. L. Benes, R. F. Byrnes, and N. Spulber (eds.), *The Second Soviet Yugoslav Dispute* (Bloomington: Indiana University Press, 1960); also in R. Bass and E. Marbury (eds.), *The Soviet-Yugoslav Controversy, 1948–58* (Prospect, N.Y.: Prospect Books, 1959), and R. B. Farrell, *Yugoslavia and the Soviet Union, 1948–1956* (Hamden, Conn.: Shoe String Press, 1956). The issues in the 1948 conflict are analyzed by A. B. Ulam in *Titoism and the Cominform* (Cambridge: Harvard University Press, 1952). See, further, on this topic, E. Halperin, *The Triumphant Heretic* (London: Heineman, 1958), and H. F. Armstrong, *Tito and Goliath* (London: Gollancz, 1951).

CHAPTER SEVEN

Rumania

The General Setting

FEW COUNTRIES in the world display as complex a geographic pattern over a relatively small area (91,700 square miles) as Rumania. Carpathian by the nature of its relief and Danubian through its hydrographic network, Rumania is also a maritime land by virtue of its 152 miles of shore line on the Black Sea. Geographically the country does not belong entirely either to Central, Eastern, or Southern Europe; rather it combines features of the mountainous Alpine system of Central Europe and the vast East European plain. Mountains, hills, and plains each comprise approximately one-third of Rumania's total area. In altitude they range respectively between 2,500–12,000 feet, 650–2,500 feet, and 0–650 feet. These features also are reflected in the climate which is subject to Atlantic, Mediterranean, and Russian Steppe influences. The western part is generally Atlantic in character, while the eastern and southern areas are distinctly more continental. Mediterranean aspects are significant only in the southwest. The principal hydrographic feature is the presence of the Danube which empties into the Black Sea after flowing through southwestern and southern Rumania. However, two geographic factors are particularly deserving of our attention: Rumania's natural resources and her proximity to Russia.

Silver and gold were mined in pre-Roman times; crude oil—one of the country's main sources of wealth—was known to exist from as early as the fourteenth century; coal and natural gas are also to be found in large quantities. The plain is one of the most fertile in Europe, particularly the "granary" of the Baragan. Timber resources are enormous.

These riches and location have tempted powerful neighbors throughout Rumanian history. Hungarians, Turks, Poles, and Russians have constantly sought and frequently succeeded in establishing control over individual Rumanian provinces or the country as a whole. These constant foreign pressures are reflected in the demographic and political configuration, and in the general economic development.

Rumania is a multinational and multireligious state. While the overwhelming majority of the population is Rumanian (15,000,000 out of a total of 17,500,000), significant minorities, Hungarian (1,500,000), German (400,000) and Jewish (150,000), have played important roles in the country's development. The Hungarian minority still poses political problems to the regime. The smaller minority groups, Gipsies, Ukrainians, Serbians, Russians, Czechs and Slovaks, Tatars, Turks, and Bulgarians, while politically insignificant, are symbolic reminders of long periods of foreign domination. The overwhelming majority, 80 percent, of the population is Rumanian Orthodox; other religious groups include Roman Catholics, Calvinists, Lutherans, Jews, Unitarians, Mohammedans, and other minor denominations. The political role of the dominant Orthodox Church is inconsequential, in conformity with the long-standing tradition of subservience to the state.

The majority of the people are still engaged in agriculture, nearly 70 percent being active in either farming or forestry. Historically the peasantry and bureaucracy were Rumanian, the industrial working class and industrial entrepreneurs Rumanian, German, Hungarian, or Jewish and the commercial class primarily Jewish and Hungarian. Since 1948 these distinctions have gradually disappeared until no meaningful occupational pattern based on demographic considerations may now be determined. Whereas it would be difficult to assert that the homogenization of the multinational and multireligious Rumanian society has been achieved under Communism, it is evident that traditional conflicts caused by these factors have markedly declined even in the case of such antagonistic groups as the Hungarians and Rumanians in Transylvania. In fact most of Rumania's inhabitants appear to be united, at least in the common effort of exploiting the country's vast economic resources for building a prosperous industrial society, and of minimizing the unfortunate geopolitical factor of proximity to the Soviet Union.

The failure of Rumania's previous rulers to utilize the vast natural resources for the people's benefit and the resulting maintenance of an essentially feudal political and socioeconomic order provides the theoretical justification for Communism. Russia's historic interference in Rumanian affairs, particularly the ruthless economic exploitation of the country after World War II, accounts for its nationalist, anti-Russian character. Rumania's economic development beyond the agricultural stage may indeed be attributed to the gigantic efforts and determination of the Communist regime. The industrialization of society, tentatively begun in the late nineteenth century, had reached only a minimal level on the eve of World War II. In terms of gross industrial output, a seven-fold increase over 1939 was recorded in 1963. While progress was more spectacular in producer goods (1963 was 10 times 1939) it was also noticeable in consumer goods (1963, 4 times 1939). The most dramatic achievements were in mining and construction, and in the development of elaborate steel mills, chemical, and electric products industries. The electrification of rural areas was achieved under communist rule. Industrial employment has more than doubled. The basic programs of social insurance, workmen's compensation and other essential benefits of industrial society were introduced only in recent years. Agricultural techniques have been drastically altered, particularly upon completion of collectivization in 1962. This remarkable economic progress was, however, obscured by the inordinate exploitation of Rumanian industrial and agricultural production by the Soviet Union in the years immediately following World War II and the survival of the early Communist tradition of economic subservience and dependency on the U.S.S.R. throughout the fifties. This Russian domination was the inevitable consequence of Stalinist imperialism and, from the Rumanian standpoint, of geographic proximity to the Soviet Union. Emancipation from the U.S.S.R., within the limits of what is geopolitically and economically possible, is however the story of Rumanian Communism, at least since Stalin's death. All aspects of political evolution must be focussed on this basic issue.

Constitutional Development and Government

The record shows that during the years immediately after the establishment of the Communist regime in 1945 the state machinery and apparatus as well as all basic laws, including the constitution itself, were rigidly patterned on Russian prototypes. Recent changes in Russo-Rumanian relations notwithstanding, the pattern adopted in the immediate postwar period has remained basically unchanged. It is indeed striking that until the summer of 1965 the political life operated within the framework of laws and institutions that were functioning in 1952, and often earlier. This apparent anomaly is explained partly through the "continuity" theory propounded by the Rumanian regime's claim that the current programs and policies for socialist Rumania were formulated by the Communist party in 1945. Consequently, the institutions established at that time and in subsequent years were the work of men with foresight who laid the institutional foundations for socialism. A corollary explanation also provided by the regime is that major restructuring of governmental organization is warranted only at an advanced stage of socialist construction. Consequently, even upon the proclamation of the Socialist Republic of Rumania in the summer of 1965 the traditional Communist institutions and laws remained virtually unaltered. Indeed, the political, cultural and socioeconomic balance sheet—the Constitution of the Socialist Republic of Rumania of 1965—differs only in minor respects from its antecedent, the Constitution of the Rumanian People's Republic of 1952.

Whereas the present regime regards itself as the heir to the best in Rumania's historic tradition, it has constantly rejected constitutional or even institutional connections with the "old regime." All pre-1948 constitutions, starting with that of 1866 and including that of 1923 and, of course, the Carol II Constitution of 1938, were instruments for ratification of the political supremacy of the bourgeois-landlord interests headed by the reactionary monarchy. Polemical aspects aside, these constitutions were indeed unrepresentative of Rumanian conditions, essentially meaningless imitations of foreign prototypes that did not apply to nineteenth- and twentieth-century Rumania. The same considerations apply also to the Communist constitutions, at least in the lack of correspondence between the letter of the document and the reality. The constitution of 1948 was an ad hoc document, anticipating future changes. As a blueprint for the radical transformation of the socioeconomic order and installation of tested Soviet institutions it is, however, worthy of investigation. Its most notable feature was the omission of Article 126 of the Soviet constitution proclaiming the political supremacy of the Communist party. This deficiency was remedied in 1952 when the objective factors for "legalizing the then prevailing political, economic, and social conditions and the fundamental rights and liberties of the working people" were proclaimed to exist and thus justify the adoption of a new constitution.

That lengthy document, recognizing the party's position as the ultimate repository and executor of all state power, described the existing state institutions and granted all basic civil rights when compatible with "the interest of those who work" and with the "strengthening of the regime of people's democracy." It also provided for almost universal suffrage, insured educational and cultural opportunities to all, and outlined the immediate and long-range goal of the regime—the construction of socialism. The same basic principles are also incorporated in the 1965 constitution. The two documents are substantially alike, differing only in detail reflecting the changes that have occurred in Rumania since 1952. Thus, the latest constitution records the socialist transformation of agriculture, alterations in the country's socioeconomic and political structure, and broadening of the civil rights of its citizens.

The institutional framework of the new constitution is essentially that of 1952. Technically, the supreme organ of state power is the Grand National Assembly, the sole legislative body, elected on the basis of one deputy per 40,000 inhabitants. This assembly which in practice merely approves the decisions of the party, also goes through the formality of electing the State Council (the Presidium until 1961) and appoints the Council of Ministers. The aforementioned governmental institutions are important only to the extent that they carry out the decisions of the party. Nevertheless, as executors of party decisions and through the overlapping of key party and governmental posts in the same individuals, their role is crucial to understanding the Rumanian state. The Presidium technically exercises broad supervision over the Council of Ministers. Its members include the President—the head of the Rumanian People's Republic—three vice-presidents, who, like the President, are senior members of the party's Central Committee, and fifteen "leading cultural and political figures" whose functions are essentially honorific or advisory. The Council of Ministers, on the other hand, is a large body of approximately twenty-five heads of various administrative departments, six vice-prime ministers and three first vice-prime ministers without specific cabinet positions. In effect it is the primary administrative institution of the country. Its functions are broad and its efficiency remarkable. The state apparatus expands vertically and horizontally under its collective control or that of individual ministers except that local and regional matters not directly connected with the central government are entrusted to the people's councils. These are popularly elected bodies whose autonomy is limited and functions restricted to routine regional or local administrative matters.

At all levels the government is subject to supervision and reprimand by the Procurator General, the head of the Procuratura, and guardian of the "people's legality." Heading the General Procuratura and the local procuraturas subordinated to it, this official is *de facto* the most powerful administrative and judicial officer, as the findings of his office and subordinate institutions normally result in indictments and convictions by the judiciary. The judiciary, consisting of a pyramid of courts under the Supreme Court, as a rule merely confirms the recommendations of public prosecutors in matters concerning violations of administrative edicts, improper functioning of governmental offices and, for that matter, legal infractions of all kinds.

The range of current Rumanian legislation is indeed all-encompassing. Apart from an extensive assortment of laws specifically concerned with criminal offenses against the state, a variety of codes of civil procedure have been promulgated in recent years. The penal code, elaborated gradually after 1948 and assuming its more-or-less definitive form by 1958, was initially intended to give legal sanction to arbitrary administrative and police actions of a regime determined to destroy all opposition to the Communist revolution. The range of crimes against "the security of the state" included both political and economic infractions, with emphasis on the former. As in all "people's democracies" during the Stalinist years, minor offenses such as comments on the policies of the regime or listening to foreign radio stations were classified as political crimes and condemned with draconic punishments. With the stabilization of the political situation and general relaxation of pressure in recent years the politically punitive legislation, while still on the books, has been enforced less and less. By contrast emphasis has been placed on economic infractions, primarily the loosely defined "economic sabotage." Since 1963, however, the regime has officially reduced the number of criminal offenses against the state in all fields with a resultant decrease in the number of applications of the penal code. The Code of Civil Procedure containing certain elements of prewar legislation has assumed greater significance in the sixties. Its provisions, concerned with normal property and related issues, reflect the problems of a growing industrial society and the changes that occurred in the process of "socialist transformation" of the economy and society.

The Rumanian Communist Party: Leadership and Policies

The entire process of control, policy-making, legislation, and administrative action—in short the entire political life of the country—focuses on the Rumanian Communist party. This organization, with a membership of over 1,300,000, has proven to be a formidable instrument for attaining the goals first formulated in 1945 and redefined in subsequent years. Much maligned and abused by Kremlinologists and other observers of Eastern European developments until its declaration of independence from Moscow in April 1964, the Rumanian Communist party has demonstrated a degree of cohesion and efficiency unsurpassed in the Soviet bloc. The traditional view that a tiny organization of ideologically retarded stooges of Moscow was brought into power by the Soviet armies in 1944 must be subject to careful revision. It is true that the Rumanian Communist party, founded and outlawed shortly after World War I, played no significant role in either the international Communist movement or in Rumanian political life before 1944. But it is equally true that during the "period of illegality" and external Stalinist control the internationalist, "cosmopolitan" group of intellectuals was divorced from the proletarian, Rumanian, and incarcerated elements who were to become the leaders of the Communist regime after 1952. This dichotomy is crucial to any understanding of contemporary Rumania. It is now evident that the leaders of the celebrated Grivitza Strike of railwaymen of 1933, including Gheorghe Gheorghiu-Dej and Chivu Stoica, formed the nucleus of a patriotic, Rumanian-oriented, group isolated by their imprisonment from the international movement and Rumanian political life. Thus, while the leadership of the Communist party was either decimated by Stalin's purges or, if Stalinist or opportunist, welcomed asylum in Moscow, the Rumanian Communist movement lost its organization as well as its identity. Nevertheless, if the number of activists in Rumania was small and consisted primarily of second- or third-rank members of the party, free or in prison, the "democratic," antifascist elements associated with Communist ideology retained some popularity among left-wing intellectuals and even a substantial part of the proletariat. If direct contacts were negligible between the incarcerated and the free, a common bond equated with agrarian and industrial antifascism and antifeudalism was evident.

A noteworthy, but actually unnoticed development was the assumption of major offices in both the party and government apparatus by a substantial number of the imprisoned Rumanian contingent immediately after Rumania's "liberation" of August 23, 1944. Gheorghiu-Dej, as First Secretary, was theoretically the most prominent man in the Communist party, a fact accented by his presentation of the party's program at its first meaningful conference in 1945. But in effect, Gheorghiu-Dej and his primary associates' power was negligible. Whether the Soviet army and political officers had—as alleged—sought the liquidation of the party members by the Rumanian fascist regime is open to question. The fact remains, however, that for strategic reasons it became imperative to have "home front" antifascists join the Soviet-trained, housed, and politically indoctrinated contingents comprising the Tudor Vladimirescu brigade and the political émigré fighters headed by the trusted and subservient Ana Pauker. Unquestionably, Ana Pauker and her Moscow-oriented cohorts Vasile Luca and Iosif Chisinevski were more powerful in the formative years of the Rumanian Communist state than were Gheorghiu-Dej and his proletarian associates. Moreover, the so-called Moscow group sought to replace Gheorghiu-Dej's proletarians by another Rumanian group with fewer direct ties with the working class by birth or occupation. Thus, the necessary link between the nonethnic, Moscow-directed, leadership and the Rumanian masses was to be forged through the more pliant intellectuals and bureaucrats—men like Miron Constantinescu or Teohari Georgescu—than the tough proletarians. It is also evident now that Ana Pauker and her associates were no match for Gheorghiu-Dej and his. Gheorghiu-Dej, the technically indispensable front man, was quietly consolidating his own forces, rallying around himself the younger members of the party, the technocrats and economic experts, and all those who for one reason or another were hostile to the Moscow group, to Stalin's exploitation of the country's wealth, or to coffee-house Communism. By stressing the theme of socialist transformation of Rumania and appealing to the national interest rather than the international concept which meant total subordination to the Soviet Union, Gheorghiu-Dej cautiously steered a course toward exploiting those "objective conditions" that would eventually permit his opponents' removal from power.

In this struggle, Gheorghiu-Dej committed no errors. He accepted the principles of Stalinist repression both within and outside the party as prerequisites for ultimate success. The ruthless transformation of the "old order" was essential to the attainment of the "objective condition" for "building socialism"; a disciplined, dedicated, trustworthy nucleus of followers was needed within the organization. In this respect, Gheorghiu-Dej and his retinue may indeed be described as Stalinist and, in a sense, opportunist. In practical political terms, however, any other course would have been fatal. But a careful reading of Gheorghiu-Dej's main speeches between 1945 and 1952 reveals more than abject adulation of Stalin and the Soviet Union. Whenever feasible he stressed the need for Rumania's socialist transformation under the leadership of the party, albeit under the broad umbrella of Stalin's protection and example. The moment of truth came in 1952 when the "objective conditions" for seizure of power within the party presented themselves.

Numerous explanations have been given for the downfall of the triumvirate of Ana Pauker, Vasile Luca and Teohari Georgescu, ranging from Gheorghiu-Dej's exploitation of Stalinist anti-semitism to punishment of right- and left-wing deviationism with Stalin's approval. In retrospect it would appear that Gheorghiu-Dej acted at a time when retaliation by the Kremlin would have been impossible, and in any event he offered enough to Stalin to avert his wrath. It must not be forgotten that the internal coup occurred during the Korean War and that Gheorghiu-Dej assured Moscow of the continuation of the traditional pro-Russian policies. Indeed, Stalin could hardly have acted against a friendly regime that was strengthened by the centralization of power in the hands of a hard core of dedicated Communists devoted to socialist transformation and eliminating the bottlenecks created by the unpopular Luca and Pauker. It is indeed doubtful that anyone but the most initiated members of Gheorghiu-Dej's entourage suspected in 1952 that the new leadership would eventually pursue a course of national Communism in defiance of Moscow. Titoism could hardly have been expected from the orthodox Gheorghiu-Dej who had condemned heresy in the past. But it is evident now that Gheorghiu-Dej had Titoist proclivities from as early as 1948 and that the then prevailing rumors of Stalin's suspicions to that effect may indeed have been accurate. Still, subsequent actions and words must have convinced Moscow that Gheorghiu-Dej was above reproach —if not suspicion—and hence acceptable in 1952.

What would have happened in Rumania had Stalin not died in 1953 is a matter of speculation. The Gheorghiu-Dej team was, after all, still hampered in its activities by Chisinevski and, to a lesser extent by Miron Constantinescu, and the party machinery was hardly the well-oiled, efficient unit that it is today. In the eyes of the party and the Rumanian masses the new leadership was no great improvement over the old. For that matter it was not less feared. But Stalin's death permitted Gheorghiu-Dej to implement tentatively his ideas on socialist construction and seek direct popular support for the policies of the party. These policies were defined as the attainment of socialism in Rumania in accordance with the principles adopted at the Conference of 1945. Reaching this goal became the *raison d'être* of the Communist regime and of the Rumanian people. The New Course adopted in 1953, designed to relax the extreme economic and political pressures exerted upon Rumania by Stalin and in turn upon the population by the party, was indicative of a change in both tactics and orientation. Whereas there would be no abandonment of authoritarianism, the arbitrary persecution and economic abuse identified with the deposed "deviationists," and by implication with Moscow, would not be tolerated. Henceforth at least part of the national production would be used for Rumania's growth. At the same time, the new leadership was seeking to reduce its economic dependence on the Soviet Union and members of the Soviet bloc by exploring trade possibilities with the West. These cautious maneuvers, occurring under the umbrella afforded by the "spirit of Geneva" and the Kremlin's attempted reconciliation with Yugoslavia, brought a noticeable change in Gheorghiu-Dej's position by 1955. Rather, it led to a clear formulation of the principles that were ultimately incorporated in the celebrated Statement of 1964.

With the hindsight characteristic of Kremlinologists, it was discovered that Gheorghiu-Dej's report to the party's Second Congress in December 1955 did indeed contain the quintessence of current Rumanian doctrine and politics. In the past, the same speech had received a somewhat different interpretation, namely, admission of failure for which the antiparty group headed by Ana Pauker was held responsible. Whereas this evaluation is not totally inaccurate it ignores the very essence of Gheorghiu-Dej's statement: the tentative formulation of a doctrine of national Communism according to which every member of the socialist camp should erect the socialist society in accordance with specific national problems and interests, with specific national resources, with specific historic conditions. Cooperation with the socialist community remained an essential requirement for the attainment of each nation's aims but individual countries should be allowed to determine the extent of such collaboration and have an equal voice in formulating international Communist policies. International relations with fellow socialist nations—described as "relations of the new type"—had to be based on the Marxist-Leninist principle of interaction between socialist patriotism and proletarian internationalism, "on mutual respect for state sovereignty and equal rights of all members of the socialist camp." Also significantly, Gheorghiu-Dej applauded the principle of peaceful coexistence and tentatively formulated the current doctrine: "The Rumanian People's Republic abides by the principles of respecting the national sovereignty and equality of rights of all nations, of non-aggression and peaceful settlement of all problems, of peaceful coexistence among countries with different social systems, and of non-interference in internal affairs." In sum then, the program enunciated in December 1955 called for the rapid building of socialism in Rumania by whatever means were deemed proper by the party.

It is to the credit of the leadership of the Rumanian Communist party that regardless of the vicissitudes of international relations, both within the socialist camp and between the socialist camp and the West, that it was able to carry out its program with the now generally acknowledged and admired effectiveness. It is indeed the extraordinary unity of the leadership and its ability to pursue difficult policies in difficult times that singles out the Rumanian experiment as a major success in the Communist world. Through exceptionally skillful exploitation of its opportunities, through masterful maneuvering within and without the camp, and above all, through masterful timing, Gheorghiu-Dej and his associates could implement the promise of a nationally determined independent course by 1964. And this despite the grave geopolitical handicap of extreme proximity to the Soviet Union.

The unity of the party is attributable ultimately to a common opposition to Russian exploitation of Rumania's wealth. The organization that Gheorghiu-Dej was creating by 1955 consisted primarily of technocrats, economists, workers, and nationalist left-wing intellectuals who accepted his leadership and program as best suited to Rumania's interests. Hungary's experience of 1956 clearly convinced these elements and the masses that "liberation" would not occur and enormously enhanced the strength of a party advocating the improvement of national conditions, the building of an effective, industrialized society through use of the vast Rumanian natural resources for the benefit of the Rumanian people. Rumanian Communism was preferable to Russian-imposed exploitation whose purpose was to strengthen the Soviet Union. It was indeed easy for the party leadership to purge the last opponents to Gheorghiu-Dej's group in 1957. The downfall of Chisinevski and Constantinescu—identified with Moscow—represented the removal of the last obstacles to complete control by the anti-Pauker national Communists.

Evaluation of party and government activities between 1957 and 1962 was hampered by the inability of observers to recognize the manifestations that actually implemented the 1955 doctrine. Working on the assumption that Gheorghiu-Dej was merely another Pauker and subservient Stalinist, foreign analysts classified Rumania as the satellite *par excellence*. By 1962, however, it became evident that extremely significant changes had occurred in Rumania proper and in the camp as a whole, largely as a consequence of unheralded but decisive actions by the Rumanian Communist party.

Proceeding cautiously so as not to arouse Moscow's suspicions and wrath, the party pursued a vigorous program of industrialization and expansion of international economic relations with the West. In this drive toward economic advancement and greater independence the party cleverly exploited the contradictions facing Moscow in relations with the West—in the spirit of peaceful coexistence—and with China, the principal opponent of such policies. Convinced that the Kremlin could not take reprisals against a state advocating all of Moscow's policies, particularly coexistence and unity of the socialist camp, the Rumanians assumed the same posture as Khrushchev's team, but for different purposes. While constantly subscribing to Moscow's pronunciamentos and fully endorsing Russian views on international affairs, Gheorghiu-Dej and his associates were expanding their economic ties with the West. Concurrently, as champions of the unity of the camp, they entertained friendly relations with China. Moreover, between 1957 and 1960 the regime pursued a vigorous policy of economic development both in industry and agriculture on the assumption that an economically powerful Rumania would be in a better position to gain advantages from Moscow and the support of the Rumanian people.

But this course was fraught with uncertainty. As long as Khrushchev could coerce the Soviet bloc into common military and economic action through the Warsaw Pact and Council for Mutual Economic Assistance (COMECON), both weapons required to contain the hostile NATO and Common Market, the possibility of emancipation from Soviet domination was remote. It must have been a frustrating, but not altogether unexpected, experience for Gheorghiu-Dej to have the remarkable list of economic achievements presented at the Third Congress of the party in December 1960 received with major reservations by Moscow, the West, and the Rumanian masses. The spectacular increases in industrial production, the growth of industry, the massive building program, and all other economic indicators were minimized by Moscow which, like its economically advanced partners Czechoslovakia and East Germany, still regarded Rumania as an underdeveloped country. As such, it could hardly claim equal status with advanced members of the bloc and would have to accept COMECON-dictated formulae for economic integration. The prescribed solutions would have prevented the full economic development envisaged by the Rumanian party and the frustration of the goals formulated in 1945, restated in 1955, and again in 1960. The attitude of the West was not substantially different. Rumania was a second-rate industrial nation, a satellite of Moscow, a poor risk for economic investment. Nor was the regime's popularity substantially greater in Rumania itself. The authoritarian Stalinist methods utilized to insure unflinching execution of the party program were hardly compensated by improved housing and living conditions. The peasantry, staunchly opposed to total collectivization of agriculture, was particularly unfriendly. Still, the architects of party policies were unmoved by all these considerations and decided to doggedly pursue their master plan. By establishing economic ties with Western nations whenever possible, by distributing more of the economic gains to the Rumanian people, and by holding to their claims that the country's progress toward socialism justified acceptance of its plans by other members of COMECON, the Rumanian leadership was biding its time. Political foresight reaped its rewards in the fall of 1962 when the Cuban confrontation weakened Moscow's position in the bloc and toward the West and China. In the disarray following the withdrawal of the missiles from Cuba, the exacerbation of the Sino-Soviet conflict, and the determination of the United States to encourage divisive forces in the Russian empire and Communist world in general, the Rumanian leadership made the decisive moves.

First, in March 1963, it rejected economic integration under COMECON. Subsequently it adopted a position of neutrality in the Sino-Soviet conflict while increasing economic and political ties with the West. Finally, it translated party goals into historic terms by equating them with the Rumanians' traditional national aspirations for a prosperous, independent, democratic country. All these steps were clearly designed to complete the country's socialist transformation so as to permit optimum exploitation of the national wealth to the country's own advantage and transform Rumania into a truly independent and prosperous Communist state. Since 1963 the Rumanian party has pursued these policies vigorously in the face of continuous pressure by the Soviet Union and its devoted partners in the bloc who naturally resented the Rumanian course of independence and collaboration with both the West and China. Indeed, the Statement of April 1964 was a response to these pressures, an unequivocal restatement of the principles enunciated by Gheorghiu-Dej at the Second Party Congress in 1955. And these policies have been pursued relentlessly even after Gheorghiu-Dej's death in March 1965 and during the current intensification of the Vietnam crisis.

The Rumanian Communist Party: Continuity and Change

The Rumanian course was ultimately determined by changes in the international situation. However, the imaginative exploitation of the "objective factors" that permitted its adoption and execution must be credited to the Rumanian Communist party. The party, the only political organization in existence, has been for a long time regarded as one of the weakest yet most ruthless among the world Communist organizations. The party was indeed

weak during the period of internecine conflict that culminated
in the purge of the Pauker group and subsequent consolidation
of power by Gheorghiu-Dej and his associates. As previously
explained, the organization had no meaningful history in pre-
1944 Rumania. Its gaining and maintaining political power after
World War II was possible only through Russian armed support.
It is clear that the destruction of the traditional political parties,
including the powerful National Peasant party, was as fundamental an aim of the Communists as the forcible seizure of
political power under the pretense of holding free elections in
1946. Nor can there be any argument about the cynical realism
surrounding the alliance with the Social Democratic party and
other minor socialist and left-wing groups in a Popular Democratic Front to facilitate the execution of a *coup d'état* legalized
through electoral intimidation and fraud.

The lack of popular support and identification of the victorious leadership with Soviet interests was certainly rooted in mass
opposition to the ruthlessness and radical nature of the party's
program as well as to Russian aims and policies in Rumania. In
the eyes of the Rumanians there was little difference between
Gheorghiu-Dej and Ana Pauker in 1947. Still, Ana Pauker was
more suspect on account of her Jewish origin and long-standing
identification with the hated Soviet Union. It is also evident
that the party's membership increase from less than 1,000 to
nearly 1,000,000 in five years was primarily through the forced
enrollment of industrial workers and the adhesion of opportu-
nistic functionaries, intellectuals, and others seeking material
advantage through identification with the organization. But the
membership was unreliable, untrained, and obviously unable to
win the confidence of the masses. In the early postwar years
important developments occurred only in the party top echelons.
As far as the rank and file was concerned periodical purges
directed by one faction or another merely increased the opportunism or fears of the membership with disastrous effects on
the party's morale. In 1952, however, following the seizure of
power by Gheorghiu-Dej and his entourage the process of purification began in earnest. By 1955 the size of the organization
declined from approximately 1,000,000 to 540,000. The smaller
cadres may have been better disciplined and more devoted to

Gheorghiu-Dej's platform but they still were not a powerful organization. Popular support for the party was virtually nil and the new leadership was as despised as the old, regardless of promises of a brighter future. Few indeed could have anticipated the evolution of the party's current policies in 1952—or, for that matter in 1955. If Gheorghiu-Dej was known, his nationalist sentiments were either ignored or discounted. His closest associates were either inconspicuous or held in contempt; in any case, they were regarded as stooges of a foreign power. Chivu Stoica, the Chief of State, was considered a party hack, while Alexandru Moghioros, and Emil Bodnaras, both members of the Politbureau, rated as unimaginative pawns of Moscow. Many leading architects of the present course who were even then in the Gheorghiu-Dej camp were unknown and guilty by association. Yet it was this nucleus that brought discipline into the party organization and formulated the policies previously described. Their internal modus operandi was unspectacular. Purges were minimal but the selection process was improved and the social composition of the membership broadened to bring closer identification between the members and the masses affected by the policies. Indeed, the greatest merit of the leadership that emerged in 1952 and has consolidated and expanded its hold since that time, has been its determined attempt to secure the confidence of the population through realization of the promises contained in the party programs. Evidently, despite opposition to certain aspects of the Party's aims and methods the leadership has attained its goals to a surprising extent. And this because gradually, as conditions permitted, the party has displayed remarkable intelligence in its appraisal of the interests of the Rumanian people and carried out corresponding policies—without altering its fundamental aims.

Whereas as late as 1955 the Central Committee regarded the relatively high membership, 55 percent of the workers, as disproportionately low for a Communist party, by 1965 it has gained sufficient popular support to consider a lowering of the proportion of industrial workers (44 percent) to insure better representations by other social classes. It is noteworthy that in the latest report on the composition of the organization issued in April 1965, the Central Committee in providing data on social composition (44 percent workers, 33 percent peasants, and 23 percent intellectuals and professional people), stressed the need for adding well-trained individuals, particularly technocrats and members of the teaching profession. The changes are designed to convince the population that the party acts in the best national interest and seeks closer identification with the people at large. Moreover, by allowing greater flexibility in acceptance of new members the new recruitment policy holds out to all the possibility of membership and promise of privileges that were once reserved to this elite. The gradual expansion in membership, currently reported at 1,378,000 members and candidate members, attests to the effective implementation of these goals.

It is truly a remarkable phenomenon that the once-feared and detested Rumanian Communist party is now considered a competent leader and exponent of the national interest. This change is largely the result of a marked decline in the severity of the police state, substantial economic progress, and assumption of a nationalistic posture. Indeed, the party—posing as the heir and executor of the traditional goals of national independence and prosperity—is at least tolerated by all except those who still nurture the utopian dream of total liberation from Communism. The assumption by the party of the historic mantle and the efficient execution of the legacy is, of course, the organization's most effective trump card at home. The new nationalism with its implied territorial revisionism with respect to Bessarabia and Northern Bukovina, has been popular with the traditionally anti-Russian masses. Similarly, the resistance to economic integration into COMECON according to the Russian, Czech, and East German formula, has further enhanced the party's popularity, particularly as this resistance has resulted in effective exploitation of the country's resources, more rapid industrialization, and greater economic benefits for the Rumanians.

The economic and cultural rapprochement with the West is also applauded at home inasmuch as renewal of such ties has been interpreted as symbolic of political relaxation and as a significant departure from Stalinism. The presentation on the Rumanian stage of plays by Ionesco, Brecht and other major Western writers, the granting of passports for travel to Western

Europe, and allowing Western tourists and expatriates to visit the country freely have been instrumental in altering the domestic image of the Communist party. These basic measures, part of the general "humanization" of the regime, have more than counteracted unfavorable reaction to high prices, continuing economic controls, total collectivization of agriculture, and infinite bureaucratic chicanery.

It is noteworthy, however, that the traditional forms of party organization as well as the instruments for dissemination and enforcement of party decisions and policies affecting matters other than governmental organs as such have remained virtually unchanged since 1945. The party still utilizes mass organizations, party units in the armed forces, and secret police for the abovementioned purposes even though these auxiliary organizations' functions and powers have undergone major alterations. The importance of mass organizations other than the Union of Communist Youth (UTC) has declined. While the UTC remains a training ground for future party cadres, the People's Democratic Front or the League of Democratic Women have been *de facto* placed in mothballs. The Front still makes its customary appeals and conducts electoral campaigns and propaganda whenever elections are scheduled by constitutional or political requirements. However, these campaigns have become more perfunctory, primarily because the need for constant indoctrination has become less urgent. The rallying of women's support for the party has undergone a similar fate. While greater acceptance has clearly reduced the need for activity, these organs are maintained on a standby basis. Under these circumstances the instruments of control, the army and secret police, have also faded into the background. The army is now primarily concerned with national defense rather than potential suppression of an anti-Communist revolution. The secret police appears to be more active in evaluating the response of the population to current party policies than in acquiring information for punitive action against the previously omnipresent "conspirator" and "counterrevolutionary."

In sum then, the Rumanian party and government, by adopting and executing pragmatic, feasible, and palatable domestic and foreign policies has strengthened its position enough to win the acceptance of the Rumanian people and the cautious approval of nations regarding these policies as advantageous to their own national interests. While the domestic opponents have been generally won over, such foreign critics as the U.S.S.R. and its loyal allies have been virtually handcuffed by Rumanian exploitation of the Sino-Soviet conflict and the still valid doctrine of peaceful coexistence.

Nevertheless, Russian opposition to Rumania's independent course cannot be ignored. The Russians are irate over Rumania's sabotage of COMECON and allusions to Moscow's seizure of Bessarabia and Bukovina. Encouragement of Hungarian counterrevisionism in Transylvania, relocation of the Rumanian inhabitants of Bessarabia, and general coolness toward Bucharest are all indicative of the Kremlin's displeasure with the Rumanian regime. Still, the current Rumanian course is likely to be altered only through radical changes in the relations of the major powers. Repudiation of the doctrine of peaceful coexistence, a Sino-Soviet or even a Russo-American rapprochement may terminate the Rumanian experiment. Even if somewhat remote, these possibilities cannot be ruled out by the cautious but deliberate leadership of the Rumanian Communist party.

Summary and Conclusions

Although handicapped by proximity to the Soviet Union and, paradoxically, by its natural resources coveted by Russia and historically by powerful neighbors, Rumania has been able to emancipate itself from the position of a Russian satellite in recent years. The process of emancipation—the so-called "Rumanian course"—has been characterized by maximum use of the country's natural resources in building a viable industrial economy and by exploitation of the political dilemmas facing the Soviet Union in its relations with the West and Communist China.

The Rumanian course is theoretically based on the Rumanian Communist party's determination to adhere to the program that was first formulated in 1945. As revised and reinterpreted in subsequent years, the party's task is to fulfill both the historical and Communist legacies which are equated with the creation of an economically powerful, internationally respected, democratic, independent Greater Rumania.

The dangers inherent in this ambitious program, most intimately connected with Russian opposition to the establishment of independent states within the Russian bloc, are fully recognized by the current Rumanian leadership and account for all of its political actions, at least since the death of Stalin. As all major decisions are ultimately made by a small group of men, the Rumanian Communist party has not found it necessary to broaden its basis of political support either within party organizations themselves or among the masses other than in seeking general endorsement for its policies. The prevention of free discussion within the party organization has been justified in terms of the need for secrecy in the formulation of essentially anti-Russian policies by Gheorghiu-Dej and his associates. This accounts on the one hand for the authoritarian, Stalinist, methods of control prior to 1963, and on the other for the unity and hegemony of the ruling group. Indeed, purges have been minimal compared to other Communist parties, while factionalism and related manifestations are virtually unknown. Moreover, the skillful timing and execution of the various steps toward realization of the "national communist goals" have resulted in the party's leadership gaining at least the tacit support of the masses.

Aware of the geopolitical proximity of the Soviet Union and of the dangers of excessive liberalization, the Rumanian Communist regime has shown but little interest in political experimentation. Organizationally, the political and economic structure of the country has remained virtually unaltered since the establishment of the Rumanian People's Republic in 1947. The formal establishment of the Socialist Republic of Rumania—recognizing the socioeconomic evolution of the last twenty years—is not likely to result in any meaningful modification of the institutional framework or in the principle of democratic centralism. The major changes which have occurred in recent years and are likely to occur in the future have been and will be dictated by the top echelons of the Rumanian Communist party on the basis of their appraisal of "objective conditions," both national and international. The support of party members and of the masses will be sought not through extending their political rights but through further identification of the general goals with those of the leadership and through further satisfaction of the economic —and cultural—desiderata of the Rumanian people.

BIBLIOGRAPHICAL NOTE

Primarily because of a lack of interest in Rumanian affairs and of spectacular events in Rumania's political evolution before 1963, no studies comparable to those on Hungary, Poland, and Yugoslavia may be recommended.

The basic survey covering all relevant topics—political, economic, cultural, geographic, and demographic—is Stephen Fischer-Galati, *Romania* (New York: Praeger, 1957). This volume is, however, dated inasmuch as it contains no information after 1956. Specific Rumanian problems, primarily political, have been the subject of later studies. The best analysis of general political developments is contained in Ghita Ionescu, *Communism in Rumania, 1944–1962* (London: Oxford University Press, 1964). This study too is somewhat out of date since the author was unable to cover the major changes that occurred in the crucial years 1963–1965. Some insight into recent developments may, however, be gained from David Floyd, *Rumania: Russia's Dissident Ally* (New York: Praeger, 1965).

No systematic studies are available on the Rumanian government, constitutional development, or even Communist party. The reader can only be referred to basic statements by leaders of the Rumanian Communist party which have appeared in Western languages. Most valuable are the collected speeches of Gheorghe Gheorghiu-Dej, available in German, under the title *Artikel und Reden* (Bucharest: Editura Politica, 1959, 1961, and 1962), and Nicolae Ceausescu, *Report to the Ninth* Congress of the *Rumanian Communist Party* (Bucharest: Meridiane, 1965). English versions of the Rumanian constitutions of 1952 and 1965 have also been published.

Economic and other statistical data have been published annually in recent years in the *Rumanian Statistical Pocket Book*. Critical studies on the Rumanian economy are virtually nonexistent except for those prepared by John Michael Montias, the distinguished American economist. The most valuable of these is "Unbalanced Growth in Rumania," *The American Economic Review*, Vol. LIII, No. 2 (May 1963), pp. 562–571.

Briefer surveys of monthly or annual developments may be found in *East Europe*, the monthly review of East European affairs published by the Free Europe Committee; the *Rumanian Review*, the monthly publication issued by the Rumanian Embassy in Washington; and the *New International Yearbook*, published annually by the Funk & Wagnalls Company, New York.

INDEX

68 69 70 71 7 6 5 4 3